# been there and back to nowhere

Geschlecht in transnationalen Orten
Gender in transnational spaces
postproduction documents 1988 – 2000

**Ursula Biemann**

b_books Berlin

b_books  Lübbenerstrasse 14, D-10997 Berlin, Tel. +49 30-6117844, b_books@txt.de

Herausgegeben/published by  Ursula Biemann
Lektorat/Editor  Stephan Geene
Lektorat/Copyeditor Deutsch  Monica Caviezel
Lektorat/Copyeditor English  Kimi Lum

Grafik/Graphic design  Ilia Vasella, Zürich
Druck/Printer  Grafica Novanta, Milano

Auslieferung  Vice Versa, Dorotheenstrasse 4, 12557 Berlin, Tel. +49 30-61609237, Fax +49 30-61609238
Distribution U.S.A.  Autonomedia, POB 568 Williamsburgh Station, Brooklyn, NY 11211-0568
Phone & Fax 718-9632603, info@autonomedia.org / www.autonomedia.org

© Ursula Biemann und b_books, Mai 2000
ISBN 3-933557-12-7

5 Introduction / Einführung

17 Diaspora, Border and Transnational Identities **by Avtar Brah**
28 Disapora, Grenze und transnationale Identitäten

41 Survival and Exploraterrarism. Re-mapping the posthuman space by Yvonne Volkart
56 Überleben und Exploraterrarismus. Den posthumanen Raum neu kartographieren

69 **Border Project**
88 Performing the Border – Video Script
133 Performing the Border Gender, transnational bodies, and technology
146 Performing the Border Geschlecht, transnationale Körper und Technologie
162 Interview with Bertha Jottar / Border Swings by Bertha Jottar

173 **Lexicon Hispanica**

183 **Global Food**

195 **Interstices / Zwischenräume**

211 **Mediated Identities / Mediale Identitäten**
242 Videos by Sikay Tang and Simin Farkhondeh

253 **Afghan Collection**

263 **Platzwechsel**
266 Ethno-x-centric Reflections on the National Expo and the National Museum
272 Ethno-x-zentrische Überlegungen zu Landesausstellung und Landesmuseum

277 **Kültür**
279 Outsourcing and Subcontracting
293 Auslagerung und Zulieferung

309 **Writing Desire**
333 Interview with Rosi Braidotti

335 **Trafficking and Trading**

357 Project Information / Projektinformation
362 Biographies

To my grandmother May Ellen
who was sold to Switzerland for child labor

**Acknowledgements** With regard to the collective effort required for this publication, I am especially thankful for the graphic collaboration of Ilia Vasella, the editorial work of Stephan Geene, Monica Caviezel, and Kimi Lum, and above all, the critique and encouragement of Yvonne Volkart throughout this process. In addition, I would like to thank Bertha Jottar, Simin Farkhondeh and Sikay Tang for letting me include their video works, Avtar Brah for the permission to reprint excerps of her book, and Mendes Bürgi and Dorothee Richter for allowing me to reprint my texts. Finally, I would like to acknowledge some of those who, through their interest, example, or friendship, have made this endeavor meaningful: Lyana Amaya, Jörg Bader, Gabriel Baur, Fritz Biemann, Mary Biemann, Daniel Biemann, Benjamin Buchloh, Sabeth Buchmann, Ron Clark, Alexis Danzig, Colin Deland, Rosalyn Deutsche, Mauricio Diaz, Mark Dion, Ayse Durakbasa, Maria Guerra, Sylvia Kafehsy, Gülsün Karamustafa, Mary Kelly, Barbara Krüger, Maritza Le Breton, Renate Lorenz, Pierrette Malatesta, Trinh T. Minh-ha, Heinz Nigg, Meral Özbek, Catherine Queloz, Yvonne Rainer, Walter Riedweg, Martha Rosler, Gita Saghal, Jayce Salloum, Annette Schindler, Lilian Schneiter, Berta Sichel, Shelly Silver, Connie Solfrank, Kaatje Sprenger, Jo Schmeiser, Thomas Schmutz, Susanne Steiner, Marion von Osten, Brian Wallis.

# _INTRODUCTION

This book is about cultural displacement, my own and others'. The stories it tells take place against the background of the last twelve years, and that background increasingly becomes the foreground as the narrative proceeds. By narrative I mean the gradual unfolding of ideas which become necessary to think at a particular moment in time and in a specific set of personal and political circumstances. The stories also describe the passage from the critically detached aesthetics of institutional criticism in the art space to the recognition of one's subjective involvement in the shaping of personal and representational, and thus cultural, relations. At present, if the politics of location are considered so important, it is because this concept is not confined to one geographical location with its cultural specificity but allows biographical determining factors to be relevant components. These factors reflect specific social, educational, economic, and professional motivations as well as personal relations, desires, and collective fantasies. They are all culturally situated and define the ground from which artistic practice emerges. The theoretical texts and art projects in this book, then, present a range of positions and strategies developed in the postcolonial context of particular biographies and cultural sites.

I was first introduced to a postcolonial critique during my art studies in New York. This critical discourse had entered the art world consciousness in a decisive way only by the mid-to late eighties when minority artists had started to apply considerable pressure to enter art institutions. Aesthetic politics related to ethnicity and minority identities made their appearance in exhibitions like *The Decade Show* in 1990, when it was proclaimed that the avant-garde was no longer to be found at the forefront but in the margins. By then, Trinh Minh-ha's first book *Woman Native Other* had come out, a formally and intellectually groundbreaking critique on the ethnographic I/eye and one which became a permanent item in my backpack over a prolonged period of time, and James Clifford's *Predicament* on collecting art and culture and the impact of cultural displacement in institutional terms, published in 1988, was particularly influential to artists who came from institutional criticism because until then critique was directed mainly at the institution of high art. Yet this evidence that the avant-garde had multiple fronts led to the art institution being henceforth understood as one among many institutional sites to be scrutinized and, certainly, not as the only one where vital cultural debates might take place.

To operate both inside and outside the art context in pursuit of a language that could mediate these worlds was one of the major challenges at the end of the eighties, when the art museum still played a decisive role in setting aesthetic and political standards. This dilemma has decreased in recent years, since lately the international artist and media activist community has become increasingly networked and thus many of the most relevant cultural events have begun taking place outside the major art institutions.

In my own work, though, the conflict is apparent in the double track my art practice has engaged in, and I'm not saying these are mutually exclusive. On the one hand, I conducted an institutional critique of art and ethnography representing major Western institutions of knowledge and cultural coding in the projects *Lexicon Hispanica* and *Afghan Collection* and later in *Platzwechsel*. Here I continued and expanded the concerns already articulated by site-specific and context art. Whether intentionally or not, this strategy followed a model of the artist as a scientist, a distanced observer who categorizes and interprets the object of investigation.

On the other hand, as important as I assessed the work of redefining Western parameters which have exercised authority over the valuation and devaluation of cultural productions in the past, I still did not find the scientific role model all that interesting, not even a simulation of it. Thus my approach became more like the artistic attitude of a social agent who conducts a conceptual critique but wants to position herself in the social and political context. This attitude implied that I would go into the field to collect samples of cultural significance and articulate them materially and discursively.

In the pursuit of my commitment to a feminist critique of global conditions engendered by corporate ideology I became deeply involved in the U.S.-Mexican border situation. Unlike the institutional ethnography work, this long-term social and economic research was perceived as a radical abandonment of any workable art definition. Finding a form to relate it to the art context, and I don't mean just aesthetically, was a bit like poking around in the dark. When I began research on the position of women in the international labor division in 1986, the border of Mexico existed mainly as a socio-economic debate. I drew my information from NGO reports, from labor organizations, and academic texts written by anthropologists, economists, and sociologists. Gill Perez told me that I had to make up my mind between doing Marx or Tolstoy. I had a hard time making this decision, instead I kept looking for ways of expressing tough information in a cultural and aesthetic language that would challenge the Western standards of representation both visually and institutionally. The *Border Project* set out to articulate culturally the different gender theories and global economy. If this project kept me interested for so long, it's because it touched on many of the core issues around which these last years have centered for me as a (gendered) cultural producer. It's easier, or maybe more urgent, for a female artist to search for a synthesis of this kind. For a woman the question of positionality is never only a professional decision (particularly not one which would require deciding between two master narratives) because she is always already positioned in the image-language signification system. Just how strongly enmeshed I was in these cultural processes became apparent when I displaced myself again.

At the end of 1991 I left New York and returned to Europe. The wall had come down, promising uncertain cultural reformulations. The politically engaged years of the New York art scene were clearly over; it was time to move on. But starting over in Europe, where the liberalization of the world market and the globalization frenzy seemed to overrule cultural objectives and critical dialogue, was a bit of a cultural shock. The Youth Movement of the early eighties had not stimulated the art scene in Zurich in any fundamental way. At the time, the main political activities on a cultural level were being instigated and carried out by film and video activists. The artists concentrated their energies on squatting an empty factory building to gain cultural work space, but their art practice remained within bourgeois parameters. I was faced with an art community that settled for art production in a conventional studio-gallery constellation. For someone coming from a critical post-studio art education who saw the role of the artist not so much as the producer but as the mediator and who had some time ago shifted her focus from work to text, this approach could hardly qualify as an adequate positioning in the wider social context. Indeed this approach would concede to the art market as the ultimate institutional frame and concentrate itself entirely on production as if the paradigmatic shifts in the sixties known as postmodernism had never taken place. My only option was to forge ties with an institution that defined cultural work more broadly and was already engaged in activities linking social, cultural and political concerns. The project *Interstices-Interespacios* was my first collaborative community project which was conceived and realized with Femia, a local center for culture and education for migrant women. Whereas the *Border Project* dealt with the larger conditions framing women's lives on the line between the industrial and the developing world, this community project was more concerned with psychological and social aspects of identity as a result of cultural displacement. This project was an opportunity for me to come to terms with my own personal migration experience, since my moves to Mexico and New York in 1982 and my return to Zurich in 1991 had stirred up my cultural self-definition.

In (German-speaking) Europe, postcolonial critique hadn't entered the art world until the mid-nineties with a number of symposia in Germany and with the *steirische herbst/Inclusion-Exclusion* in Austria. Clementine Deliss' exhibition *Lotte or the transformation of the object*, which took place in Graz at the end of 1990, was a singular precursor. What had been discussed in the U.S. in terms of politics of representation, hybrid identity, dislocation, intertextuality, and self-positioning, was handled here under the crude headings of "problems with foreigners" and "racism." Yet the stubborn focus on race and difference doesn't do justice to the complex cultural and social conditions of today's diaspora societies. Rather it reproduces the binary oppositions (us/them) that underlie the colonial concept of culture. *Interstices* and the following projects were conceived to contribute greater subtlety to the aesthetic and discursive field and to formulate positions which attempt to dissolve the fundamentally static notion of cultural identity or at least to present it as ambivalent.

The Western art world has particular manners in dealing with non-Western artists and their productions. The nineties saw enormous changes as corporations and the art world alike reached out in pursuit of total expansion. The struggles and negotiations that accompany these changes make their appearance in two other collaborative projects *Mediated Identities* and *Kültür - a gender project from Istanbul*. It didn't suffice any longer to articulate a critique on prevailing representations of the other. Extending my privileged invitation to extra-European cultural producers and negotiating these relationships as part of the art project turned out to be a more effective form of institutional critique.

Also, there was a growing need to locate questions of gender and other categories of identity within the context of the wider transformations of the public sphere, particularly of urban reality. *Kültür* focused on the way female bodies circulated in this transnational space, how gender relations were being regulated in representation, in the public sphere of the city, in the subcontracting economy, in migration laws. This project manages to link, in more efficient terms, the gender-specific social and economic analysis to the institutional critique of the art context. The participation in an International Art Biennial in Istanbul in 1997, an event that resulted directly from the global dream of a city competing for financial capital while using in this competition radical marginalization measures against the local female population that had been subcontracted for the Western economy, becomes the point where my two concerns finally merge perfectly.

With the recent euphoria over the use of digital media in art and cultural spaces, a comprehensive, gendered analysis of global capital with regard to the culture and information industry seems more relevant than ever. One consequence of this has been my returning to the Mexican border town Ciudad Juarez to see how NAFTA has affected the situation of women in the high-tech industry. With the video *Performing the Border* I attempt to combine a materialist perspective on international division of labor with a more discursive approach to the kinds of subjectivity, identity, and sexuality that are forming in these transnational zones. The Mexican artist Bertha Jottar, who has participated in the Border Art Workshop in Tijuana for a number of years and now lives in New York, makes relevant contributions to the discursive understanding of the border concept in both the video and the interview printed in this book. As important as a deconstruction of existing representations has been to my practice, I find it essential to go on site, understand people's lives and the places they inhabit, and produce my own version of images. It's very obvious that the subjectivities produced by the new technologies and hypermobility in the North are radically different from the ones transnationalism produces in the South. And when we see ourselves confronted with a strong identity-effacing tendency in the corporate high-tech discourse, while subjects in the South are being overdetermined by sexualizing and racializing identity markers, what perhaps at this point becomes vitally important is to insist on singularity, specificity, and locationality. In the essay *Performing the Border* I try to think through the different kinds of subjectivities produced on the border through representations, work conditions, the public sphere, and the kinds of trajectories women trace in the move through these transnational spaces.

In her text *Diaspora, Border and Transnational Identities* Avtar Brah theorizes concepts of diaspora, border, and politics of location as a new grid for a historicized analysis of contemporary transnational movements of people, information, culture, communities, and capital. Her concept of diaspora that refers to multi-locationality within and across territorial, cultural, and psychic boundaries is very helpful and future-oriented in that it never plays out one minority positioning against another but allows for the theorization of identity in a way adequate to the complexity of diaspora societies.

In her essay *Survival and Exploraterrarism* Yvonne Volkart addresses gendered borders in a number of video works, some of which focus on the border along Eastern Europe while others transcend many national and cultural borders simultaneously. She discusses the specific aesthetics developed by the artists that map identity for an existence in the posthuman space where various topographies (TV room, Belgrade, gallery space, peep show, discos) become the basis for biographical inscriptions that transcend their spatial and personal conditions. Whenever the artist aspires to the realization of becoming a subject, she observes that the location in its real and symbolic significance plays a central role: places of desire/places of survival. Ann-Sofi Sidén, for instance, examines the situation of prostitutes from various countries in Eastern Europe on the German-Czech border. Sidén chose Dubi as a particular location for her research even though the conditions found here are merely symptomatic for a whole chain of entanglements.

My own investigations on the border have made clear that international labor in the South is not only feminized but also sexualized, that female workers are literally addressed in their sexuality, and that prostitution is in fact a structural part of global capitalism. As I have elaborated in the border essay, the notion of the self undergoes transformations that affect questions of boundaries, gender, and sexual relations and this is particularly so in the electronic landscape. On a more discursive level, *Writing Desire* examins electronic communications technologies in terms of the boundaries between private fantasy and the public sphere and their capitalization. Among the many signs pointing to the commercialization of sexual relations, the project examines more closely the accelerating development of the trafficking of women and the bride market, the point where the virtual and physical movement of female bodies conflates.

My present research and video project, in collaboration with Simin Farkhondeh, focuses explicitly on the sexualization of international labor and migration, tracing women's trajectories in the trafficking for sexual exploitation. *Trafficking and Trading* (working title) will take a look at the trafficking of women from a global perspective. Former U.S. military rest & recreation (R&R) areas in the Philippines and Burmese brothels in Thailand are sites where military, state, and private structures in the handling of this new cargo become apparent.

All these projects have been realized in collaboration with other cultural producers whom I thank sincerely for their contributions of texts and artworks and for bringing this book closer to being the kind of cultural practice it stands for.

# _EINLEITUNG

In diesem Buch geht es um kulturelle Verschiebung, um meine und die von anderen. Die Geschichten in diesem Buch erzählen vom Transfer von einem kulturellen Ort an einen anderen. Sie finden vor dem Hintergrund der letzten zwölf Jahre statt, und dieser Hintergrund wird im Verlauf der Erzählung zunehmend zum Vordergrund. Unter Erzählung verstehe ich das graduelle Entfalten von Ideen, die zu einem bestimmten Moment und unter einem spezifischen Set von persönlichen und politischen Umständen notwendig werden. Gleichzeitig beschreiben die Geschichten den Übergang von einer kritisch distanzierten Ästhetik institutioneller Kritik im Kunstraum zu einer Position, die die eigene subjektive Involvierung anerkennt und die versteht, dass sie persönliche und repräsentationelle und somit auch kulturelle Beziehungen mitgestaltet. Wenn die Politik des Ortes gegenwärtig so wichtig scheint, dann deshalb, weil Verortung sich nicht auf einen geografischen Ort mit seinen kulturellen Eigenheiten beschränkt. Vielmehr bezieht sie biografisch bestimmende Faktoren als wesentliche Komponente mit ein, welche eine Sozialisierung und Bildung, ökonomische und professionelle Motivationen sowie persönliche Beziehungen, Begehren und kollektive Fantasien wiedergeben. Sie alle sind kulturell situiert und bestimmen den Grund, aus dem künstlerische Praxis hervorgeht. Die theoretischen Texte und Kunstprojekte in diesem Buch stellen also postkoloniale Positionen und Strategien dar, die sich in bestimmten Biografien und kulturellen Schauplätzen entwickelt haben.

Ich begegnete postkolonialen Theorien erstmals während meines Kunststudiums in New York. Dieser kritische Diskurs ist erst Mitte bis Ende der 80er-Jahre in das Kunstwelt-Bewusstsein eingedrungen, als minoritäre KünstlerInnen anfingen, beachtlichen Druck auf die Kunstinstitutionen auszuüben. Ästhetische Politik ethnischer und minoritärer Identitäten proklamierte in Ausstellungen wie *The Decade Show* 1990 die Avantgarde sei nicht länger vorne, sondern an den Rändern zu finden. Zu dem Zeitpunkt war Trinh Minh-ha's erstes Buch *Woman Native Other* erschienen, eine formal und intellektuell durchschlagende Kritik des ethnografischen Ich/Auge (I/eye), die über geraume Zeit zum permanenten Artikel in meinem Rucksack wurde. Von James Cliffords *Predicament* (1988) über das Sammeln von Kunst und Kultur und die Auswirkung von kultureller Verschiebung in institutioneller Hinsicht liessen sich vor allem jene KünstlerInnen inspirieren, die institutionelle Kritik betrieben, denn bis anhin war jene Kritik vor allem auf die Institution der Hochkunst ausgerichtet. Doch wegen der offensichtlichen Tatsache, dass die Avantgarde mehrere Fronten hatte, musste die Kunstinstitution künftig als einer unter vielen institutionellen Orten verstanden werden, die gründlich zu untersuchen waren, und sicher nicht als der einzige Ort, an dem wichtige kulturelle Debatten stattzufinden hatten. Gleichzeitig innerhalb und ausserhalb des Kunstkontextes zu handeln, auf der Suche nach einer Sprache, die zwischen diesen Welten vermitteln konnte, das war eine der hauptsächlichen Herausforderungen, als das Kunstmuseum Ende der 80er-Jahre noch eine entscheidende Rolle im Setzen von ästhetischen und politischen Standards spielte. Dieses Dilemma nahm in den letzten Jahren ab, als sich – dank einer zunehmend international vernetzten Community von KünstlerInnen und AktivistInnen – viele der relevantesten kulturellen Veranstaltungen ausserhalb der grossen Kunstinstitutionen abspielten.

Dieser Konflikt findet sich in der Doppelspurigkeit meiner Kunstpraxis wieder, und ich meine damit nicht, dass sich beide Bereiche gegenseitig ausschliessen. Zum einen betrieb ich in den Projekten *Lexicon Hispanica, The Afghane Collection* und später in *Platzwechsel* eine institutionelle Kritik an Kunst und Ethnografie als wichtige westliche Institutionen von Wissen und kulturellem Kodieren. Damit führte ich die bereits in der ortspezifischen Kunst und in der Kontext-Kunst artikulierten Anliegen weiter und erweiterte sie. Ob gewollt oder nicht – diese Strategie entspricht einem Modell des Künstlers oder der Künstlerin als WissenschafterIn, als einer distanzierten BeobachterIn, die den Gegenstand der Untersuchung kategorisiert und interpretiert. Wenn es auch sehr wichtig ist, die westlichen Parameter neu zu definieren, an denen in der Vergangenheit kulturelle Produktionen gemessen wurden, war doch das wissenschaftliche Modell nicht allzu interessant für mich, nicht einmal als Simulation. Ich bevorzugte die Haltung der künstlerischen, sozialen Agentin, die eine konzeptuelle Kritik formuliert, sich aber im sozialen und politischen Kontext situiert. Diese Haltung heisst: nach draussen gehen, um kulturelle Merkmale zu sammeln und sie materiell und diskursiv zu artikulieren.

Meiner Verpflichtung gegenüber feministischer Kritik an den Auswirkungen der globalen, neoliberalen Ideologie folgend, begann meine langjährige Auseinandersetzung mit der US-mexikanischen Grenzsituation. Im Gegensatz zur institutionellen Ethnografie-Arbeit wurde diese soziale und ökonomische Recherche als radikale Abweichung von jeder brauchbaren Kunstdefinition wahrgenommen. Eine Form zu finden, sie mit dem Kunstkontext in Beziehung zu setzen – und zwar nicht nur ästhetisch –, diese Aufgabe liess mich ein bisschen im Dunkeln tappen. Soweit mir bekannt war, als ich diese Recherche zur Position der Frau in der internationalen Arbeitsteilung 1986 begann, beschränkte sich die Debatte um die mexikanische Grenze vor allem auf sozioökonomische Aspekte. Ich bezog meine Informationen aus Berichten von NGOs (Nichtregierungsorganisationen), von Arbeitsorganisationen und aus akademischen Texten von AnthropologInnen, ÖkonomInnen und SoziologInnen. Gill Perez sagte mir, ich müsse mich entscheiden, ob ich auf Marx oder Tolstoi machen will. Mir ist die Entscheidung zwischen einem theoretischen oder einem metaphorischen Ansatz immer schwer gefallen. Stattdessen suchte ich nach Wegen, wie ich harte Informationen in eine kulturelle und ästhetische Sprache verarbeiten konnte, die westliche Standards von Repräsentation visuell und institutionell kritisch hinterfragen würden. Das *Border Project* nahm sich vor, Gender-Theorien und globale Ökonomie kulturell miteinander zu artikulieren. Dieses Projekt hat mich deshalb so lange Zeit interessiert, weil es zentrale Punkte berührt, um die es mir als Kulturproduzentin in den letzten Jahren ging. Für eine Künstlerin ist es einfacher oder vielleicht dringender, eine solche Synthese zu suchen, denn die Frage der Positionierung ist für eine Frau nie nur eine berufliche Entscheidung (vor allem keine, die zwischen zwei Meistererzählungen – Marx oder Tolstoi – zu wählen hätte), da sie im Bedeutungssystem von Bild und Sprache immer schon positioniert ist. Wie stark ich in diese kulturellen Prozesse eingebunden war, zeigte sich, als ich mich selbst verlagerte.

Ende 1991 verliess ich New York und kehrte nach Europa zurück. Die Mauer war weg und dies versprach auch eine kulturelle Aufbruchstimmung. Ausserdem waren die politisch engagierten Jahre der New Yorker Kunstszene vorbei; es war Zeit zu gehen. Doch als ich in Europa ankam, wo die Liberalisierung des Weltmarkts und der Globalisierungswahn jegliche kulturellen Ziele und jeglichen kritischen Dialog zu beherrschen schien, erlitt ich erst einmal einen Kulturschock. Die Kunstszene, die ich in Zürich vorfand, war von der Jugendbewegung der frühen 80er-Jahre offensichtlich wenig stimuliert worden. Die politischen Aktionen auf kultureller Ebene waren damals vor allem von Film- und VideoaktivistInnen ausgelöst worden, während sich die KünstlerInnen hauptsächlich auf die Besetzung eines leeren Fabrikgebäudes konzentrierten, um kulturellen Arbeitsraum zu gewinnen. Ihre Kunstpraxis blieb innerhalb der bürgerlichen Parameter. Ich sah mich einer Kunstszene gegenüber, die sich mit einem konventionellen Atelier-Galerie-Modus abzufinden schien. Für jemanden, der von einer kritischen post-studio-Bildung herkam und die Rolle der Künstlerin nicht so sehr als diejenige einer Produzentin, sondern als die einer Vermittlerin sah und sich zudem längst vom Kunstwerk zum Text bewegt hatte, konnte diese Vorgehensweise wohl kaum eine interessante Positionierung im weiteren sozialen Kontext darstellen, da sie zum einen den Kunstmarkt als den institutionellen Rahmen akzeptiert und zum anderen die Produktion derart in den Mittelpunkt stellt, als hätten die Wandlungsprozesse in den 60er-Jahren, die man als Postmodernismus bezeichnet, nie stattgefunden. So blieb mir nur die Option, mich mit Institutionen in Verbindung zu setzen, die ein breiteres Verständnis von kultureller Praxis zeigten und durch ihre Aktivitäten bereits soziale, kulturelle und politische Anliegen verbanden. Das Projekt *Zwischenräume – Interespacios* war mein erstes kollaboratives Community-Projekt, das ich mit Femia, einem Zentrum für Bildung und Kultur für Migrantinnen in Zürich konzipierte und realisierte. Während sich das *Border Project* mit den weiteren Rahmenbedingungen der Frauen an der Grenze zwischen Industrie- und Entwicklungsländer befasste, konzentrierte sich dieses Gemeinschaftsprojekt mehr auf die psychologischen und sozialen Aspekte von Identität als Resultat von kultureller Verschiebung. Dieses Projekt war auch eine Gelegenheit, mich mit meiner eigenen Migrationserfahrung zu beschäftigen, denn meine Ausreise nach Mexiko und New York 1983 und die Rückkehr nach Zürich 1991 hatten beide Male mein kulturelles Selbstverständnis durcheinander geworfen.

Im deutschsprachigen Europa hielt die postkoloniale Kritik in der Kunst erst Mitte der 90er-Jahre Einzug mit einer Reihe Symposia in Deutschland und mit dem Projekt des steirischen herbst, *Inklusion-Exklusion* in Österreich. Clementine Deliss' Ausstellung *Lotte oder die Transformation des Objekts*, die Ende 1990 in Graz stattfand, bildete eine Ausnahme. Was in den USA als Politik der Repräsentation, der hybriden Identitäten, der Dislozierung, der Intertextualität und der Selbstpositionierung diskutiert wurde, lief hier unter der groben Rubrik von "Ausländerproblemen" und "Rassismus". Doch der sture Fokus auf Rasse und Differenz wird den komplexen kulturellen und sozialen Bedingungen heutiger Diaspora-Gesellschaften nicht gerecht. Er reproduziert noch die binären Oppositionen (uns/die), die dem kolonialen Konzept zugrunde liegen. *Zwischenräume* und die folgenden Projekte wurden als Beitrag zu einer feineren Differenzierung im ästhetischen und diskursiven Feld konzipiert und formulieren Positionen, die den fundamental statischen Begriff von kultureller Identität aufzulösen versuchen oder ihn zumindest als ambivalent präsentieren.

Die westliche Kunst hat gewisse Gepflogenheiten im Umgang mit nicht-westlichen KünstlerInnen und ihren Produktionen entwickelt. Die 90er-Jahre sahen enorme Veränderungen, als sich Konzerne und

Kunst gleichermassen in eine Phase totaler Expansion begaben. Der Kampf und die Verhandlungen, die diese Veränderungen begleiten, tauchen in zwei weiteren kollaborativen Projekten auf: *Mediale Identitäten* und *Kültür – ein Genderprojekt aus Istanbul*. Es genügte nicht mehr, eine Kritik der bestehenden Repräsentationen des Anderen zu formulieren. Das Privileg einer europäischen Künstlerin an internationalen Ausstellungen teilzunehmen, an aussereuropäische KulturproduzentInnen weiterzureichen und diese Beziehung als Teil des Kunstprojektes zu verhandeln, erwies sich als eine effektivere Form der institutionellen Kritik.

Zudem gab es ein wachsendes Bedürfnis, Fragen des Geschlechts und anderer Kategorien von Identität in den weiteren Transformationen des öffentlichen Raums zu verorten, vor allem in der städtischen Realität. *Kültür* befasst sich damit, wie Geschlechterbeziehungen in der Repräsentation reguliert werden, in der Öffentlichkeit der Stadt, in einer Unterhändler-Ökonomie, in Migrationsmassnahmen. Dieses Projekt verbindet eine geschlechterspezifische soziale und ökonomische Analyse mit der institutionellen Kritik des Kunstkontextes. Die Teilnahme an der Internationalen Kunst Biennale in Istanbul in 1997, eine Veranstaltung, die direkt aus dem Globalisierungswunsch einer Stadt resultiert, die sich aggressiv um finanzielles Kapital bewirbt, die sich aber mit radikalen Marginalisierungsmassnahmen gegen die lokale weibliche für die westliche Ökonomie arbeitende Bevölkerung stellt, verzahnte meine beiden Hauptanliegen.

Die euphorische Anwendung digitaler Medien in Kunst- und Kulturräumen lässt eine umfassende geschlechterspezifische Analyse des globalen Kapitals in Bezug auf die Kultur- und Informationsindustrie wichtiger werden. Die Rückkehr in die mexikanische Grenzstadt Ciudad Juarez, mit dem Ziel, den Einfluss von NAFTA auf die Situation der Frauen in der Hightech-Industrie zu erforschen, ist eine Konsequenz davon. Mit dem Video *Performing the Border* versuche ich, eine materialistische Perspektive der internationalen Arbeitstrennung mit einem diskursiveren Umgang mit der Art von Subjektivität, Identität und Sexualität, die sich in diesen transnationalen Zonen bilden, zu kombinieren. Die Künstlerin Bertha Jottar, die sich jahrelang am Border Art Workshop in Tijuana beteiligte und jetzt in New York lebt, steuert Wesentliches zum diskursiven Verständnis des Grenzkonzeptes bei, im Video sowie in diesem Buch.

So wichtig mir die Dekonstruktion existierender Repräsentationen in meiner Kunstpraxis gewesen ist, so notwendig finde ich es auch, vor Ort zu gehen, das Leben der Leute sowie die bebauten und bewohnten Räume zu verstehen und eine eigene Version von Bildern herzustellen. Es ist klar, dass die Subjektivitäten, die durch die neuen Technologien und durch die Hypermobilität im industriellen Norden produziert werden, sich radikal von denen unterscheiden, die der Transnationalismus im Süden produziert. Und wenn wir uns im neoliberalen Hightech-Diskurs einer stark identitätsnivelierenden Tendenz gegenübersehen, während die Subjekte im Süden durch sexualisierende und ethnifizierende Marker überdeterminiert werden, wird es zu diesem Zeitpunkt wichtig, auf Singularität, Spezifität und Lokalität zu insistieren. Im Essay *Performing the Border* versuche ich die unterschiedlichen Formen von Subjektivität, die an der Grenze entstehen, genauer zu untersuchen. Ich versuche zu verstehen, wie sie durch Repräsentationen, aber auch durch reale Lebens- und Arbeitsbedingungen geformt werden.

In ihrem Text *Diaspora, Grenze und transnationale Identitäten* bringt Avtar Brah am Anfang dieses Buches Konzepte von Diaspora, Grenze und der Politik des Ortes mit in einer historisierten Analyse aktueller transnationaler Bewegungen von Personen, Information, Kultur, Gemeinschaften und Kapital zusammen. In ihrem Konzept von Diaspora bezieht sie sich auf eine multiple Verortung sowohl innerhalb territorialer, kultureller und psychischer Grenzen als auch in ihrer Überschreitung. Dieses Konzept ist zugleich hilfreich und zukunftsorientiert, weil es eine minoritäre Position nie gegen eine andere ausspielt, sondern Identität so theoretisiert, dass sie der Komplexität von Diaspora-Gesellschaften gerecht wird.

In ihrem Essay *Überleben und Exploraterrarismus* analysiert Yvonne Volkart geschlechterspezifische Grenzen in einer Reihe von Videoarbeiten, von denen sich die einen auf die europäische Ostgrenze beziehen und sich andere gleichzeitig über verschiedene nationale und kulturelle Grenzen hinwegsetzen. Sie führt die spezifischen Ästhetiken vor, mit denen die KünstlerInnen Identitätsentwürfe für eine Existenz im posthumanen Raum kartografieren, wo verschiedene Topografien (Fernsehzimmer, Belgrad, Galerie-Raum, Peepshow, Discos) zur Grundbedingung personen- und ortsübergreifender biografischer Einschreibung und Partizipation werden. Wo KünstlerInnen mit der Realisierung des Begehrens nach Subjektwerdung operieren, spielen auch Orte in ihrer realen und symbolischen Bedeutung eine zentrale Rolle. Ann-Sofi Sidén z. B. untersucht die Lebensbedingungen von Prostituierten aus verschiedenen Ländern Osteuropas an der deutsch-tschechischen Grenze. Sie wählte Dubi als spezifischen Ort für ihre Recherche, obwohl jene Situation lediglich ein Symptom in einer ganzen Reihe von Verkettungen ist.

Meine eigenen Untersuchungen an der Grenze haben gezeigt, dass internationale Arbeit im Süden nicht nur feminisiert ist, sondern auch sexualisiert; dass die weibliche Arbeitskraft in ihrer Sexualität interpelliert (angerufen) wird und dass Prostitution ein struktureller Teil globalen Kapitalismus ist. Wie ich im Border-Essay ausführe, unterzieht sich der Begriff des "Selbst" Wandlungen, die Fragen von Grenze, Geschlecht und sexuellen Beziehungen betreffen, und dies ist speziell in der elektronischen Landschaft so. Auf diskursiver Ebene untersucht das Projekt *Writing Desire* elektronische Kommunikationstechnologien auf die Grenze zwischen privaten Fantasien und öffentlicher Sphäre und auf deren Kapitalisierung hin. Unter den Anzeichen einer wachsenden Kommerzialisierung von emotionellen und sexuellen Beziehungen geht das Video der beschleunigten Entwicklung des Brautmarktes nach, wo sich virtuelle und reale Bewegungen von weiblichen Körpern überlagern.

Meine jetzige Recherche für ein Video-Projekt in Zusammenarbeit mit Simin Farkhondeh konzentriert sich auf die Sexualisierung internationaler Arbeit und Migration und zeichnet die illegalen transnationalen Wege der Frauen nach, die in die Prostitution verkauft werden. In *Trafficking and Trading* (Arbeitstitel) soll Frauenhandel aus einer globalen Perspektive angeschaut werden. Ehemalige "Rest & Recreation" Zonen der Amerikanischen Armee in den Philippinen oder burmesische Bordelle in Thailand sind Orte, an denen die militärischen, staatlichen und privat organisierten Strukturen sichtbar werden.

All diese Projekte sind in Zusammenarbeit mit anderen KulturproduzentInnen entstanden, denen ich meinen warmen Dank für ihre Kunst- und Textbeiträge ausspreche und dafür, dass sie das Buch näher an die Art von Kulturpraxis bringen, für die es steht.

# _DIASPORA, BORDER AND TRANSNATIONAL IDENTITIES
Avtar Brah

As we approach the beginning of the twenty-first century we witness a new phase of mass population movements. There has been a rapid increase in migrations across the globe since the 1980s. These mass movements are taking place in all directions. The volume of migration has increased to Australia, North America and Western Europe. Similarly, large-scale population movements have taken place within and between countries of the "South". More recently, events in Eastern Europe and the former Soviet Union have provided impetus for mass movements of people. Some regions previously thought of as areas of emigration are now considered areas of immigration. Economic inequalities within and between regions, expanding mobility of capital, people's desire to pursue opportunities that might improve their chances in life, political strife, wars, and famine are some of the factors that remain at the heart of the impetus behind these migrations. People on the move may be labour migrants (both "documented" and "undocumented"), highly qualified specialists, entrepreneurs, students, refugees and asylum seekers or the household members of previous migrants. In 1990, the International Organisation for Migration estimated that there were over 80 million such "migrants". Of these, approximately 30 million were said to be in "irregular situations" and another 15 million were refugees or asylum seekers. By 1992, some estimates put the total number of migrants at 100 million, of whom 20 million were refugees and asylum seekers (Castles and Miller 1993). The notion of "economic migrant" as referring primarily to labour migrants was always problematic, not least because it served to conceal the economic proclivities of those who were likely to be placed outside such a definition, for example industrialists or commercial entrepreneurs. However, these new migrations call this construct even more seriously into question as global events increasingly render untenable such distinctions as those held between the so called "political" and "economic" refugees.

These population movements are set against major re-alignments in the world political order. New transnational configurations of power articulate with fundamental transformations in the political economy of late twentieth-century capitalism. Globalising tendencies set in motion centuries ago acquire new meanings in a world characterised by the increasing dominance of multinational capital; the flexible specialisation of labour and products; and the revolutionising impact of new technologies in production, distribution and communication. The emergent new international division of labour depends quite crucially upon women workers. Indeed, whether working in electronics factories or textile sweatshops, performing outwork from their homes, or (rather more atypically) holding jobs in the commanding heights of the economy – women have become emblematic figures of contemporary regimes of accumulation. It is not surprising, therefore, that women comprise a growing segment of the migrations taking place in all regions and of all types of migrations. This feminisation of migration is especially noticeable in particular instances. For example, women form the majority of Cape Verdian workers migrating to Italy, Filipinos to the Middle East or Thais to Japan. Similarly, women predominate in a number of refugee movements (Castles and Miller 1993).

These recent migrations are creating new displacements, new diasporas. In the context of a proliferation of new border crossings the language of "borders" and of "diasporas" acquires a new currency. Various new scholarly journals have one or the other of these terms in their titles. Yet, surprisingly, there have been relatively few attempts made to theorise these terms. This is partly because, as James Clifford (1994) rightly observes, it is not easy to avoid the slippage between diaspora as a theoretical concept, diasporic "discourses" and the distinct historical "experiences" of diaspora. They seem to invite a kind of "theorising", Clifford continues, that is always embedded in particular maps and histories. Yet, perhaps this embeddedness is precisely why it becomes necessary to mark out the conceptual terrain that these words construct and traverse if they are to serve as theoretical tools.

This text is precisely such an attempt to explore the analytical purchase of these terms. It delineates specific features which may serve to distinguish diaspora as a theoretical concept from the historical "experiences" of diaspora. Inter alia I suggest that the concept of diaspora should be understood in terms of historically contingent "genealogies" in the Foucauldian sense; that is, as an ensemble of investigative technologies that historicise trajectories of different diasporas and analyse their relationality across fields of social relations, subjectivity and identity. (...)

Inscribed within the idea of diaspora is the notion of "border". The second part of this text is organised around the theme of borders. I address border as a political construct as well as an analytical category, and explore some of the strengths and limitations of the idea of "border theory", especially as it has been mobilised via Gilles Deleuze and Felix Guattari's concept of "deterritorialisation" and applied to the analysis of literary texts.

The concepts of border and diaspora together reference the theme of location. This point warrants emphasis because the very strong association of notions of diaspora with displacement and dislocation means that the experience of *location* can easily dissolve out of focus. The third section is centred on this topic and explores the contradictions of and between location and dislocation. As a point of departure, I use the long-standing feminist debate around issues of home, location, displacement and dislocation, which came up with the concept of a *politics of location* as locationality in contradiction. Self-reflexive autobiographical accounts often provide critical insights into the politics of location (...)

The concepts of *diaspora, border* and *politics of location* together offer a conceptual grid for historicised analyses of contemporary trans/national movements of people, information, cultures, commodities and capital. The three concepts are immanent. Part four of this essay discusses a new concept that I wish to propose, namely that of *diaspora space* as the site of this immanence. Diaspora space is the intersectionality of diaspora, border, and dis/location as a point of confluence of economic, political, cultural and psychic processes. It addresses the global condition of culture, economics and politics as a site of "migrancy" and "travel" which seriously problematises the subject position of the "native". My central argument is that diaspora space as a conceptual category is "inhabited" not only by those who have migrated and their descendants but equally by those who are constructed and represented as indigenous. In other words, the concept of diaspora space (as opposed to that of diaspora) includes the entanglement of genealogies of dispersion with those of "staying put". (...)

## Thinking through the concept of diaspora

First, a note about the term *diaspora*. The word derives from the Greek *dia*, "through", and *speirein*, "to scatter". According to Webster's Dictionary in the United States, diaspora refers to a "dispersion from". Hence, the word embodies a notion of a centre, a locus, a "home" from where the dispersion occurs. It invokes images of multiple journeys. The dictionary also highlights the word"s association with the dispersion of the Jews after the Babylonian exile. Here, then, is an evocation of a diaspora with a particular resonance within European cartographies of displacement; one that occupies a particular space in the European psyche, and is emble-matically situated within Western iconography as the diaspora par excellence. Yet, to speak of late twentieth-century diasporas is to take such ancient diasporas as a point of departure rather than necessarily as "models", or as what Safran (1991) describes as the "ideal type". The dictionary juxtaposition of what the concept signifies in general as opposed to one of its particular referents highlights the need to subject the concept to scrutiny, to consider the ramifications of what it connotes or denotes and to consider its analytical value.

At the heart of the notion of diaspora is the image of a journey. Yet not every journey can be understood as diaspora. Diasporas are clearly not the same as casual travel. Nor do they normatively refer to temporary sojourns. Paradoxically, diasporic journeys are essentially about settling down, about putting down roots "elsewhere". These journeys must be historicised if the concept of diaspora is to serve as a useful heuristic device. The question is not simply about *who travels* but *when, how, and under what circumstances*? What socio-economic, political and cultural conditions mark the trajectories of these journeys? What regimes of power inscribe the formation of a specific diaspora? In other words, it is necessary to analyse what makes one diasporic formation similar to or different from another: it is possible, for instance, that the diaspora in question was constituted by conquest and colonisation, as has been the case with several European diasporas. Or it might have resulted from the capture or removal of a group through slavery or systems of indentured labour, as, for example, in the formation respectively of African and Asian diasporas in the Caribbean. Alternatively, people may have had to desert their home as a result of expulsion and persecution, as has been the fate of a number of Jewish groups at various points in history. Or they may have been forced to flee in the wake of political strife, as has been the experience of many contemporary groups of refugees such as the Sri Lankans, Somalis and Bosnian Muslims. Perhaps the dispersion occurred as a result of conflict and war, resulting in the creation of a new nation state on the territory previously occupied by another, as has been the experience of Palestinians since the formation of Israel. On the other hand, a population movement could have been induced as part of global flows of labour, the trajectory of many, for example, African-Caribbeans, Asians, Cypriots or Irish people in Britain.

If the circumstances of leaving are important, so, too, are those of arrival and settling down. How and in what ways do these journeys conclude and intersect in specific places, specific spaces and specific historical conjunctures? How and in what ways is a group inserted within the social relations of class, gender, racism, sexuality or other axes of differentiation in the country to which it migrates? The manner in which a group comes to be "situated" in and through a wide variety of discourses, economic processes, state policies and institutional practices is critical to its future. This "situatedness" is central to how different groups come to be relationally positioned in a given context. I emphasise the question of relational positioning, for it enables us to begin to deconstruct the regimes of power which operate to differentiate one group from another, to represent them as similar or different, to include or exclude them from constructions of the "nation" and the body politic; it enables us to begin to deconstruct the very forces which inscribe people as juridical, political, and psychic subjects. It is axiomatic that each empirical diaspora must be analysed in its historical specificity. But the issue is not simply about the need for historicising or addressing the specificity of a particular diasporic experience, important though this is. Rather, the *concept* of diaspora concerns the historically variable forms of *relationality* within and between diasporic formations. It is about relations of power that draw similarities and differences between and across changing diasporic constellations. In other words, the concept of diaspora centres on the *configurations of power, which differentiate diasporas internally as well as situate them in relation to one another*.

Diasporas, in the sense of distinctive historical experiences, are often composite formations made up of many journeys to different parts of the globe, each with its own history, its own particularities. Each such diaspora is an interweaving of multiple strands of journeys, a text of many distinctive and, perhaps, even disparate narratives. This is true, among others, of the African, Chinese, Irish, Jewish, Palestinian and South Asian diasporas. For example, South Asians in Britain have a different, albeit related, history from South Asians in Africa, the Caribbean, Fiji, South East Asia or the USA. Given these differences, can we speak of a "South Asian diaspora" other than as a mode of description of a particular cluster of migrations? The answer depends crucially upon how the relationships between these various components of the cluster are conceptualised.

I would suggest that it is the *economic, political and cultural specificities linking these components that are signified by the concept of diaspora*. This means that these multiple journeys may configure into one journey via a confluence of narratives as it is lived and re-lived, produced, reproduced and transformed through individual as well as collective memory and re-memory. It is within this confluence of narrativity that a "diasporic community" is imagined differently under different historical circumstances. By this I mean that the identity of the diasporic imagined community is far from fixed or predetermined. It is constituted within the crucible of the materiality of everyday life; in the everyday stories we tell ourselves individually and collectively.

All diasporic journeys are composite in another sense too. They are embarked upon, lived and re-lived through multiple modalities: modalities, for example, of gender, "race", class, religion, language and generation. As such, all diasporas are differentiated, heterogeneous, contested spaces, just as is implicated in the construction of a common "we". It is important, therefore, to be attentive to the nature and type of processes in and through which the collective "we" is constituted. Who is empowered and who is disempowered in a specific construction of the "we"? How are social divisions negotiated in the construction of the "we"? What is the relationship of this "we" to the respective "others"? Who are these others? This is a critical question. It is generally assumed that there is a single dominant other whose overarching omnipresence circumscribes constructions of the "we". Hence, there tends to be an emphasis on bipolar oppositions: black/white, Jew/Gentile, Arab/Jew, English/Irish, Hindu/Muslim. The centrality of a particular binary opposition as the basis of political cleavage and social division in a given situation may make it imperative to foreground it. The problem remains, however, as to how such binaries should be analysed. Binaries can all too readily be assumed to represent ahistorical, universal constructs. This may help to conceal the workings of historically specific socio-economic, political and cultural circumstances that mark the terrain on which a given binary comes to assume its particular significance. That is, what are actually the effects of institutions, discourses and practices may come to be represented as immutable, trans-historical divisions. As a consequence, a binary that should properly be an object of deconstruction may gain acceptance as an unproblematic given.

It is especially necessary to guard against such tendencies at the present moment, when the surfacing of old and new racisms, violent religious conflicts and the horrors of "ethnic cleansing" make it all too easy to slide into an acceptance of contextually variable phenomena as trans-historical universalisms that are then presumed to be an inevitable part of human nature. On the contrary, the binary is a socially constructed category whose trajectory warrants investigation in terms of how it was constituted, regulated, embodied and contested, rather than taken as if it had always already been present. A bipolar construction might be addressed fruitfully and productively as an object of analysis and a tool of deconstruction; that is, as a means of investigating the conditions of its formation, its implication in the inscription of hierarchies and its power to mobilise collectivities.

The point is that there are multiple others embedded within and across binaries, albeit one or more may be accorded priority within a given discursive formation. For instance, a discourse may be primarily about gender and, as such, it may centre upon gender-based binaries (although, of course, a binarised construction is not always inevitable). But this discourse will not exist in isolation from others, such as those signifying class, "race", religion or generation. The specificity of each is framed in and through fields of representation of the other. What is at stake, then, is not simply a question of some generalised notion of, say, masculinity and femininity, but whether or not these representations of masculinity and femininity are racialised; how and in what ways they inflect class; whether they reference lesbian, gay, heterosexual or some other sexuality; how they feature age and generation; how and if they invoke religious authority. Binaries, thus, are intrinsically different and unstable. What matters most is how and why, in a given context, a specific binary – e.g. black/white – takes shape, acquires a seeming coherence and stability, and configures with other constructions, such as Jew/Gentile or male/female. In other words, *how these signifiers slide into one another in the articulation of power*.

We may elaborate the above point with reference to racialised discourses and practices. The question then reformulates itself in terms of the relationship at a specific moment between different forms of racism. Attention is shifted to the forms in which class, gender, sexuality or religion, for instance, might figure within these racisms, and to the specific signifier(s) – colour, physiognomy, religion, culture, etc. – around which these differing racisms are constituted. An important aspect of the issue will be the relational positioning of groups by virtue of these racisms. How, for instance, are African, Caribbean, South Asian and white Muslims differentially constructed within anti-Muslim racism in present-day Britain? Similarly, how are blacks, Chicanos, Chinese, Japanese or South Koreans differentiated in the USA within its racialised formations? What are the economic, political, cultural and psychic effects of these differential racialisations on the lives of these groups? What are the implications of these effects in terms of how members of one racialised group might relate to those of another? Do these effects produce conditions that foster sympathetic identification and solidarity across groups, or do they create divisions? Of central concern in addressing such questions are the power dynamics, which usher in racialised social relations and inscribe racialised modes of subjectivity and identity. My argument is that these racisms are not simply parallel racisms but are intersecting modalities of *differential racialisations marking positionality across articulating fields of power*. (...)

If, as Khachig Tölölian (1991) suggests, contemporary diasporas are the "exemplary communities of the transnational moment", and the term now overlaps and resonates with meanings of words such as migrant, immigrant, expatriate, refugee, guest worker or exile, then the concept of diaspora that I am seeking to elaborate is *an interpretive frame referencing the economic, political and cultural dimensions of these contemporary forms of migrancy*. As such, it interrogates other discourses surrounding the social relations of migrancies in this phase of late twentieth-century capitalism. (...)

## Diaspora and minority

In Britain there has been a tendency to discuss diaspora primarily along a "majority/minority" axis. This dichotomy surfaced in post-war Britain as an element underpinning the processes of racialisation. The term "minority" was applied primarily to British citizens of African, Caribbean and Asian descent – a postcolonial code that operated as a polite substitute for "coloured people". The elaboration of the discourse of "minorities" marks the fraught histories, now widely documented, of immigration control, policing, racial violence, inferiorisation and discrimination that has become the hallmark of daily life for these groups. This discourse also resonates with older connotations of the term in classical liberal political theory, where women, subjugated colonial peoples and working classes tend to be associated with the status of being a "minor in tutelage" (Spelman 1988; Lloyd 1990; Philips 1991). Even when the majority/minority dichotomy is mobilised in order to signal unequal power relations, as is the case in studies that document discrimination against "minorities", its usage remains problematic. This is partly because the numerical referent of this dichotomy encourages a literal reading, reducing the problem of power relations to one of numbers, with the result that the repeated circulation of the discourse has the effect of naturalising rather than challenging the power differential. Moreover, conceptualising social relations primarily in terms of dichotomous oppositions, as I have pointed out above, fails to take full account of the multidimensionality of power. (...)

The concept of diaspora that I wish to propose here is embedded within a multi-axial understanding of power; one that problematises the notion of "minority/majority". A multi-axial performative conception of power highlights the ways in which a group constituted as a "minority" along one dimension of differentiation may be constructed as a "minority" along another. And since all these markers of "difference" represent articulating and performative facets of power, the "fixing" of collectivities along any singular axis is seriously called into question. (...)

# The local and the global of diaspora

A combination of the local and the global is always an important aspect of diasporic identities. But the relationship between these elements varies. The diasporas proliferating at the end of the twentieth century will, in some respects, be experienced quite differently in this age of new technologies and rapid communications compared with the time when it took months to travel or communicate across the seas. The impact of electronic media, together with growing opportunities for fast travel, invests Marshall McLuhan's idea of "the global village" with new meanings. Simultaneous transmission to countries linked by satellite means that an event happening in one part of the world can be "watched together" by people in different parts of the globe. Electronic information "super-highways" usher in new forms of communication unimaginable only two decades ago. These developments have important implications for the construction of new and varied "imagined communities". Having said this, it does not necessarily follow that there will be a single overarching one-way process of cultural homogenisation, not least because global consumption of visual or other forms of culture is mediated in complex ways (Hall et al. 1992).

The effects are not totally predictable, for there can be many and varied readings of the same image. The same image can elicit a diversity of meanings, signalling the effects of personal biography and cultural context on processes of meaning production. In other words, the compression of time and space and the consequent "shrinking" of the world can have contradictory outcomes. There are, on the one hand, possibilities for greater awareness of global inequalities leading to transnational modes of cooperation in the development of strategies to combat such inequalities. New forms of political solidarity and activism could emerge to meet the challenges of this era. There could be the release of much creative energy, resulting in transformation in politics, art, music, literature and other forms of cultural production. On the other hand, globalism today is the very means of encoding the changing post-Cold War world order. It is the vehicle for securing cultural hegemony in the age of "G-Eightism" now that, as of July 1994, Russia has been admitted to the political, if not yet the economic, inner sanctum of the Group of Seven. This globalism of late capitalism inscribes the economic and political terrain against which all these new migrations are taking place, a terrain with which both the old and new diasporas must contend. I develop this point further in the next section. *Diasporic identities are at once local and global. They are networks of transnational identifications encompassing "imagined" and "encountered" communities.* (...)

# Thinking through borders

Embedded within the concept of diaspora is the notion of the border, and, indeed, it is not possible to address the concept of diaspora without considering its relationship to the idea of borders. It is to this construct that I now turn.

Borders: arbitrary dividing lines that are simultaneously social, cultural and psychic; territories to be patrolled against those who are construed or constructed as outsiders, aliens, the Others; forms of demarcation where the very act of prohibition inscribes transgression; zones where fear of the other is the fear of the self; places where claims to ownership – claims to "mine", "yours" and "theirs" – are staked out, contested, defended and fought over.

Gloria Anzaldua's theorisation of border and borderlands provides important insights. Two are especially important for my purposes here. First, she uses these terms as a means of reflecting upon social conditions of life at the Texas/US Southwest-Mexican border where, as she says, "the Third World grates against the first and bleeds" (Anzaldua 1987: 3). She also invokes the concept of the border as a metaphor for psychological, sexual, spiritual, cultural, class and racialised boundaries. If understood in terms of my discussion of "difference", the Anzaldua text speaks of borders simultaneously as social relation, the everyday lived experience, and subjectivity/identity. Borders are arbitrary constructions. Hence, in a sense, they are always metaphors. But, far from being mere abstractions of a concrete reality, metaphors are part of the discursive materiality of power relations. Metaphors can serve as powerful inscriptions of the effects of political borders.

Each border embodies a unique narrative, even while it resonates with common themes with other borders. Such metaphoric materiality of each border calls attention to its specific features: to the geographical and/or psychic territories demarcated; to the experi-ences of particular groups of people who are sundered apart or affected in other ways by the creation of a certain border zone; or the old and new states which may be abolished or installed by the drawing of particular boundaries. How is a border regulated or policed? Who is kept out and why? What are the realities for those stigmatised as undesirable border-crossers? The realities, for instance, of proclaiming a gay or lesbian identity in a social context saturated with homophobia and heterosexism, as Anzaldua shows. Or the realities of present-day labour migrants negotiating the immigration apparatus of the state: difficulties of gaining visas, confronting immigration checks, detentions and deportations and in some circumstances even facing the possibility of losing one's life.

The USA-Mexico border typifies the conditions of contemporary migrancy. It encapsulates certain common thematics, which frequently come into play whenever "overdeveloped" countries institute measures to selectively control the entry of peoples from economically "underdeveloped" segments of the globe. This border speaks the fate of formerly colonised people presently caught up in the workings of a global economy dominated by transnational capital and mediated by politics of "G-Sevenism" or "G-Eightism". These new regimes of accumulation are characterised by "flexibility" (or what perhaps will increasingly be referred to as "adaptability", the term favoured by the G7 summit in July 1994) in labour processes, labour markets, commodities and patterns of consumption. There is an intensification in the segmentation of the labour market into a comparatively small sector of highly skilled core staff at the managerial and professional level, and a much larger group of employees who are often called "peripheral" workers but whose labour is in fact central to the functioning of the global economy. The core staff holds well-paid, full-time, permanent jobs with good promotion and re-training prospects. They are expected to be flexible and adaptable and, when required, geographically mobile, but any inconvenience that this may generate is offset by the security of entitlement to pensions, insurance and other benefits. The so-called "peripheral" employees working in the "secondary labour market" are generally poorly paid, and they comprise two distinct sub-groups. The first of these consists of full-time employees performing skilled or semi-skilled jobs. High turnover rates are fairly typical of this type of employment. The second group, which includes a wide variety of part-timers, temporary staff, fixed-term contract holders, job sharers, and home workers, provides an even greater level of flexibility. Not surprisingly there is in this secondary labour market a predominance of women, immigrant and migrant workers (both male and female) and their descendants, as well as other low-paid categories of worker. The late twentieth-century forms of transnational movement of capital and people usher in new kinds of diasporic formations. The rapid rate of technological, commercial and organisational innovation is accompanied by a proliferation of new methods of production, new markets, new products and services and new systems of financing. The accelerated mobility of capital to wherever profitability can be maximised within domestic boundaries or overseas has a particular bearing on population movements. A combination of offshore and onshore relocation of jobs, alongside a continuing demand for migrant labour for certain kinds of low-paid work in the economically advanced "cores" is resulting in an eruption of new borders while the old borders are being subjected to processes of entrenchment or erosion (Sassen 1988; Rouse 1991; Miles 1993). (...)

The growing polarisation of the labour market in the United States has increased demand for Mexican workers to fill the lowest layers of jobs in agriculture, on the assembly line and in the service sector. At the same time, new legal restrictions designed to regulate the flow of migrants have been imposed in the face of intensification of racism and growing political pressure against a background of job losses in certain sectors of the economy. Racism is also fuelled by the fact that certain elements of capital find it increasingly more lucrative to locate some aspects of the labour process in Mexico. Mexican workers now suffer resentment for "taking our jobs" in the USA and in Mexico. These (ropes of resentment construct the worker as an embodiment of capital rather than its contradiction. Thus there emerges the paradox of the "*undocumented worker*" – *needed to service the lower rungs of the economy, but criminalised, forced to go underground, rendered invisible; that is, cast as a phantom, an absent presence that dwells as a shadow in the nooks and crannies wherever low-paid work is performed*. (...)

## The idea of "border theory"

Increasingly, the idea of "border theory" is invoked to refer to scholarship that addresses "borders" both in their geographical and analytical sense. The concept of "deterritorialisation" proposed by Gilles Deleuze and Felix Guattari has been used in a number of analyses of literary texts presumed to constitute "border writing" (Lloyd 1990; Hicks 1991; Calderon and Salvidar 1991). Deleuze and Guattari have identified "deterritorialisation" as a distinctive feature of what they call "minor literature" – that is, literature with its primary characteristics defined in opposition to canonical writing. Minor literature, they contend, is marked by "the deterritorialisation" of language, the connection of the individual to a political immediacy, and the collective assemblage of enunciation" (Deleuze and Guattari 1986 (l975): 13). The concept of deterritorialisation is understood to be the description of the displacement and dislocation of identities, persons and meanings with the moment of alienation and exile located in language and literature. It refers to the effects of a rupture between signifier and signified, so that "all forms come undone, as do all the significations, signifiers, and signifieds to the benefit of an unformed matter of deterritorialised flux, of nonsignifying signs" (ibid.). While the attraction of such a term in analysing literary texts is understandable, its generalised applicability is much more problematic. The literary trope of "border writing" can be important in elucidating certain aspects of border encounters. As Emily Hicks suggests, border writing articulates a textual strategy of translation as opposed to representation She argues that it enacts non-synchronous memory and offers the reader the possibility of practising multidimensional perception. The reader enters a multi-layered semiotic matrix, and experiences multi-lingual, cross-cultural realities. I agree with Hicks that "border writing" offers a rich, multi-faceted and nuanced depiction of border histories. My cautionary note here is aimed at the tendency to conflate "border theory" with the analysis of "border writing", especially when the latter is used as a synonym for literary texts. Literary texts constitute but one element of border textualities, the concept of "territory" as well as its signifieds and significations is a contested site in diaspora and border positionalities, where the issue of territorialisation, deterritorialisation or reterritorialisation is a matter of political struggle. The outcomes of these contestations cannot be predicted in advance. In other words, *the move from a literary text to the "world as text" is much more fraught, contradictory, complex and problematic than is often acknowledged.* (...)

## Diaspora space and the creolisation of theory

The concepts of diaspora, borders and multi-axial locationality together offer a conceptual grid for historicised analyses of con-temporary trans/national movements of people, information, cultures, commodities and capital. The concept of diasporas presupposes the idea of borders. Correspondingly, the concept of border encapsulates the ideas of diasporising processes. The two are closely intertwined with the notion of the politics of location or dislocation. The three concepts are immanent. I wish to propose the concept of diaspora space as the site of this immanence. Diaspora space is the intersectionality of diaspora, border and dis/location as a point of confluence of economic, political, cultural and psychic processes. It is where multiple subject positions are juxtaposed, contested, proclaimed or disavowed; where the permitted and the prohibited perpetually interrogate; and where the accepted and the transgressive imperceptibly mingle even while these syncretic forms may be disclaimed in the name of purity and tradition. Here, tradition is itself continually invented even as it may be hailed as originating from the mists of time; what is at stake is the infinite experientality, the myriad processes of cultural fissure and fusion that underwrite contemporary forms of transcultural identities. These emergent identities may only be surreptitiously avowed. Indeed, they may even be disclaimed or suppressed in the face of constructed imperatives of "purity". But they are inscribed in the late twentieth-century forms of syncretism at the core of culture and subjectivity (Hall 1990; Coombes 1992).

The concept of diaspora space references the global condition of "culture as a site of travel" (Clifford 1992) which seriously problematises the subject position of the "native". Diaspora space is the point at which boundaries of inclusion and exclusion, of belonging and otherness, of "us" and "them", are contested. My argument is that diaspora space as a conceptual category is "inhabited", not only by those who have migrated and their descendants, but also by those who are constructed and represented as indigenous. In other words, the concept of diaspora space (as opposed to that of diaspora) includes the entanglement, the intertwining of the genealogies of dispersion with those of "staying put". The diaspora space is the site where *the native is as much a diasporian as the diasporian is the native*. However, by this I do not mean to suggest an undifferentiated relativism. Rather, I see the conceptual category of diaspora space in articulation with four modes of theorising difference, proposed earlier, where "difference" of social relation, experience, sub-jectivity and identity are relational categories situated within multi-axial fields of power relations. The similarities and differences across the different axes of differentiation – class, racism, gender, sexuality, and so on – articulate and disarticulate in the diaspora space, marking as well as being marked by the complex web of power.

In the diaspora space called "England", for example, African-Caribbean, Irish, Asian, Jewish and other diasporas intersect among themselves as well as with the entity constructed as "Englishness", thoroughly re-inscribing it in the process. Englishness has been formed in the crucible of the internal colonial encounter with Ireland, Scotland and Wales; imperial rivalries with other European countries; and imperial conquests abroad. In the post-war period this Englishness is continually reconstituted via a multitude of border crossings in and through other diasporic formations. These border crossings are territorial, political, economic, cultural and psychological. This Englishness is a new ensemble that both appropriates and is in turn appropriated by British-based African-Caribbean-ness, Asian-ness, Irish-ness and so on. Each of these formations has its own specificity, but it is an ever-changing specificity that adds to as well as imbues elements of the other. What I am proposing here is that border crossings do not occur only across the dominant/dominated dichotomy, but that, equally, there is traffic within cultural formations of the subordinated groups, and that these journeys are not always mediated through the dominant culture(s). In my scheme such cultural ensembles as British Asian-ness, British Caribbean-ness or British Cypriot-ness are crosscutting rather than mutually exclusive configurations. The interesting question, then, is how these British identities take shape; how they are internally differentiated; how they interrelate with one another and with other British identities; and how they mutually reconfigure and decentre received notions of Englishness, Scottishness, Welshness, or Britishness. *My argument is that they are not "minority" identities, nor are they at the periphery of something that sees itself as located at the centre, although they may be represented as such.* Rather, through processes of decentring, these new political and cultural formations continually challenge the minoritising and peripheralising impulses of the cultures of dominance. Indeed, it is in this sense that Catherine Hall (1992) makes the important claim that Englishness is just another ethnicity.

I have argued that feminist theorisation of the politics of location is of critical relevance to understanding border positionalities. This, however, is not to minimise the importance of other theoretical and political strands in illuminating diasporising border processes. In-sights drawn from analyses of colonialism, imperialism, class and gay and lesbian politics, for instance, are equally indispensable. Earlier, we noted the growing currency of the term "border theory" to reference analytical perspectives that, inter alia, address some of these aspects. This term jostles with others, such as "post-colonial theory" and "diaspora theory". Here, I am less concerned about the overlaps or differences between and across these conceptual terrains. The point I wish to stress is that these theoretical constructs are best understood as constituting *a point of confluence and intersectionality* where insights emerging from these fields inhere in the production of analytical frames capable of addressing multiple, intersecting axes of differentiation. In other words, it is a space of/for theoretical crossovers that foreground processes of power inscribing these inter-relationalities, a kind of *theoretical creolisation*. Such creolised envisioning is crucial, in my view, if we are to address fully the contradictions of modalities of enunciation, identities, positionalities and standpoints that are simultaneously "inside" and "outside". It is necessary in order to decode the polymorphous compoundedness of social relations and subjectivity. The concept of diaspora space, which I have attempted to elaborate here, is firmly embedded in a theoretical creolisation of the type described above.

This text is a shortened version of Chapter 8 of Avtar Brah's book *Cartographies of Diaspora. Contesting identities* London and New York: Routledge 1998

# _DIASPORA, GRENZE UND TRANSNATIONALE IDENTITÄTEN
Avtar Brah

Zu Beginn des 21. Jahrhunderts werden wir ZeugInnen einer neuen Phase umfangreicher Migrationsbewegungen, die in den achtziger Jahren begonnen hat und die sich auf alle Regionen der Erde erstreckt. Die Migration geht nicht nur nach Australien, Nordamerika und Westeuropa, sondern spielt sich auch innerhalb und zwischen den Ländern des "Südens" ab. Bis vor kurzem noch haben Ereignisse in Osteuropa und der ehemaligen Sowjetunion Massenauswanderungen provoziert. Inzwischen sind einige Regionen mit einer hohen Auswanderungsquote zu Einwanderungsgebieten geworden. Wirtschaftliche Ungleichgewichte innerhalb und zwischen den Regionen, flüssigere Kapitalströme, der Wunsch nach einer Verbesserung der Lebenschancen, politische Konflikte, Kriege und Hunger sind einige der Ursachen der Migration. Bei Menschen, die auswandern, kann es sich um ArbeitsmigrantInnen ("dokumentierte" wie "undokumentierte") handeln, um hochqualifizierte SpezialistInnen, UnternehmerInnen, StudentInnen, Flüchtlinge und Asylsuchende oder auch um deren Angehörige. Die *International Organisation of Migrants* schätzt, dass die Zahl der "MigrantInnen" im Jahr 1990 bei über 80 Millionen lag. Von diesen seien ungefähr 30 Millionen in "ungewöhnlichen Situationen" und weitere 20 Millionen Flüchtlinge und Asylsuchende (Castles and Miller 1993). Der Begriff des "Wirtschaftsflüchtlings", bezogen auf Menschen, die Arbeit suchen, war immer problematisch. Nicht zuletzt deshalb, weil er die wirtschaftlichen Interessen all jener verschleiert, die eher ausserhalb dieser Definition liegen, beispielsweise Konzernchefs oder UnternehmerInnen. Die neuen Migrationsbewegungen stellen das Konstrukt des "Wirtschaftsflüchtlings" noch stärker in Frage. Die globalen Entwicklungen heben die Unterscheidung zwischen Flüchtlingen aus "politischen" und aus "wirtschaftlichen" Gründen auf.

Die Migrationsbewegungen stehen in Zusammenhang mit radikalen Umwälzungen innerhalb der politischen Weltordnung. Neue transnationale Machtverhältnisse verändern im ausgehenden 20. Jahrhundert die politische Ökonomie des Kapitalismus. Tendenzen zur Globalisierung, die bereits vor Jahrhunderten angestossen wurden, erhalten neue Bedeutung in einer Welt, die durch die zunehmende Dominanz multinationalen Kapitals geprägt wird. Arbeit und Produktion werden flexibler und spezialisierter organisiert, während neue Technologien die Produktion, den Vertrieb und die Kommunikation revolutionieren. Die heraufziehende internationale Arbeitsteilung beruht in hohem Masse auf weiblichen Arbeitskräften. Egal ob sie im elektrotechnischen Bereich, in Textilfabriken oder in Heimarbeit produzieren, oder ob sie (was eher untypisch ist) führende Posten in der Wirtschaft innehaben – Frauen sind die emblematischen Figuren der zeitgenössischen Akkumulation. Es überrascht daher nicht, dass Frauen ein stetig wachsendes Segment der Migrationsbewegungen darstellen. In manchen Fällen fällt die Verweiblichung der Migration besonders auf. Frauen bilden die Mehrheit der Arbeitskräfte, die von den Kapverden nach Italien auswandern, der Filipinos, die in den Mittleren Osten und der ThailänderInnen, die nach Japan gehen. Auch bei vielen Flüchtlingsbewegungen sind die Frauen in der Überzahl (Castles and Miller 1993).

Diese Migrationswellen erzeugen neue Verschiebungen, neue Diasporas. Die Bewegungen über Grenzen hinweg geben den Konzepten der "Grenze" und der "Diaspora" eine aktuelle Bedeutung, und eine Vielzahl von Wissenschaftsmagazinen führt auch den einen oder anderen dieser Begriffe in ihrem Titel. Überraschenderweise wurden aber bislang kaum Ansätze unternommen, diese Begriffe theoretisch zu bestimmen. Zum Teil mag das seinen Grund darin haben, dass es, wie James Clifford (1994) zutreffend feststellt, äusserst schwierig ist, das theoretische Konzept der Diaspora von "Diskursen" der Diaspora und bestimmten historischen "Erfahrungen" der Diaspora zu trennen. Clifford zufolge scheinen all diese Konzepte eine Art der "Theoretisierung" zu verlangen, die stets in bestimmte Kartographien und Geschichten eingebettet ist. Dieses Eingebettetsein ist aber vielleicht gerade der Grund, der es notwendig erscheinen lässt, jenes konzeptuelle Terrain zu bestimmen, das diese Begriffe konstruieren und überschreiten, sollen sie als theoretische Werkzeuge brauchbar sein.

Dieser Text ist ein solcher Versuch, die analytische Kraft dieser Begriffe auszuloten. Er geht bestimmten Merkmalen nach, anhand derer sich das theoretische Konzept der Diaspora von den historischen "Erfahrungen" der Diaspora unterscheidet. Unter anderem schlage ich vor, den Begriff Diaspora im Foucaultschen Sinne historisch kontingenter "Genealogien" aufzufassen, d.h. als Ensemble investigativer Technologien. Diese erlauben es, die Erscheinungsweise unterschiedlicher Diasporas zu historisieren und ihr Beziehungsgefüge im Hinblick auf soziale Verhältnisse, Subjektivität und Identität zu untersuchen. Das Konzept der Diaspora beinhaltet meiner Auffassung nach eine Kritik am Diskurs fixierter Ursprünge. Zugleich berücksichtigt es den Wunsch nach Heimkehr, was allerdings nicht dasselbe ist wie der Wunsch nach "Heimat". Diese Unterscheidung ist wichtig. Nicht zuletzt deshalb, weil nicht alle Diasporas die Ideologie der "Rückkehr" unterstützen. Der Diaspora ist der Begriff der "Grenze" eingeschrieben, weshalb sich der zweite Teil meiner Ausführungen dem Thema der Grenze widmet, die für mich einerseits ein politisches Konstrukt und andererseits eine analytische Kategorie darstellt. Dabei werde ich einige der Stärken und Schwächen von "Grenztheorien" untersuchen, wie sie im Zusammenhang mit der Analyse literarischer Texte, insbesondere am Beispiel von Gilles Deleuzes und Felix Guattaris Konzept der "Deterritorialisierung", deutlich werden.

In der Verknüpfung von Grenze und Diaspora klingt das Thema der Verortung an. Dieser Aspekt ist zu betonen, weil Diaspora meist mit Vertreibung oder Verdrängung assoziiert wird, und so die Erfahrung des Ortes aus dem Blick gerät. Die Widersprüche zwischen Verortung und Ortlosigkeit werden im letzten Teil meines Textes anskizziert. Als Ausgangspunkt dient mir hier die alte feministische Debatte über Heim, Ort, Verschiebung und Vertreibung und die Idee einer "Politik des Ortes". (...)

In ihrer Verknüpfung bilden die Konzepte Diaspora, Grenze und Politik des Ortes ein konzeptuelles Raster, das die historisch informierten Analysen zeitgenössischer trans/nationaler Bewegungen von Menschen, Informationen, Kulturen, Waren und Kapital sichtbar macht. Im vierten Teil dieses Aufsatzes möchte ich ein neues Konzept zur Diskussion stellen: den Raum der Diaspora. Dieser bildet die Schnittstelle von Diaspora, Grenze und Ort/losigkeit, jenen Raum, wo ökonomische, politische, kulturelle und psychische Prozesse zusammenfliessen. Die globale kulturelle, wirtschaftliche und politische Situation erscheint im Rahmen dieses Konzepts als "Zustand der Migration" und "Reise"; die Vorstellung des "Einheimischen" wird in Frage gestellt. Meine zentrale These lautet, dass der Raum der Diaspora nicht nur von den MigrantInnen einschliesslich ihrer Angehörigen "bewohnt" wird, sondern auch von denjenigen, die als einheimisch konstruiert und repräsentiert werden. Anders als die Diaspora verknüpft der Raum der Diaspora Genealogien der Streuung mit denen des "Nicht-vom- Fleck-Weichens".

## Das Konzept der Diaspora durchdenken

Zuerst eine Bemerkung zum Begriff "Diaspora". Das Wort entstammt dem Griechischen und leitet sich ab von dia, "durch", und speirein, "streuen". Dem Webster's Dictionary zufolge bezieht sich Diaspora auf eine "Verstreuung aus" [dispersion from]. Damit impliziert dieser Begriff ein Zentrum, einen Fixpunkt, ein "Heim", und zugleich verschiedene Bilder vom Reisen. Das Wörterbuch betont ausserdem die Verbindung des Begriffs mit der Verstreuung der Juden nach dem babylonischen Exil. In den europäischen Kartographien der Verschiebung, aber auch in der europäischen Psyche nimmt diese Diaspora einen besonderen Platz ein. Sie hat eine geradezu emblematische Funktion. Für aktuelle Überlegungen über die Diaspora sind diese Vorstellungen aber nicht sehr hilfreich. Sie bilden lediglich den Ausgangspunkt, stellen aber keine "Modelle" oder "Idealtypen", wie es Safran (1991) genannt hat, dar. Die im Wörterbuch erkennbare Gegenüberstellung des Allgemeinbegriffs mit einer bestimmten historischen Ausprägung zeigt die Notwendigkeit, das Konzept der Diaspora auf seine analytischen Wert hin zu untersuchen und die Verzweigungen zwischen seinen Konnotationen und seinen Denotationen zu beachten.

Wesentlich für den Begriff der Diaspora ist die Vorstellung der Wanderung, der Reise, wobei aber nicht jede Reise in eine Diaspora mündet. Es geht nicht um das Reisen an sich oder um zeitweise Aufenthalte an anderen Orten. Paradoxerweise hat das Reisen im Zeichen der Diaspora das Ziel, sich woanders niederzulassen und Wurzeln zu schlagen. Diese Reisen müssen historisch betrachtet werden. Die Frage lautet nicht einfach: wer reist, sondern auch wann, wie und unter welchen Umständen? Durch welche sozioökonomischen, politischen und kulturellen Voraussetzungen werden diese Reisen bestimmt? Welche Machtbeziehungen strukturieren eine bestimmte Diaspora? Es gilt, anders formuliert, darum herauszufinden, warum eine diasporische Formation einer anderen ähnelt oder sich von ihr unterscheidet. Ist die Diaspora, wie so viele europäische Diasporas, durch Eroberung und Kolonisierung entstanden, oder ging sie, wie bei den afrikanischen und karibischen Diasporas, aus Gefangennahme und Verschickung von Menschen durch Sklaverei oder ungewollte Arbeitsverhältnisse hervor? Menschen können aber auch durch Vertreibung und Verfolgung dazu gezwungen worden sein, ihre Häuser zu verlassen. Das war das Schicksal vieler jüdischer Gemeinschaften in unterschiedlichen Epochen. Oder sie wurden, wie die aktuelle Beispiele aus Sri Lanka, Somalia und Bosnien-Herzegowina zeigen, infolge politischer Unruhen zur Flucht gezwungen. Die Verstreuung der Menschen kann durch Konflikte und Kriege ausgelöst worden sein, sie kann zur Schaffung eines neuen Nationalstaates geführt haben, der auf dem Grund vormals besetzten Territoriums eines anderen Staates errichtet wurde. Ein Beispiel dafür wären die Palästinenser seit der israelischen Staatsgründung. Migrationswellen können aber auch durch globale Bewegungen von Arbeitskräften ausgelöst worden sein. Das lässt sich bei den afrikanisch-karibischen, asiatischen, zypriotischen oder irischen Einwanderern nach Grossbritannien beobachten.

Nicht weniger wichtig als die Umstände, die zum Verlassen eines Landes geführt haben, sind die Umstände der Ankunft und Niederlassung. Wie und auf welche Weise kommen diese Migrationsbewegungen zu einem Ende und wie überlagern sie sich an bestimmten Orten, in bestimmten Regionen und zu bestimmten historischen Momenten? Wie und auf welche Weise wird eine Gruppe in dem Land, in das sie einwandert, in die Klassen- und Geschlechterverhältnisse, in Rassismus und Sexualität einregistriert oder nach anderen Kategorien der Differenzierung bestimmt? Die Form, in der eine Gruppe durch eine Vielzahl von Diskursen, ökonomischen Prozessen, staatlichen Politiken und institutionalisierten Praktiken "situiert" wird, ist für ihre Zukunft von entscheidender Bedeutung. Diese "Situiertheit" ist zentral für die Frage, wie verschiedene Gruppen in einem bestimmten Kontext relational positioniert werden. Die Frage der relationalen Positionierung möchte ich besonders betonen, weil sie uns ermöglicht, die Machtregimes zu dekonstruieren, die über die Differenzierung der Gruppen untereinander operieren, die sie als ähnlich oder unterschiedlich darstellen, die sie in die Konstruktionen der "Nation" und des Staatswesens einschliessen oder daraus ausschliessen, und die sie als juridische, politische und psychische Subjekte fixieren. Als Axiom gilt, dass jede empirische Diaspora in ihrer historischen Spezifität analysiert werden muss. Das bedeutet allerdings mehr als nur die Spezifität einer bestimmten diasporischen Erfahrung historisch zu erfassen, sichtbar zu machen, so wichtig das auch ist.

Das Konzept der Diaspora bezieht sich vielmehr auf die historische Variabilität der Beziehungen innerhalb und zwischen diasporischen Formationen. Es erstreckt sich auf die Machtbeziehungen, die zwischen wechselnden diasporischen Konstellationen Ähnlichkeiten und Unterschiede erzeugen. Mit anderen Worten, das Konzept der Diaspora bezieht sich auf die Machtkonfigurationen, die Diasporas intern differenzieren und sie zugleich in Beziehung zueinander setzen.

Die Diaspora im Sinne einer historischer Erfahrung ist oftmals eine Ballung vieler gegenläufiger Bewegungen, von denen jede ihre eigene Geschichte, ihre eigenen Besonderheiten aufzuweisen hat. Die Migrationsbewegungen ergeben einen Text nicht nur unterscheidbarer, sondern auch disparater Erzählungen. Erkennen lässt sich das am Beispiel der afrikanischen, chinesischen, irischen, jüdischen, palästinensischen und südasiatischen Diasporas. So haben die Südasiaten in Grossbritannien eine andere Geschichte als in Afrika, der Karibik, auf den Fidschis, in Südostasiens oder den USA, obwohl ihre Geschichten in Beziehung zueinander stehen. Lässt sich bei Berücksichtigung dieser Unterschiede dann noch von einer "südasiatischen Diaspora" im Sinne eines einheitlichen Ensembles sprechen? Die Antwort auf diese Frage hängt in hohem Masse davon ab, wie man sich die Beziehungen zwischen den verschiedenen Elementen dieses Ensembles denkt.

Meiner Auffassung nach bezeichnet das Konzept der Diaspora die ökonomischen, politischen und kulturellen Spezifika, welche diese Elemente oder Geschichten miteinander verknüpfen. Die verschiedenartigen Wanderungsbewegungen verdichten sich zu einer Bewegung, indem ihre Erzählungen verbunden werden: Sie werden gelebt, durch individuelle wie kollektive Erinnerungsleistungen beschworen, bearbeitet und umgearbeitet. In dieser erzählerischen Verdichtung wird die "diasporische Gemeinschaft" in unterschiedlichen historischen Verhältnissen unterschiedlich geschildert. Damit meine ich, dass die Identität der vorgestellten diasporischen Gemeinschaft weder fix noch vorgegeben ist, sondern im Schmelztiegel der konkreten Alltagsabläufe gebildet wird, eben in den alltäglichen Geschichten, die wir uns individuell und kollektiv erzählen.

Diasporische Migrationen sind noch in einem weiteren Sinne Verknüpfungen. Sie bestehen aus verschiedenen Modalitäten wie Gender, "Rasse", Klasse, Religion, Sprache und Generation. Jede Diaspora ist ein differenzierter, heterogener und umkämpfter Raum, sogar dann, wenn ihr die Konstruktion eines gemeinschaftlichen "Wir" zugrunde liegt. Es ist daher wichtig, auf die Natur und den Typus jener Prozesse zu achten, in denen und durch die das kollektive "Wir" gebildet wird. Wer wird bei der spezifischer Konstruktion des "Wir" ermächtigt, und wer entmächtigt? Wie werden bei der Konstruktion des "Wir" soziale Unterteilungen verhandelt? In welcher Beziehung steht das "Wir" zu den "Anderen"? Und wer sind diese Anderen? Das ist eine ganz entscheidende Frage. Allgemein wird davon ausgegangen, dass es ein einziges beherrschendes Anderes gibt, dessen Allgegenwärtigkeit die Konstruktion des "Wir" bestimmt. Daraus resultiert die Betonung bipolarer Gegensätze wie schwarz/weiss, Jude/Nicht-Jude, englisch/irisch, Hindu/Muslim. Liegt es in der Funktion einer bestimmten binären Opposition, politische Spaltungen herbeizuführen und soziale Trennungen zu fixieren, dann muss ihr Charakter sichtbar gemacht werden. Dennoch bleibt die Frage bestehen, wie solche Binarismen analysiert werden sollen. Man kann davon ausgehen, dass Binarismen ahistorische, universale Konstrukte repräsentieren. Sie verdecken den Einfluss historischer, sozioökonomischer, politischer und kultureller Faktoren, also genau die Grundlagen, auf denen bestehende Gegensätze ihre Bedeutung entfalten. Dadurch können Trennungen, die durch Institutionen, Diskurse und Praktiken herbeigeführt werden, als unbewegliche, transhistorische Fakten erscheinen. In der Folge werden Binarismen, die eigentlich dekonstruiert werden sollten, als unhinterfragte Grössen akzeptiert.

Die Wachsamkeit derartigen Tendenzen gegenüber ist gerade heute am Platz. Alte und neue Rassismen, gewalttätige religiöse Konflikte und der Schrecken "ethnischer Säuberungen" verleiten dazu, kontextuell abhängige Phänomene als transhistorische Universalien zu interpretieren, die dann als Wesensbestandteil der menschlichen Natur begriffen werden. Binarismen sind aber gesellschaftlich konstruierte Kategorien, deren Entstehen, Wirkungsweise und Ausprägungen untersucht werden müssen, statt sie als immer schon vorhanden anzunehmen. Eine bipolare Konstruktion sollte in fruchtbarer und produktiver Weise als Objekt der Analyse und Instrument der Dekonstruktion begriffen werden. Es gilt ihre Entstehungsbedingungen offenzulegen, ihre Funktion bei der Herausbildung von Hierarchien sowie ihre Macht, Kollektive zu mobilisieren.

In den Binarismen verbirgt sich eine Vielzahl Anderer, eine Tatsache, die unter den Tisch fällt, wenn innerhalb einer diskursiven Formation einem bestimmten Begriff Priorität eingeräumt wird. So können in einem Diskurs über Gender auf Gender gestützte Binarismen im Vordergrund stehen (was nicht heissen soll, dass binäre Konstruktionen unvermeidlich sind). Doch ist ein solcher Diskurs nicht unabhängig von anderen Diskursen zu sehen, beispielsweise solchen über Klasse, "Rasse", Religion oder Generation. Die Spezifität eines jeden Diskurses wird durch die weiteren Repräsentationsfelder umrissen und bezeichnet. Es geht nicht um eine allgemeine Repräsentation von beispielsweise Männlichkeit und Weiblichkeit, sondern ob und wie diese Repräsentationen rassisch konnotiert werden; wie und auf welche Weise sie die Klassenzugehörigkeit berühren; ob sie sich auf lesbische, schwule, heterosexuelle oder andere Sexualitäten beziehen; wie Alter und Generation in ihnen aufscheinen; und wie und ob sie religiöse Autorität beanspruchen. So betrachtet sind Binarismen ihrem Wesen nach differenziert und instabil. Entscheidend ist, wie und warum ein bestimmter Binarismus - beispielsweise schwarz/weiss - in einem bestimmten Kontext Gestalt annimmt, warum und wodurch er Kohärenz und Stabilität gewinnt und sich zugleich mit anderen Binarismen wie Jude/Nicht-Jude oder männlich/weiblich verzahnt.

Der eben genannte Punkt lässt sich im Hinblick auf rassisch konnotierte Diskurse und Praktiken noch weiter ausführen. So stellt sich beispielsweise die Frage nach dem Verhältnis zwischen unterschiedlichen Rassismen zu einem bestimmten Zeitpunkt beziehungsweise nach der Erscheinungsweise von Kategorien wie Klasse, Gender, Sexualität oder Religion innerhalb dieser Rassismen. Relevant sind auch die Signifikanten - Farbe, Physiognomie, Religion, Kultur usw. -, welche diese Rassismen organisieren. Ein weiterer entscheidender Aspekt dieser Problematik ist die Beziehung, die durch Rassismus zwischen einzelnen Gruppen geschaffen wird. Wie unterscheiden sich beispielsweise die Konstruktionen von afrikanischen, karibischen, südasiatischen und weissen Muslimen innerhalb des antimuslimischen Rassismus im gegenwärtigen Grossbritannien? Oder auch: Wie werden Schwarze, Chicanos, ChinesInnen, JapanerInnen oder SüdkoreanerInnen innerhalb der rassisch konnotierten Formationen der USA unterschieden? Was sind die ökonomischen, politischen, kulturellen und psychischen Auswirkungen dieser unterschiedlichen rassischen Zuschreibungen auf das Leben innerhalb dieser Gruppen? Was sind die Implikationen dieser Auswirkungen im Hinblick auf das Verhältnis der Mitglieder der unterschiedlichen Gruppen zueinander? Führen sie zu Identifikation und Solidarität oder provozieren sie Abgrenzung? Zur Beantwortung solcher Fragen muss der Machtdynamik Rechnung getragen werden, welche die sozialen Beziehungen rassisch prägt und rassisch konnotierte Formen von Subjektivität und Identität begünstigt. Nach meiner Auffassung handelt es sich bei diesen Rassismen nicht um Parallelphänomene, sondern um Verknüpfungen, um differentielle rassische Zuschreibungen von Positionen innerhalb genau gegliederter Machtfelder.

Nach einer Formulierung von Khachig Tölölian (1991) handelt es sich bei den zeitgenössischen Diasporas um die "exemplarischen Gemeinschaften des transnationalen Moments". Tatsächlich klingen im Begriff Diaspora Begriffe wie MigrantIn, ImmigrantIn, Ausgebürgerter, Flüchtling, GastarbeiterIn oder ExilantIn an. Das Konzept der Diaspora, wie ich es zu skizzieren suche, bildet einen Interpretationsrahmen, um auf die ökonomischen, politischen und kulturellen Dimensionen dieser zeitgenössischen Form der Migration aufmerksam zu machen. Es dient dazu, andere Diskurse über die Migration in der letzten Phase des Kapitalismus im 20. Jahrhundert zu hinterfragen.

## Diaspora und Minderheit

In Grossbritannien bestand immer die Tendenz, das Phänomen Diaspora entlang der Achse "Mehrheit/Minderheit" zu erklären. In den Nachkriegsjahren strukturierte dieser Gegensatz rassische Zuschreibungen. Mit "Minderheit", einem postkolonialen Codebegriff, der einen höflichen Ersatz für das Wort "Farbige" bildete, wurden vor allem britische BürgerInnen afrikanischer, karibischer und asiatischer Herkunft bedacht. Besieht man sich den Diskurs über die "Minderheiten" genauer, so stösst man auf die inzwischen ausführlich dokumentierten üblen Machenschaften der Einwanderungskontrolle und Polizei, auf rassistische Gewalt, Abwertung und Diskriminierung - all dem, was zu den Alltagserfahrungen der MigrantInnen gehört. Der Diskurs über die Minderheiten deckt sich zum Teil mit der klassischen liberalen Theorie, die Frauen, unterjochten Kolonialvölkern und der Arbeiterklasse den Status "Unmündiger" (Spelman 1988; Lloyd 1990; Philips 1991) zuerkannte. Der Gegensatz Mehrheit/Minderheit bleibt aber auch da problematisch, wo es um die Diskriminierung von "Minderheiten" geht und darum, auf ungleiche Machtverhältnisse hinzuweisen. Die Problematik rührt daher, dass der numerische Bezug dieser Dichotomie eine buchstäbliche Lektüre nahelegt, mit dem Ergebnis, dass die Wiederholung des Diskurses eher zu einer Festschreibung der Machtunterschiede führt als zu ihrer Infragestellung. Darüber wird die Vielschichtigkeit der Macht ignoriert, wenn gesellschaftliche Verhältnisse rein im Sinne dichotomer Gegensätze begriffen werden.

In meinem Konzept der Diaspora bildet sich die Macht in allen Dimensionen/Schichten ab. Dadurch wird die Beschränkung auf den Gegensatz Mehrheit/Minderheit hinfällig. Begreift man die Macht als multiaxiale, performative Kraft, dann zeigt sich, dass eine bestimmte Gruppe, die entlang einer Differenzierungsachse als "Minderheit" konstruiert wird, entlang einer anderen Achse als "Mehrheit" erscheinen kann. Die Markierungen von "Differenz" sind nichts anderes als strukturelle und performative Machtfacetten.

## Das Lokale und das Globale der Diaspora

Ein zentrales Merkmal diasporischer Identitäten ist die Verbindung lokaler und globaler Elemente, deren Verhältnis zueinander sich allerdings verändern kann. Die Diasporas am Ende des 20. Jahrhunderts führen zu anderen Erfahrungen als ihre historischen Vorläufer. Benötigten die Kommunikation oder das Reisen früher oft Monate, vollziehen sie sich im technologischen Zeitalter in rasantem Tempo. Der Einfluss der Komunikations- und Transporttechnologien gibt Marshall McLuhans Idee vom global village einen ganz neuen Sinn. Die gleichzeitige Ausstrahlung von Ereignissen in Ländern, die durch Satelliten vernetzt sind, führt dazu, dass Leute überall auf der Welt "gemeinsam zusehen", wenn irgendwo etwas geschieht. Elektronische Datenautobahnen ermöglichen neuartige Formen der Kommunikation, die noch vor zwanzig Jahren undenkbar waren. Diese Entwicklungen haben entscheidende Auswirkungen auf die Konstruktion "imaginierter Gemeinschaften". Das soll aber nicht heissen, dass als automatische Folge dieser Prozesse an ihrem Ende eine kulturelle Homogenisierung steht. Das ist allein deshalb nicht möglich, weil der globale Konsum von visueller oder anderer Kultur auf vielschichtige Weise vermittelt ist (Hall et al. 1992).

Der Verlauf dieser Prozesse lässt sich nicht vorherbestimmen, weil sich ein Bild auf die unterschiedlichste Weise interpretieren lässt. Es kann eine Fülle von Bedeutungen hervorrufen, die den Einfluss des Persönlichen, Biografischen und des kulturellen Kontextes auf die Bedeutungsproduktion belegen. Mit anderen Worten, die Verdichtung von Zeit und Raum und die daraus folgende "Schrumpfung" der Welt kann widersprüchliche Auswirkungen haben. Einerseits besteht die Möglichkeit, dass das Bewusstsein für globale Ungleichgewichte zunimmt und dass es dadurch zu länderübergreifenden Kooperationen kommt, die solche Ungleichgewichte zu beseitigen suchen. Es können neue Formen der politischen Solidarität und des Aktivismus entstehen, um den aktuellen Herausforderungen zu begegnen. Es kann zur Freisetzung kreativer Energien kommen, und in deren Folge zu Umwälzungen innerhalb der Politik, in Kunst, Musik, Literatur und anderen Formen kultureller Produktion. Andererseits bündelt die Globalisierung das Instrumentarium zur Schaffung einer neuen Weltordnung nach Ende des Kalten Krieges, zur Sicherung der kulturelle Hegemonie der G 8, nachdem Russland im Juli 1994 den Status eines politischen, allerdings nicht wirtschaftlich eingebundenen Mitgliedslandes erhalten hat. Der globale Charakter des Spätkapitalismus bestimmt das politische und wirtschaftliche Terrain, auf dessen Grundlage die neue Migration erfolgt; auf diesem Terrain haben sich sowohl die alten als auch die neuen Diasporas zu behaupten. Im nächsten Abschnitt möchte ich diesen Aspekt genauer entwickeln: Diasporische Identitäten sind zugleich lokal und global. Es sind Netzwerke transnationaler Identifikationen, die sowohl "imaginierte" als auch "materielle" Gemeinschaften umfassen.

## Durch Grenzen denken

Im Begriff der Diaspora ist die Vorstellung von der Grenze enthalten. Tatsächlich kann man nicht über die Diaspora sprechen, ohne ihre Beziehung zur Grenze mitzudenken. Mit diesem Konstrukt werde ich mich im folgenden beschäftigen.

Grenzen: willkürliche Trennlinien, die zugleich sozial, kulturell und psychisch verlaufen; Territorien, die patrouilliert werden, um diejenigen fernzuhalten, die zu Aussenseitern, zu Fremden, zu den Anderen werden; Demarkationen, bei denen das Verbot die Übertretung ins Leben ruft; Zonen, in denen die Furcht vor dem Anderen Furcht vor sich selbst ist; Orte, an denen Besitzansprüche – Ansprüche auf "meins", "deins" und "ihres" – geltend gemacht, bestritten, verteidigt und umkämpft werden.

Gloria Anzalduas Theoretisierung von Grenzen und Grenzregionen eröffnet entscheidende Einsichten, von denen zwei an dieser Stelle besonders wichtig sind. Zum einen gebraucht sie diese Begriffe, um die Lebensbedingungen an der südwestlich-texanischen Grenze zwischen den USA und Mexiko zu reflektieren - dort, wo sich, wie sie schreibt, "die Dritte Welt an der Ersten reibt und blutet" (Anzaldua 1987, S. 3). Zum anderen zitiert sie die Grenze als Metapher für psychologische, sexuelle, spirituelle, kulturelle, klassen- und rassenbezogene Grenzen. Im Licht meiner Auffassung von "Differenz" interpretiert, erstreckt sich der Begriff Grenze in Anzalduas Text gleichzeitig auf gesellschaftliche Beziehungen, auf Alltagserfahrungen und auf Subjektivität/Identität. Grenzen sind arbiträre Konstruktionen und in gewisser Weise immer Metaphern, wobei Metapher hier nicht im Sinne einer reinen Abstraktion der konkreten Realität aufzufassen ist, sondern als Teil der diskursiven Materialität von Machtbeziehungen.

Jede Grenze hat ihre eigene Geschichte, auch wenn darin Themen anklingen, die für alle Grenzen verbindlich sind. Die metaphorische Materialität einer Grenze lenkt die Aufmerksamkeit auf ihre spezifischen Eigenheiten: auf demarkierte geographische und/oder psychische Territorien; auf die Erfahrungen bestimmter Gruppen, die durch die Errichtung eines Grenzbereichs auseinanderdividiert werden oder anderweitig betroffen sind; und auf die alten und neuen Staaten, die durch Grenzziehungen verschwinden oder entstehen. Wie wird eine Grenze reguliert und bewacht? Wer wird draussen gehalten und warum? Mit welchen Realitäten sind diejenigen konfrontiert, die als unerwünschte GrenzübertreterInnen stigmatisiert werden? Unter Realitäten verstehe ich in diesem Zusammenhang den bei Anzaldua vertretenen Anspruch auf schwule oder lesbische Identität innerhalb eines gesellschaftlichen Zusammenhangs, der durch Homophobie und Heterosexismus geprägt ist. Oder die Realitäten heutiger ArbeitsmigrantInnen, die sich mit den staatlichen Einwanderungsbehörden herumzuschlagen haben, die Schwierigkeiten bei der Ausstellung von Visa oder mit Einwanderungskontrollen haben, die interniert oder deportiert werden oder auch ihr Leben verlieren.

Die aktuelle Situation der MigrantInnen zeigt sich exemplarisch an der Grenze zwischen Nordamerika und Mexiko. Hier stösst man auf jene Probleme, die immer dann auftauchen, wenn die "überentwickelten" Länder den Zutritt von Völkern aus wirtschaftlich "unterentwickelten" Gebieten der Erde regulieren. Diese Grenze versinnbildlicht das Verhängnis einst kolonialisierter Menschen, die sich heute in einer globale, durch transnationales Kapital und die Politik der G 7- oder G 8-Gruppe dominierte Ökonomie versetzt finden. Haupteigenschaft der neuen Regimes der Akkumulation ist die "Flexibilität" (oder das, was in zunehmenden Masse als "Anpassungsfähigkeit" bezeichnet wird; so lautete der Lieblingsausdruck beim Gipfel der G 7 im Juli 1994) im Arbeitsprozess, auf den Arbeitsmärkten, in der Güterproduktion und im Konsumverhalten. Die Segmentierung des Arbeitsmarktes schreitet immer weiter voran, so dass ein vergleichsweise kleiner Kern gut ausgebildeter Kräfte auf der Managementebene einer wesentlich grösseren Gruppe von Angestellten gegenübersteht, die oft als "peripher" eingestuft werden, deren Arbeitskraft für das Funktionieren der globalen Ökonomie aber von zentraler Wichtigkeit ist. Die Kerngruppe verfügt über gutbezahlte, ausgelastete und dauerhafte Berufe mit Aufstiegschancen und Weiterbildungsmöglichkeiten. Von ihr wird erwartet, dass sie flexibel und anpassungsfähig und, falls erforderlich, geographisch mobil ist. Jede Unannehmlichkeit, die eine solche Existenz mit sich bringen könnte, wird durch die Sicherheit bei den Renten, Versicherungen und andere Vergünstigungen wettgemacht. Dagegen werden die "peripheren" Angestellten, die im "zweiten Arbeitsmarkt" tätig sind, in der Regel schlecht bezahlt. Sie lassen sich in zwei Gruppen unterteilen, von denen die erste aus Vollzeit-Angestellten besteht, die qualifizierte oder halb-qualifizierte Tätigkeiten ausführen. Für diese Art der Beschäftigung ist eine hohe Frequenz beim Jobwechsel die Regel. Die zweite Gruppe, zu der TeilzeitarbeiterInnen, Saisonangestellte, Beschäftigte auf Honorarbasis oder im Job-Sharing und HeimarbeiterInnen gehören, muss noch flexibler sein. Es überrascht kaum, dass in diesem Bereich vor allem Frauen MigrantInnen und ausländische Arbeitskräfte (männlich und weiblich) sowie ihre Kinder arbeiten.

Die transnationalen Bewegungen von Kapital und Arbeitskräften führen im ausgehenden 20. Jahrhundert zu neuen diasporischen Formationen. Die rasante Beschleunigung bei technologischen, geschäftlichen und organisatorischen Innovationen geht einher mit neuartigen Produktionsweisen, neuen Märkten, Produkten, Dienstleistungen und Finanzierungssystemen. Die erhöhte Mobilität des Kapitals, das zur Profitmaximierung an beliebige Orte im In- und Ausland fliesst, hat starke Einflüsse auf Bevölkerungsbewegungen. Die Verlegung von Standorten und Arbeitsplätzen sowie die stete Nachfrage nach ArbeitsmigrantInnen, die in den ökonomisch entwickelten "Zentren" schlechtbezahlte Jobs machen führt zur Entstehung neuer Grenzen, während die alten Grenzen befestigt werden oder verschwinden (Sassen 1988; Rouse 1991; Miles 1993).

In den USA hat die zunehmende Polarisierung des Arbeitsmarktes die Nachfrage nach mexikanischer Arbeitskräften steigen lassen. Diese machen Niedriglohnjobs in der Landwirtschaft, am Fliessband und im Dienstleistungsbereich. Gleichzeitig wurden Gesetze und Verordnungen erlassen, um angesichts des zunehmenden Rassismus sowie wachsender politischer Unzufriedenheit über Entlassungen in bestimmten Wirtschaftszweigen den "Migrantenstrom" zu regulieren. Der Rassismus erhält auch dadurch Nahrung, dass es manche Investoren lukrativer finden, Arbeitsprozesse nach Mexiko auszugliedern Mexikanische ArbeiterInnen sind mit dem Vorwurf konfrontiert, "uns die Jobs wegzunehmen". Diese Ressentiments führen dazu, dass der Arbeiter als Verkörperung des Kapitals erscheint, und nicht im Widerspruch dazu gesehen wird. Schliesslich geht aus dieser Konstellation der "undokumentierte Arbei ter" hervor: benötigt für die Dreckarbeit, aber zugleich kriminalisiert. In die Schattenwirtschaft gedrängt und unsichtbar gemacht ist er abwesend anwesend: ein Phantom, das überall dort, wo schlecht bezahlte Arbeit verrichtet wird, die Schlupfwinkel und Ritzen verdunkelt.

## Die Idee der "Grenztheorie"

Untersuchungen, bei denen es im analytischen wie geographischen Sinn um "Grenzen" geht, laufen in zunehmendem Masse unter dem Begriff "Grenztheorie". Das von Deleuze und Guattari vorgeschlagene Konzept der "Deterritorialisierung" hat in eine Vielzahl von Texten Eingang gefunden, die als *border writing* (Lloyd 1990; Hicks 1991; Calderon und Salvidar 1991) bezeichnet werden. Für Deleuze und Guattari ist die "Deterritorialisierung" das Merkmal eines Schreibens, das sie als "kleine Literatur" bezeichnet haben - eines Schreibens, dessen Eigenschaften der kanonischen Literatur widerspricht. Deleuze und Guattari zufolge deterritorialisiert die "kleine Literatur" die Sprache, aber auch die Verbindung zwischen dem Individuum und der politischen Unmittelbarkeit einschliesslich dem kollektiven Gemenge von Aussagepositionen (Deleuze und Guattari 1986). Mit dem Konzept der Deterritorialisierung soll die Verschiebung von Identitäten, Personen und Bedeutungen beschrieben werden; sein vorherrschendes Moment sind die in Literatur und Sprache abgespeicherten Erfahrungen von Entfremdung und Exil. Deterritorialisierung bezeichnet den Bruch zwischen Signifikant und Signifikat, so dass "alle Formen aufgehoben werden. Dasselbe gilt von den Bedeutungen, Signifikanten und Signifikaten, die entbunden werden zugunsten einer formlosen, deterritorialisierten Masse: zu Zeichen, die nichts bezeichnen" (ebd.). Während die Anziehungskraft eines solchen Begriffs für die Textanalyse unmittelbar einleuchtet, ist seine allgemeine Anwendung problematisch. Die literarische Trope des *border writing* kann bestimmte Aspekte von Grenzbewegungen erhellen. Nach Emily Hicks begründet *border writing* eine Textstrategie, die nicht auf Repräsentation, sondern auf Übersetzung fusst. Dabei würde das nicht-synchrone Gedächtnis angesprochen; die LeserInnen erhielten die Möglichkeit, vieldimensionale Wahrnehmungen zu machen, und sich in eine vielschichtige semiotische Matrix zu begeben, um multilinguale, interkulturelle Wirklichkeiten zu erfahren. Ich stimme mit Hicks darin überein, dass *border writing* eine facettenreiche und nuancierte Darstellung von Grenzgeschichten bietet. Ich möchte nur vor der Tendenz warnen, die Theorie der Grenze mit der Analyse von Texten über Grenzen zu vermischen. Das gilt vor allem dann, wenn letztere als Synonym für literarische Texte überhaupt herhalten müssen. Nach meiner Auffassung sind literarische Texte lediglich ein Element der umfassenden Textualität der Grenze. Der Begriff des "Territoriums" einschliesslich seiner Signifikate und Bedeutungen bezieht sich auf ein Kampfgebiet. Fragen der Territorialisierung, Deterritorialisierung und Reterritorialisierung implizieren politische Auseinandersetzungen, sobald es um Diaspora und Grenze geht. Das Ergebnis dieser Auseinandersetzungen lässt sich allerdings nicht voraussehen, was bedeutet, dass der Schritt vom literarischen Text zur "Welt als Text" wesentlich gefahrvoller, widersprüchlicher, komplexer und problematischer ist als es gemeinhin dargestellt wird.

## Der Raum der Diaspora und die Kreolisierung der Theorie

In ihrer Verknüpfung bilden die Konzepte der Diaspora, der Grenze und der vielfachen Lokalitäten eine Struktur, mit deren Hilfe die historischen Bedingungen aktueller trans/nationaler Ströme von Menschen, Informationen, Kulturen, Waren und Kapital untersucht werden können. Diese Struktur, die Schnittstelle von ökonomischen, politischen, kulturellen und psychischen Prozessen, möchte ich als Diasporaraum bezeichnen. An diesem Ort werden Subjektpositionen miteinander konfrontiert, bezogen oder bestritten. Hier durchdringen sich erlaubte und verbotene, akzeptierte und transgressive Praktiken und Diskurse, auch wenn die entstehenden Mischformen im Namen von Reinheit und Tradition abgelehnt werden. Mehr noch, hier wird Tradition selbst ständig neu erfunden. Der Diasporaraum zeigt die unendlichen Wahrnehmungspotentiale, die Vielzahl kultureller Risse und Verbindungen, die den gegenwärtigen Formen transkultureller Identitäten zugrunde liegen. Diese im Entstehen begriffenen Identitäten werden vielleicht nur heimlich anerkannt, wenn sie nicht gar vom Regime konstruierter Reinheitsimperative abgelehnt oder unterdrückt werden. In jedem Fall aber sind diese Identitäten den Formen des Synkretismus eingeschrieben, die im ausgehenden 20. Jahrhundert zum Kern von Kultur und Subjektivität gehören (Hall 1990; Coombes 1992).

Der Diasporaraum offenbart die globale Situation der "Kultur als Schauplatz des Reisens" (Clifford 1992). Auf diesem Territorium wird die Subjektposition des "Einheimischen" stark in Frage gestellt. Im Diasporaraum werden die Grenzen zwischen Einschliessung und Ausschliessung, Zugehörigkeit und Anderssein, "uns" und "ihnen" bestritten. Dieser Raum wird meiner Auffassung nach nicht nur von MigrantInnen und ihren Abkömmlingen bewohnt, sondern auch von denen, die als einheimisch konstruiert und repräsentiert werden. Der Diasporaraum (im Gegensatz zur Diaspora) verknüpft die Genealogien derer, die verstreut sind, mit denen, die sesshaft sind. Die Einheimischen sind hier im gleichen Masse BewohnerInnen der Diaspora wie die BewohnerInnen der Diaspora Einheimische. Mit dieser These will ich aber keinesfalls einem undifferenzierten Relativismus das Wort reden. Ganz im Gegenteil vollziehen sich im Diasporaraum – im Rahmen von gesellschaftlichen Beziehungen und Erfahrungen, von Subjektivität und Identität – Prozesse der Differenzbildung. Der Diasporaraum ist eine von Machtbeziehungen durchzogene Matrix, in welcher sich die verschiedenen Positionen verknüpfen und entknüpfen.

So überschneiden sich beispielsweise im Diasporaraum mit dem Namen "England" afrikanisch-karibische, irische, asiatische, jüdische und andere Diasporas. Sie überschneiden sich aber auch mit jenem Konstrukt, das als "das Englische" gilt. Das Englische ist überhaupt erst im Schmelztiegel kolonialer Begegnungen mit Irland, Schottland und Wales entstanden, allerdings auch im Verlauf imperialer Auseinandersetzungen mit anderen europäischen und aussereuropäischen Mächten. Seit der Nachkriegszeit wird das Englische durch Grenzüberschreitungen, die andere diasporische Formationen involvieren, immer wieder neu gebildet. Diese Grenzüberschreitungen sind territorialer, politischer, ökonomischer, kultureller und psychischer Art. Sie fügen das Englische zu einem immer wieder neuen Ensemble zusammen, das sich unter anderem das in England situierte Afrikanisch-Karibische, Asiatische, Irische aneignet, um im Gegenzug selbst wieder Element dieser Formationen zu werden. Jede Formation hat ihre Spezifität, die sich aber in einem permanenten Wechsel befindet. Dabei kommt es meiner Auffassung nach nicht nur bei der Dichotomie von Beherrschern und Beherrschten zu Grenzüberschreitungen, sondern auch innerhalb der kulturellen Formationen der untergeordneten Gruppen selbst. Diese Austauschprozesse werden nicht immer durch die dominanten Kulturen vermittelt. Oft überschneiden sich kulturelle Ensembles wie das Englisch-Asiatische, das Englisch-Karibische oder das Englisch-Zypriotische, statt sich gegenseitig auszuschliessen. Die entscheidende Frage lautet damit, wie diese englischen Identitäten Gestalt annehmen; wie sie sich intern ausdifferenzieren; in welcher Beziehung sie zueinander und zu anderen englischen Identitäten stehen; und schliesslich wie sie vorhandene Vorstellungen des Englischen, Schottischen, Walisischen oder Britischen umarbeiten und dezentrieren.

Nach meiner These sind diese Identitäten weder "Minderheiten"-Identitäten noch liegen sie an der Peripherie von etwas, das sich selbst als Zentrum sieht, auch wenn sie in dieser Zuschreibung repräsentiert werden. Durch ihre Dezentrierung neutralisieren die neuen politischen und kulturellen Formationen den Impuls der dominanten Kultur, sie zu minorisieren und an den Rand zu drängen. In diesem Sinne kann Catherine Hall (1992) behaupten, dass das Englische nur eine Ethnizität unter vielen ist.

Zwar bin ich überzeugt, dass die feministische Theorie der Politik der *location* von entscheidender Bedeutung für das Verständnis von Grenzpositionalitäten ist, doch möchte ich die Wichtigkeit anderer theoretischer und politischer Beiträge zur Erhellung diasporisierender Grenzprozesse nicht verleugnen. Die Einsichten, die sich beispielsweise aus Analysen des Kolonialismus, des Imperialismus, der schwulen und lesbischen Politik ziehen lassen, sind gleichfalls relevant. Ich habe weiter oben auf die zunehmende Verbreitung von "Grenztheorien" hingewiesen. Dieses Konzept überschneidet sich mit anderen Theoriefeldern, wie etwa "postkolonialer Theorie" und "Diasporatheorie". Mir geht es aber weniger um die Überschneidungen oder Unterschiede zwischen diesen konzeptuellen Terrains. Vielmehr möchte ich betonen, dass diese theoretischen Konstrukte am besten als Orte des Zusammenfliessens verstanden werden. Die Einsichten und Erkenntnisse aus unterschiedlichen Feldern tragen zum Entstehen analytischer Rahmen bei, die in der Lage sind, multiple, einander überlagernde Achsen der Differenzierung aufzuzeigen. Es geht hier mit anderen Worten um einen Raum von/für theoretische *cross-overs*, um die Machtprozesse innerhalb dieser Zusammenhänge zu betonen. Es geht um eine Art theoretischer Kreolisierung. Diese kreolisierende Betrachtung scheint mir notwendig, um die Widersprüche von Ausdrucksmodalitäten, Identitäten, Positionen und Standpunkten, die gleichzeitig "innen" und "aussen" sind, sichtbar zu machen. Sie ist notwendig, um die polymorphe Zusammensetzung von Subjektivität und gesellschaftlichen Beziehungen aufschlüsseln zu können. Das Konzept des Diasporaraumes, das ich hier vorzustellen versucht habe, gründet sich auf eine theoretische Kreolisierung des eben beschriebenen Typus.

Übersetzung von Ruth Noack und Roger M. Buergel

Dieser Text ist eine gekürzte Version des 8. Kapitels von Avtar Brahs Buch *Cartographies of Diaspora. Contesting Identities,* London and New York: Routledge 1998

**Sources/Zitierte Werke:**

Anzaldua G. (1987) *Borderlands/La Frontera: The New Mestiza*, San Francisco: Sprinsters/Aunt Lute.
Castles S. and Miller M. J. (1993) *The Age of Migration: International Population Movements*, London: Macmillan.
Clifford J. (1992) *Travelling Cultures*, in L. Grossberg, C. Nelson and P. Treichler (eds) Cultural Studies, New York: Routledge.
Coombes A.E. (1992) *Inventing the Postcolonial: Hybridity and Constituency in Contemporary Curating*, "New Formations", 18.
Deleuze G. and Guattari F. (1986) *What is a Minor Literature?* In Kafka: Towards a Minor Literature, Minneapolis: University of Minnesota Press (1975).
Hall C. (1992) *White, Male and Middle Class: Explorations in Feminism and History*, London: Verso.
Hall S. (1990) *Cultural Identity and Diaspora*, in J. Rutherford (ed) Identity: Community, Culture, Difference, London: Lawrence & Wishart.
Hall S., Held D. and McGrew A. (eds) (1992) *Modernity and its Futures*, Cambridge: Polity Press.
Lloyd, D. (1990) Genet's Genealogy: *European Minorities and the Ends of the Canon*, in A. JanMohammed and D. Lloyd (eds) The Nature and Context of Minority Discourse, New York: Oxford University Press.
Miles R. (1993) *Racism after "Race Relations"*, London and New York: Routledge.
Philips A. (1991) *Engendering Democracy*, Cambridge: Polity Press.
Rouse R. (1991) *Mexican Migration and the Social Space of Postmodernism*, "Diaspora", 1(1):8-23.
Sassen S. (1988) *The Mobility of Labour and Capital: A Study in International Investment and Labour Flow*, Cambridge: Cambridge University Press.
Spelman E.V. (1988) *Inessential Woman: Problems of Exclusion in Feminist Thought*, London: The Women's Press.
Tölölian Khachig (1991) *The Nation State and its Others: In Lieu of a Preface*, "Diaspora", 1 (1): 3-7.

# _SURVIVAL AND EXPLORATERRARISM.[1]
# RE-MAPPING THE POSTHUMAN SPACE

Yvonne Volkart

> The face of humanity has been the face of man/mankind. Feminist humanity must take different forms, display other gestures; [...] feminist humanity must, in whatever way, resist representation and literal shaping and at the same time dare to break out in powerful new tropes, new figures of speech and idiomatic expressions, new turning points of historical possibilities. That is why here at the crest of the crisis, at the cusp of all tropes we need ecstatic speakers.
> Donna Haraway[2]

There are places and times that inscribe you, that have already inscribed you. It has always been so, even if they are situated outside of what you believe yourself to be. Perhaps you sense the secret connections, or you do not become aware of them until afterwards. At the moment you have only come in contact with something that for the time being has no meaning. Even as a little girl I feared the day I would turn 36. I imagined what it would be like to be a woman. It would be my last birthday in the old millennium and I was sure that I wouldn't live to see the new one, for I was convinced that a World War III would limit my opportunities or wipe everything out. I was scared I would have to suffer and that having been born too late I would be cheated out of a world in which I could have lived out my nostalgic desire for wide open spaces. How I longed to get to know the country, the countries to the East, where my mother came from. And I wanted to fly to Mars, too. I'm still alive and I'm constantly traveling and flying and getting to know strangers in order to build that which from my perspective constitutes an active and involved life.

That particular day, on March 24, 1999, I showed my students some videos, one of which had been produced by Marina Grzinic and Aina Smid for Slovenian television and was entitled *Luna 10. The Butterfly Effect of Geography*[3]. I found this video interesting then just as I do today because it represents a perspective different than the ordinary one, namely a woman's, the perspective of a person from a post-Communist country. It's about the desire for expansion, conquering the world, and the question of survival. The main title refers to the first lunar satellite launched into outer space by the Russians in the sixties; the subtitle, to the dream of winning new territories as products of the Cold War (Grzinic). At the beginning of the video we see a woman looking through a telescope – the repetition of the female viewer's own situation as observer. In a sort of framework situation the woman and a man guide us through the video's various window-like, or as Grzinic/Smid call it, hypertext-like image sequences. In them we see footage by progressive Yugoslavian filmmakers, like Emir Kusturica or Zelimir Zelnik, as well as documentary material taken from pirate radio stations, etc. Beauty remains silent while he speaks about technological "revolutions" like the Internet, wars, the role of the media, and the perspective of people from the East. Although he plays the role of a pontificating male authority figure, he at times appears wearing nothing but his underpants or turns into a kind of technological medium inserting numbers in a table as she dictates the words to him. Thus his body also occupies a female subordinate position. She too changes her clothing, sometimes wearing only a slip, other times a military uniform. The gender-specific and social matrices of both figures are temporary and contrary, complex and diffuse. *Luna 10* can be interpreted as a critical argument for appropriating new (wartime) technologies and media and reassigning them to women and other subaltern groups. The woman from the East has seized control of the telescope (outdated technological "prosthesis" and phallic substitute). She too wants to go to the moon, and she too will only pass on the images she sees. Her searching eye and the greenish tinge to the film are indicative of analogies to military infrared surveillance scenarios. But the screen images we are presented with are replete with contrasts. At the beginning, for example, she appears before us in a poor rural setting, her hands covered with dough. While the man recites Western technological fantasies of transgression, we see images of private domesticity, rustic simplicity, weddings, Communist parades, or three soldiers executing a woman in field. The green tinge also emphasizes the archival aspect of the footage. Spaces, bodies, identities, and technologies are represented as historical, medial, and ideological constructs. Everything becomes reciprocally involved with everything else, but there are very real spaces and bodies in which we experience everyday emotions like desire, fear, sadness, joy. Medial constructs of places and bodies don't preclude intense experience. "LIVE is a very simple program," the man in *Luna 10* sarcastically states as he sits half naked before us. His survival philosophy is simple and radical in its wish potential, "Have you queued up for the virtual bread? As it is with technological revolutions in the West, you will get only bread crumbs. Better than nothing."

On the occasion of her exhibition last winter I talked to Milica Tomic about what she had done on March 24, 1999. She had wanted to make her long-planned video *Portrait of my Mother* because the weather report had predicted it was going to be the first clear, sunny day in a long time. Her idea was to record on video the route she normally took to get from her own apartment at the center of Belgrade to her mother's apartment on the outskirts of the city. In the exhibition catalogue she writes, "Needless to say at this very time someone else was also making his final preparations to render Belgrade his object; of course, each of us in his own way and from his own perspective."

## The posthuman condition

It is important to develop these different perspectives, to look at them in relation to one another, and to insist on them – not in an attempt to patch together a pluralistic-relativistic quilt but in order to reveal the phantasms of equality and the real polarities and incompatibilities. Being able to read all the personal statements of women and men from Belgrade on the Internet and hear their rage and grief on the telephone, what did I then do with the motivation I felt to get involved? What do you do about media that reduce spaces and distances while at the same using their technologies to wage war, the deadliest of all antagonisms? What does it mean to be an actively involved art mediator who talks about gender in cyberspace and the ideological implications of new technologies while at the same time standing by and watching a number of different escalations take place? How does one deal with the fact that a critical position is utterly contradictory?

"We now see that there is room for everyone in the abyss of history. We sense that a culture is just as frail as the life of a single individual. The world, which gives the name 'progress' to its tendency towards baneful acumen, strives to combine the commodities of life with the advantages of death. It buys space and time as imaginary values of human capital and uses them to multiply its entrances," says Jacqueline, one of the fictive-real protagonists of Europe in Eva Meyer and Eran Schaerf's bi-medial radio play/video project *Europe from Afar*. Even at the end it is still not clear whether Jacqueline is a Persian, Jew, European, Christian, Arab, Israeli, actress, or an embalmed Coptic female corpse. And Piemanta, Jacqueline's grandmother/childhood classmate/double answers, "It [the world] has fully grasped the economic principle, which states that the entrances are all that count and all that pay off. We are trying to gain access to a space that will only come to be through time. Since it keeps getting bigger, it will turn into a world exhibition consisting of nothing but its own entrances."

Indeed many find the doors closed to them despite stepped-up advertising for ostensible entrances: "Would I have been hired for the media class at your college," my Polish housemate asks, "if I hadn't had a Canadian passport too?"

These are the paradoxical spaces and conditions of posthumanism, i.e. a world based on humanist ideals but caught in the contradictory process of the deconstruction and simultaneous restitution of these ideals. Even the concept of the posthuman self is so divided, ambivalent, and vague. As a metaphor for the non-natural and as an indicator for the end of humanist ideals it is used by technodeterminists and (post)feminists alike. I use it to inscribe myself in the feminist anti-essentialist and anti-androcentric tradition, on the one hand; on the other, to bring a word into play that regardless of how and where it is used is always simultaneously also some place else, i.e. always both true and false, both hype and utopia, and thus never really fixed in place – a word, therefore, that repeatedly re-embodies the paradox of place and time and the temporality of perspectives.

In these posthuman spaces the internationalization of capital, as Saskia Sassen states, goes under the name of globalization, whereas the internationalization of labor is referred to by the discriminatory and obsolete term migration.[4] While the transnationalization of the economy allows for a certain disregard for the laws of the nation states and the rights of the people therein, we are simultaneously being confronted with an increase in racism, nationalism, sexism, and fundamentalism. *Luna 10* – along with many female post- and cyberfeminist theoreticians, like Donna Haraway, Rosi Braidotti, Anne Balsamo, Carol A. Stabile, Katherine N. Hayles – shows that, despite technological determinist swagger[5] and the real shifts in borders, ideological differences like age, class, and gender have not been deconstructed even at the level of the body but are instead being reinforced and reconstituted. However, it also makes clear that there are ways of intervening in these processes, ways for a person to participate from his/her perspective. The effects on bodies and gender produced by the newly drawn borders of the North-South international division of labor is the central theme in Ursula Biemann's video work *Performing the Border*. The notion that there is no nice, easy border crossing, as Berta Jottar rightly says in

*Performing the Border*, is a point web artist Alexei Shulgin brings home unmistakably with his event. Shulgin and his "punk rock band" (an old computer) received an invitation from the Tijuana Media Center to come to Mexico and give a concert. As a Russian citizen temporary residing in the U.S., however, he wasn't granted a visa, so he gave his concert directly at the border fence. He played his keyboard on the U.S. side; the computer played on the Mexican side. "Since borders have become more permeable for products and less passable for people, Shulgin's computer is allowed to travel freely between Mexico and the USA without a visa," writes Natalie Bookchin in the press release. Shulgin names the discriminatory posthuman conditions and re-codes them into a celebration. In doing so, he can carry the exclusionary North-South and East-West relations temporarily to an absurd extreme, so that we can appreciate and enjoy them even without stressing subordination. Shulgin stages minimal acts that represent the individual will to survive as something suddenly subversive, as system-coherent answers and reactions to specific exclusionary conditions. This performance of flexibility and celebration holds a potential for political action because the idea of a party in a place not intended for such purposes takes symbolic aim at the transgression of tightly drawn borders.

Having said this, I would like to offer only an indirect and temporary answer to the above-mentioned question as to what the consequences for my identity might be if the spaces in which I move become contradictory and paradoxical. I am searching for positions like those of Shulgin and others and I am striving for collaborations in which we are prepared to take on the paradoxical nature of our different positions and perspectives as the fundamental point of departure for our own identities, life models, and spheres of action. Allow me, therefore, to respond via a discussion of works in which artists develop specific sets of aesthetics that map identity models for an existence in the posthuman space. More specifically, I would like to examine the tools used by several artists to construct "apparent spaces" (Irit Rogoff, quoting Hannah Arendt). All of them uncover the discrimination and violence in current border and technology discourses, without, however, getting caught up in maudlin victimized discussions. How does one spread hope and belief in the importance of aesthetic identity models when we all know that one fine day (nearly) everything will be destroyed and that making art will seem like an obsolete project?

It is no coincidence (but no reason for essentializing or generalizing either) that the majority of the artists I have chosen to discuss here are women. First, I as a woman represent a situated female perspective, and secondly, the affirmation of the posthuman paradoxical conditions may already be inscribed in the concept of the feminine as it is articulated symbolically. As feminist theory in general and Teresa de Lauretis in particular demonstrate, the "status [of the woman] both as object and symbol" has always been contradictory. "The female subject is both WOMAN and women." The relation between object and symbol status, which de Lauretis characterizes as "feminine," can also be applied to other subaltern groups and "unholy alliances" like man/animal or man/machine and is therefore very nearly the epitome of the embodiment of the posthumanist condition.

The central questions remain: What aesthetic strategies are being developed to address us as multiply coded, hybridized, and differential subjects so that we can re-formulate ourselves? How can we make use of the specifically situated knowledge of art and discourse producers of both genders and diverse origins to conduct identity discourses that are non-fixed and headed for new fixations? On the basis of

Yvonne Rainer's Film *The Man Who Envied Women*, de Lauretis arrives at the following conclusion, which I would like to advance as a premise of the approaches I will be discussing here, although, I might add, these women artists, with their questions on postnation, postcolonialism, etc., go beyond the topic of *Being A-woman*[6] cited by de Lauretis. "It is precisely in this space of contradictions, in the divided and duplicitous interlocking of its narrative grammar and its multiple figurative meanings, that the film addresses me, as female viewer, as *a(-)woman*. Here the film caters to my (un)feminine perspective and inscribes my subjectivity, which is inextricably linked to my gender, in what I might call an "Erkennen des Verkennens" (understanding of misunderstanding); in the personal-political contradictions of my own narrative of a-femininity."[7] For us, what is important about Teresa de Lauretis' statement is the paradoxical position the female subject finds herself in and from which point she continually reconstructs herself. Born and raised as a woman, the female subject identifies time and time again with her status as symbol and her position as woman, although it is impossible to be both at the same time because we are dealing here with phantasmatic constructs. This process of misunderstanding is at the same time the process of her multiple constructs of subjectivity, or perhaps the actual circumstances leading to them. But only if this process is deconstructed as a phantasmatic given – in the negation of this space as option, so to speak – does the female subject (as viewer) have a chance of constructing a u-topian, temporary identity. De Lauretis says, "Through the deconstruction of the narrative space the film creates a critical space in which I, as woman and a-woman, am being addressed directly." Thus, only when the subject is addressed as something completely paradoxical is it able to articulate itself in this not-fixed "critical space."

## Becoming a symptom

I would like to illustrate this process of understanding misunderstanding on the basis of Milica Tomic' video and web work "I am Milica Tomic." Tomic stands before us in a white slip; she is radiantly beautiful with a heavenly glow about her. Then, she starts to speak: I am Milica Tomic. I am a German. She repeats this 65 times substituting different languages and nations each time. I am an Austrian, I am an American, and so on. For each sentence a new wound appears, so that by the time she finishes, she is completely covered by blood-spouting gashes. After all 65 recitations everything closes back up, her body is intact once more, and the whole thing starts all over again. Having a national identity and a mother tongue are important identity-forming factors, and in our age of (not yet obsolete) nation states these constitute our feelings of home and being-in-the-world. The yearning for these identities is all but inscribed in the body; it determines the wish potential that express itself in the unmarred body. The reality, however, is also that the phantasm of the nation mutilates the bodies, that the subject articulates itself as contingent, vulnerable, and wounded body, regardless of whether one's "own" nation is particularly bloodthirsty or not. The subject, as a splinter of one of these phantasms, has always been caught in the paradox of being both body and symbol. Tomic' wounds that result directly from her words reveal that each of her performative acts of the identity recitations she is forced to make is an act of misunderstanding. Still, through her hysterical mimesis of the wish for national identity with its simultaneous deconstruction through her gaping wounds, she does not a priori dismiss her desire for (national) identity. Instead she takes this desire seriously, in respect to both its subjectivity-constituting and its traumatic-fatal productive powers and extends it, as it were, in a ritual act of speaking the understood misunderstandings ad absurdum. Her hysterical identification with the Oedipal position (she is blinded and gets castrated) in which her reduction to woman with a proper name and subject of a national state entity becomes manifest, thus her performance of a symptomatic becoming-a-wound, has the effect that we too, as viewers, are called upon to take part in this mimetic process and to identify with her role of complete vulnerability. What remains is this aesthetic space in which the woman on the screen (and on the Internet) performs as an "ecstatic speaker" (Haraway), and from which the possibilities of a much more multiple and variable space can be derived, mythic, utopian, a "tangible space for political representation and participation beyond the traditional institutions of the parliamentary systems"[8] that is both conceivable and possible.

## Topographies

Milica Tomic made her video *Portrait of My Mother (Portrait of Marija Milutinovic)* a few months later, despite the circumstances or perhaps because of them. She did indeed have to travel the route to her mother's apartment, which was located in a safe zone, every evening during the NATO bombings. Thus, she not only became the temporary protagonist of her future video turned reality, but reality also became the simulation of a fictive passage that had not yet taken place. In *Portrait of My Mother* different paths conflate: The path the daughter takes through Belgrade and the mother's journey through life, which is not disentangled from the course of Yugoslavia's history. The mother, in modern Belgrade an actress with a predilection for minimalist avant-garde aesthetics (as opposed to the dominant aesthetics of social realism), retires from acting in the eighties – during the period of forced nationalization. Suddenly, in the middle of a part she announces in an act of female self-castration that she is a bad actress. She then turns to an esoteric escapist form of Christian orthodoxy. The discussion among the three women reveals a clear parallel between the mother's life – rich in deeply personal experience and marked by her fatalistic (i.e. having politically fatal repercussions) faith under the auspices of a pro-regime church – and Serbia's reterritorialization politics. Thus Tomic' video picks up and continues from the point where her mother's life – the life of a dedicated and critical artist – was interrupted.

No images are used to illustrate Marija Milutinovic's life, however, nor is it told as a continuous story. The viewer hears the off-camera voices of the daughter, mother, and the mother's best friend as they talk about the mother's life and the current situation. Not until the very end of the 63-minute video do we see the daughter and the mother as they meet in the apartment. At this point the voices stop. The two women gaze into each other's eyes in an instant of seemingly endless silence, and embrace. Before that there was the bodiless-physical journey – on foot, by bus and taxi – through the streets of a surprisingly intact Belgrade, the silent encounters with people – strangers and relatives. Filmed from a subjective camera angle Tomic' invisible body is somehow put in motion. Interspersed at irregular intervals within this flow of visual and audio impressions are black film sequences. They are accompanied by indefinable noises, and, interrupting the women's intermittent stream of conversation, they not only seem to question everything anew but they may also constitute representation-free moments for possible entries into the videographic space. It's as if these moments urged us as female viewers to pass through these black holes and indefinable noises and to inscribe our own lives, to live our lives mentally, so to speak as bios graphein. The fact that Tomic provides us with a space for embodiment and participation is once again made clear by the installation. On both sides of the front video screening she places four slide projectors that fill the side walls with pairs of images. There are, for example, pictures of auras taken from her mother's spiritual books or instructions her mother saved from the sixties for how to insert a tampon. These reflect notions Milica had as a little girl of what the inside of the female body looked like. Topographic relations (urban space/gallery space/inside of the female body) become the basic condition determining biographic cross-person and -place inscription and participation.

## Places of survival

The location takes its meaning from its function of locating (real and virtual) bodies, i.e. forming identities. In other words, whenever the artist aspires to the realization of becoming a subject, he/she observes that the location in its real and symbolic significance plays a central role. Along the German-Czech border, for instance, Ann-Sofi Sidén examines the situation of prostitutes from various countries in Eastern Europe. She spends most of her time in Dubi. The specific location she has chosen, however, is only a symptom in a whole chain of events. For the installation *Wait a Second!* Sidén erects a series of glass booths. In each one there is a video, and the viewer – like customer at a peepshow – settles down to watch a woman as she answers Siden's (deleted) questions. In this way, Sidén simulates a real situation: On the one hand, she has a sex worker perform on the screen for a male viewer; on the other hand, this reconstruction is blatantly artificial and false (in real peepshows the booths aren't exactly transparent and the show doesn't consist of the woman simply sitting there and talking about her life). Sidén sets up the glass booths in two rows. On the left, the videos show interviews with the owners of a love hotel/boarding house and with the women who live there (Sidén also lived here during the year she spent researching this project). On the right are women living in a different brothel. The viewer doesn't notice right away that the same names keep coming up, or that people whose names were mentioned earlier are suddenly sitting in front of the camera. Concentrating on one or only a few places has the effect of making a situation seem familiar and it refracts it into several perspectives. Thus the viewer takes on a symbolic position, namely both that of the client – who may not get to see much but gets to hear all the more – as well as that of the sitting, speaking woman – who is being watched. (Sidén talks almost exclusively with prostitutes. The interview situations with a client, the owner of the love hotel, and police officers are the only exceptions.) The re-construction of the conversations of the women using transparent booths causes me as viewer to slip into a split role. I virtually become the very object that I at the same time must feel desire for but am prevented from doing so because she doesn't fulfill her fetishistic function and says shameless things. In this split role, in which the viewer suddenly is and isn't accomplice and victim, we experience, literally too close for comfort, the various frightening versions of violence and injuries told differently by each of these women. Against our will we are drawn in (just like many of these women, who were stolen and sold) and made to occupy the precarious position of people who have been humiliated. Here the difference between client and prostitute becomes blurred because they/we are all (at times we even see Sidén as agent) positioned as actors in a series of interdependent effects and economies. If we listen for several hours to the various individual circumstances, it becomes clear that there are also circumstances that keep repeating themselves (capitalization, transnationalization, discrimination against women, construction of the border as a place of consumption and transgression).

"I am interested in the figure of a broken and suffering humanity which – ambivalent and contradictory – in stolen symbolism and an endless chain of less than innocent translation draws a possibility of hope. But it also draws a never-ending series of mimetic and simulatory events that are the legacy of the huge genocides and mass destructions of ancient and modern history,"[9] writes Donna Haraway. Such posthumanist tendencies as those Haraway calls for here come to bear in Sidén's work. If one listens to the ever recurring stories the women tell, one has the impression that they are like the individual faces of a collective murmuring of other (historical and contemporary) narratives: the woman as victim, as commodity, as migrant in search of happiness, and as someone fighting for survival – brought up to date for the age of new world orders and of global flows of capital. And yet there is hope beneath the surface of many of the stories: abducted women who were able to earn money and will go back home, others who managed to stand on their own two feet and are now preparing themselves for a new existence, or those who have built up a strong social net around them or doublecrossed their double-crossers in their own ways. It becomes clear from the women's different life stories, which on the one hand are clear repetitions and on the other hand vary strongly dependent on individual horizons of experience, that these personal survival strategies are – to put it as Biemann does in *Performing the Border* – "multiple and variable."

## Mobility as a metaphor

Although *Performing the Border* is also a video that examines women on a border and reassesses the possible ways of leading one's life as a woman in subaltern circumstances, Biemann focuses on something completely different than Sidén. Sidén's approach to the women relies on her participation in their lives. She dedicates months of her time to win their trust and be able to carry out her interviews at all. Because of this physical and private involvement in the researching of the subject it is consistent of Sidén to give the embodiments and their circumstances so much weight in the exhibition space.

Biemann's approach, on the other hand, is much more theoretical and critical of the inherent capitalist structures. She focuses explicitly on the question of which role territorial borders and female bodies, i.e. gender borders, play in the context of the new international division of labor. She shows women – if I may use Saskia Sassen's imagery – as users of the transnational bridges built with international capital. The aesthetics of the video suggests without words that the border town of Ciudad Juarez is both a place of exploitation of woman in the age of transnational hi-tech companies as well as a space for constructing bodies, genders, identities, nations, and capital. Maps, fences, digitalized border landscapes and monitoring technologies visualize the territorial North-South construct and draw parallels between it and Biemann's verbal implication of the body monitoring and surveillance the women are subjected to at their workplaces. An aesthetics of mobility and fluctuation – concepts which characterize the discourse on migration, transnational capital, and industrialization – sets the video's visual rhythm, which is slackened only by intercutting of theoreticians and activists seated and speaking before the camera. The video begins with the camera's view out the window of a moving car; it ends with dancing bodies. In between we see the flux of the female masses streaming into the maquiladora, the morning bus rides, the cars and horsemen in the desert, the exhumation of corpses, the flickering television images, the virtual detonations of mine fields, the ride along the 5000-mile border, the drifting inflatable boat, the captions, the woman washing clothes by hand, the little girl walking down the street: "She is still a girl. Can she find a way to steer through these cultural ruptures?" asks the off-camera female voice. The movement of the camera, film montage, and people can be seen as the aesthetic choreographing of a discourse of migration and capital flow, a discourse that with the help of this common element manages to coordinate the different spheres and thus structurally synchronize them: the rhythm of the assembly line; the flow of the financing capital from the North; the people from the South; the foot-stomping, hand-clapping girls at the beauty contest; the female desire as it is articulated in the love songs we hear sung on the morning bus ride or in the disco; the blows and stabs delivered to the female victims. Everything is affected by these circumstances of movement and the shift of boundaries, circumstances full of contradictions. "Gender matters to capital," a caption reads. Biemann doesn't stop at revealing life on the border as a set permeated completely by sexualization – as Sidén did – but also goes on to show that the (re-)stabilization of gender is still and continually being used as a means of control, i.e. for the production of people. In other words, she makes it clear that the multis, by creating jobs for women and empowering them as consumers of an entertainment industry built especially for them, are, on the one hand, initiating a process of destruction of patriarchal structures, but, on the other hand, they are bringing this process back under control through reterritorialization.

## Places of desire

Many of these women artists choose very specific places for their projects as the point of departure and point of intersection. Mainly this has to do with the research character of the different approaches: The artist chooses a specific situation and takes a closer look around. Biemann, for example, chooses the border town of Ciudad Juarez; the artist Dorit Margreiter Short Hills, the town where her aunt and cousin live; or Sidén chooses Dubi. Each reflects a strategy for producing real contexts and for insisting on the lived realities of the embodied subjects. But all of these works also show these places as spaces in which a multitude of desires have collected, spaces, therefore, that beyond their character of authenticity are also intensely symbolic, i.e. constructed and strewn with the imaginary. Biemann's title *Performing the Border* as well as the maps and the scenes of surveillance and situations on the border clearly suggest that the naturalness of a place does not exist, that a place is always constructed, even if this in no way detracts from its character of reality. The city that Milica Tomic films and passes through is a different Belgrade from the one bombed by NATO or the one her mother talks about. Dorit Margreiter's work entitled *Short Hills* may take its name from the suburb in New Jersey where she visits her aunt and cousin – a Chinese-American family – in their home and questions them about their favorite soaps, but at the same time it sounds like the name of a soap opera itself, too. The place they live in is both real and medially constructed – an aspect that Margreiter reinforces by allowing *Short Hills* to focus mainly on the retelling of the stories of soaps as well as on her aunt's newly built TV room. Moreover she embeds her video installation physically atop a gigantic landscape model. The radio play/video *Europe from Afar* obviously toys with the phantasm of Eurocentrism by suddenly presenting Europe "from afar," despite the fact that the cosmopolitan women who are to play Europe in the video meet in Paris, so to speak in the heart of colonial Europe. Though Europe may be just an (old) construct, it is nevertheless regarded as valuable enough to be shaken out of its moribund sleep and made to perform for new utopian inscriptions. In *Europe from Afar* the theme of remapping and rebuilding, the hybrid overlapping of female bodies and territory, once again becomes evident: The video begins visually with the marking off of an athletic field and the measuring of the delicate body parts of an aging woman (Elfriede Jelinek) as she is being fitted at a tailor's for an outfit.

It seems as if the approach of a performative constructedness of places and persons is what makes it possible at all for these artists to conceive of a new construction, i.e. a re-mapping of the territorial and body-related spaces. Eva Meyer and Eran Schaerf achieve this by taking the dilapidated, hackneyed, and reterritorialized word Europe seriously, not only in its patriarchal-territorial significance as female allegory, but also in its re-mapped function as Schengenland. They throw "Europe" open in an act of artificial reconfiguration of language and images that elude all attempts to cement them, thus enabling a recasting of this space to make room for women.

In *Short Hills* Dorit Margreiter also operates with the deconstructive re-mapping of stereotypical attributes of woman and territory, or in this case woman and city. If the idea in traditional-patriarchal models was to sketch the woman as a country so that a (male) subject could occupy and subjugate it, now the objective is to create spaces in which posthuman, postcolonial female subjects can move freely. Let us take, for example, the scene in *Short Hills* in which the aunt's face is reflected in the glass of a framed photograph of Hong Kong, the city she emigrated from more than 20 years ago when she came to the U.S. to study. Here Margreiter toys subtly with the fact that her aunt used to call Hong Kong her home and, as the viewer learns during the course of the video, that she still has strong affections for the city, which she compensates by watching Hong Kong soaps. On the other hand, the comparison of woman and city is the essential patriarchal myth. In this shot Margreiter plays on these calcified formulas of the urban feminine and the original, native home, but at the same time she notes a difference. The face doesn't blend into the façades but instead reflects itself prominently in the glass. And the woman speaks; she speaks about the city and that she left it for good reasons. She doesn't visually embody this city, and she is at the same time both physically separated from and emotionally attached to it, thus aesthetically a virtual intermediate space opens out of this, a space that constitutes a reversal of attributes and in which she inscribes herself. Since the woman herself is not filmed directly by the camera, the intensification of this moment is – as the becoming-apparent-of a possible space, albeit only structurally – a mirror image, or perhaps even just an illusion. The embodiment of the woman mirrored in the glass is a reflection – also in the meditative sense – of the possibilities of aesthetic subject construction.

One of Ursula Biemann's virtual places of the appearing-on-the-scene is the nocturnal disco. From its outward appearance in the middle of the rural townscape of the border zone it initially seems just as much an implanted foreign object as the technoid maquiladora. At first Biemann shows the entertainment establishment in all its usual jarring din, then she abruptly replaces this noise with an electronic ambient sound, the flowing permeability of which has absolutely nothing to do with the women dancing to folkloristic music. The atmosphere flooded in blue and the harsh discrepancy between the bodies we see moving and exhibiting themselves and the beauty and tranquility of the music suddenly give us a sense of something else, something that isn't even present yet, hope that washes over the scene like blue light. The space of other possibilities opens up in the middle of a place where the market value is based on the empty promise that the transcendence of borders and intense encounters were possible. At the heart of simulated but nevertheless lived transcendences the sound changes and draws us as female viewers once again in a completely different way into a nocturnal orgy of embodied "ecstasies."

### Paths, Passages

To make art in the age of posthumanism also means, through actively continuing deconstructive practices with a focus on the suffix while at the same time not failing to keep in mind the negative and paradoxical nature of current conditions, to place the specific positionality of one's own perspectives in the foreground. If one recognizes the primary and universal relativity and temporality of one's own and other's positions, one no longer needs to be afraid of stereotypes or essentialisms as was often the case with involved artists in recent years. Instead one is free through imitation to foray into them; through carrying them to absurd extremes, to attempt a re-coding of them for ones own contradictory purposes. We should be skeptical of simple identity models and bliss-promising reconstruction attempts. But we also need to be wary of overworking territorialized zones. We need to pursue strategies of infiltration, invasion, and the "despite all" attitude of survival, strategies of simulation and construction that destroy every form of naturalization from the start.

It seems significant to me that of all the images I've seen recently the most hope-filled one was a long, slow-moving scene from *Europe from Afar* shot at an airport. We see an old woman dressed in the Muslim tradition seated on a luggage cart and waiting. She is watching a baby and an older child that plays with the cart, pushing it back and forth. That's all we see the whole time, this movement back and forth, and the convergence of this old person and the very young people wearing Oriental-style clothes, and in the background the pan-Western airport aesthetics. It is an image that strikes us through the piecing together of its heterogeneous elements, a quotidian image that is at the same time arresting for its contradictions. And standing out, thus, it produces a kind of pause in its motion.

---

[1] This word was coined by the writer Ginka Steinwachs and makes reference to George Sand's transgression of female borders. It is a compound of Lat. explorari: explore, Lat. terra: earth and terrorism

[2] Donna Haraway, *Ecce Homo*. Am I not a woman and inappropriate/d other: The humane in a posthumanist landscape (trans. of trans.)

[3] Marina Grzinic/Aina Smid, *Luna 10. The Butterfly Effect of Geography* (Ljubliana, 1994)

[4] Saskia Sassen, *Rethinking Immigration: An International Perspective*, in Inclusion: Exclusion. Problems of Postcolonialism and global migration. ed. Peter Weibel/Slavoj Zizek. pp. 107-116 (trans. of trans.)

[5] The exhibition catalogue *Post Human*, curated by Jeffrey Deitch, is an example of the phantasms of total practicability. This is an important exhibition not the least because it helped popularize the word postmodern.

[6] Teresa de Lauretis quotes this word from Yvonne Rainer's movie script T*he Man Who Envied Women:* "I can't live without men, but I can live without a man. [...] But I also know that something is different now. Something in the way of an unfemininity. Not a new woman, not a non-woman, or a female misogynist, or an antiwoman, and not a platonic lesbian. Unwoman is probably the wrong term, too. A-woman is better. A-womanly. A-femininity. In a footnote, however, Lauretis adds: But the feeling that it is 'towards an unfemininity' that 'feminism in its highest form' is guiding mankind is my own personal feeling and obviously not Yvonne Rainer's – at least not yet." p. 59 and p. 63 (trans. of trans.)

[7] Teresa de Lauretis, p. 59/60.

[8] Irit Rogoff, *Looking the Other Way. Participation in the visual culture*, in: Texte zur Kunst (Cologne, December 1999), p. 111 (trans. of trans.)

[9] Donna Haraway, *Ecce Homo*, p. 119 (trans. of trans.)

**page/Seite 53** Ann-Sofi Sidén: *Warte mal!* Secession Wien, 3.12.1999-16.1.2000 (mit Kat.)
**page/Seite 54 top/oben** Dorit Margreiter: *Short Hills*
**page/Seite 54 bottom/unten** Marina Grzinic/Aina Smid: *Luna 10. The Butterfly Effect of Geography* Ljubliana 1994
**page/Seite 55 top/oben** Milica Tomic: Galerie im Taxispalais, Innsbruck 13.11.1999-9.1.2000 (mit Kat.)
**page/Seite 55 bottom/unten** *Europa von weitem*, ein Film von Eva Meyer und Eran Schaerf, Komposition: Inge Morgenroth, Produktion: Bayrischer Rundfunk/Hörspiel und Medienkunst 1999

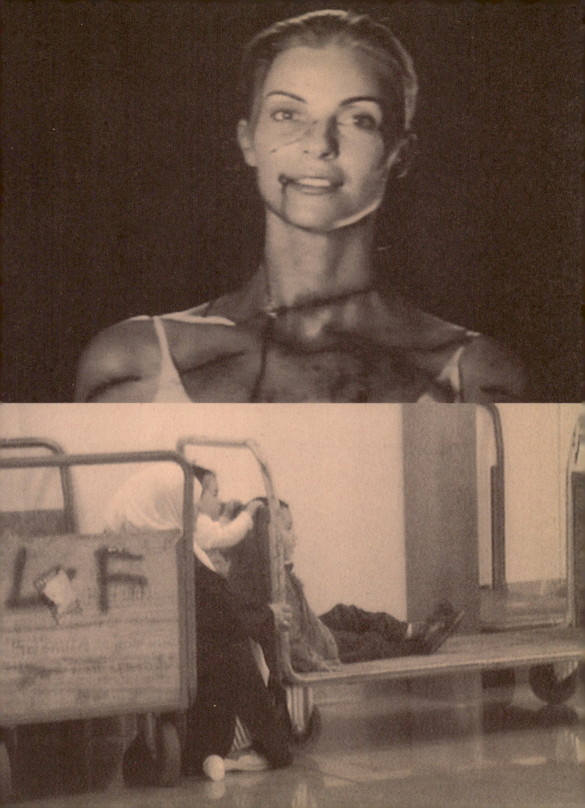

# _ÜBERLEBEN UND EXPLORATERRARISMUS[1]. DEN POSTHUMANEN RAUM NEU KARTOGRAFIEREN

Yvonne Volkart

**Das Gesicht der Humanität ist das Gesicht des Menschen/Mannes gewesen. Eine feministische Humanität muss andere Formen haben, andere Gesten zeigen; [...] Feministische Humanität muss, auf welche Weise auch immer, der Repräsentation und der buchstäblichen Gestaltung widerstehen und zugleich den Ausbruch in machtvolle neue Tropen, neue Sprachfiguren und Redewendungen, neue Wendepunkte der geschichtlichen Möglichkeiten wagen. Dafür brauchen wir, auf dem Scheitelpunkt der Krise, im Wendepunkt aller Tropen, ekstatisch Sprechende.**
**Donna Haraway**[2]

Es gibt Orte und Zeiten, die sich dir einschreiben, dir eingeschrieben haben, immer schon, obwohl sie ausserhalb dessen stehen, was du zu sein glaubst. Du ahnst die geheimen Verbindungen, oder wirst ihnen nachträglich erst gewahr. Im Moment bist du nur getroffen von etwas, das noch keine Bedeutung hat. Schon als kleines Mädchen fürchtete ich mich vor dem Tag, an dem ich 36 Jahre alt werden würde. Ich stellte mir vor, wie das sein würde, eine Frau zu sein. Es wäre mein letzter Geburtstag im alten Jahrtausend und ich war sicher, dass ich das neue nicht erleben würde, so sehr glaubte ich, dass ein 3. Weltkrieg meine Möglichkeiten verengen oder alles auslöschen würde. Ich hatte Angst davor, leiden zu müssen und als zu spät Geborene betrogen worden zu sein um jene Welt, in der ich meine Sehnsucht nach Weite hätte ausleben können. So sehr wollte ich das Land, die Länder im Osten kennenlernen, wo meine Mutter herkam. Und auf den Mars wollte ich auch. Noch lebe ich, und ich reise ständig und fliege und lerne fremde Menschen kennen, um das aufzubauen, was meine Perspektive eines engagierten Lebens ist.

An jenem Tag des 24. März 1999 zeigte ich StudentInnen unter anderem Marina Grzinics und Aina Smids für das slowenische Fernsehen produzierte Arbeit *Luna 10. The Butterfly Effect of Geography*. Das Video interessierte mich damals so wie jetzt, weil es darin um eine andere als die übliche Perspektive geht, um die einer Frau nämlich, eines Menschen aus einem postkommunistischen Land. Es handelt vom Wunsch nach Ausdehnung, Welteroberung und der Frage nach Überleben. Der Titel bezieht sich auf den ersten Mondsatelliten, den die Russen in den 60er Jahren in den Weltraum schickten, der Untertitel auf den Traum, neue Territorien als Produkte des kalten Kriegs zu gewinnen (Grzinic). Zu Beginn des Videos sehen wir eine Frau durch ein Fernrohr schauen – die Verdoppelung der eigenen Situation als weibliche Zuschauerin. Sie und ein Mann geleiten uns in einer Art Rahmensituation durch die verschiedenen window-, oder wie Grzinic/Smid sagen, hypertextartigen Bildsequenzen des Videos hindurch, welche Bilder progressiver jugoslawischer Filmemacher wie Emir Kusturica oder Zelimir Zelnik, Dokumaterial von Piratenradios u.a. zeigen. Die Schöne schweigt, während er über technische "Revolutionen" wie Internet, Kriege, die Rolle der Medien und die Perspektive der Menschen aus dem Osten spricht. Obwohl er den männlich dozierenden Part innehat, steht er manchmal in Unterhosen da, oder wird zu einer Art technologischem Medium, das Ziffern an eine Tafel schreibt, während die Frau ihm die Worte eingibt. Das heisst, sein Körper besetzt auch eine weibliche, untergebene Position. Sie wechselt ihre Kleidung ebenfalls zwischen Unterrock und Militäruniform. Die geschlechtsspezifischen und sozialen Matrixen der beiden sind temporär und widersprüchlich, komplex und gleitend. *Luna 10* kann als ein kritisches Plädoyer für die Appropriation und Umbesetzung neuer (Kriegs-) Technologien und Medien durch Frauen und andere subalterne Gruppen interpretiert werden. Die Frau aus dem Osten hat sich des Fernrohres (veraltete technologische "Prothese" und Phallussubstitut) bemächtigt. Sie will auch auf den Mond, und auch sie wird nur die Bilder übermitteln, die sie sieht. Ihr prüfender Blick und die grünliche Farbe des Films lassen Analogien zu militärischen Infrarot-Überwachungsszenarien zu. Doch die Bilder, die eingeblendet werden, sind voller Kontraste. So steht die Frau zu Beginn mit teigverklebten Händen in dörflich-ärmlicher Umgebung da. Der Mann zitiert westliche technologische Überschreitungsfantasien, wir sehen dazu Bilder privater Häuslichkeit, Ländlichkeit, Hochzeiten, kommunistische Defilées oder die Erschiessung einer Frau durch drei Soldaten auf einem Feld. Die grünliche Farbe betont das Archivartige dieses Filmmaterials. Räume, Körper, Identitäten und Technologien werden als historische, mediale und ideologische Konstruktionen dargestellt. Alles interferiert mit allem, aber es sind ganz reale Räume und Körper, in denen alltägliche Momente wie Lust, Angst, Trauer, Freude erfahren werden. Mediale Konstruktionen von Orten und Körpern schliessen intensives Erleben nicht aus. "LIVE is a very simple program" sagt der halbnackt dasitzende Mann voller Hohn in *Luna 10*. Seine Überlebensphilosophie ist simpel und radikal in ihrem Wunschpotential: "Have you queued up for the virtual bread? As it is with technological revolutions in the West, you will get only bread crumbs. Better than nothing."

Anlässlich ihrer Ausstellung im Winter unterhielt ich mich mit Milica Tomic darüber, was sie an jenem 24. März 1999 tat. Sie wollte ihr lange geplantes Video *Portrait meiner Mutter (Portrait von Marija Milutinovic)* drehen, weil es gemäss Wetterbericht das erstemal seit langem klar und sonnig zu werden versprach. Es sollte der Weg aufgenommen werden, welchen sie üblicherweise von der eigenen Wohnung im Zentrum Belgrads zur Wohnung ihrer Mutter am Stadtrand zurücklegt. Im Katalog zur Ausstellung schreibt sie: "Es erübrigt sich zu erwähnen, dass in diesen Tagen auch noch ein anderer seine letzten Vorbereitungen traf, um Belgrad zu seinem Objekt zu machen; natürlich jeder von uns auf seine Weise und aus seiner Perspektive." [4]

## Posthumane Kondition

Es ist wichtig, diese unterschiedlichen Perspektiven herauszuarbeiten, sie miteinander in Beziehung zu setzen und auf ihnen zu beharren, nicht um ein pluralistisch-relativistisches Patchwork zu entwerfen, sondern um die Phantasmen von Gleichheit und die realen Gegensätze und Unvereinbarkeiten zu enthüllen. Was habe ich mit meinem Engagement gemacht, als ich alle die persönlichen Statements der Frauen und Männer aus Belgrad im Internet lesen konnte und mir ihre Wut und Trauer am Telefon anhörte? Was tun damit, dass die Medien Räume und Distanzen schrumpfen lassen und ihre Technologien gleichzeitig Kriege führen, den tödlichsten aller Antagonismen? Was heisst es, eine engagierte Kunstvermittlerin zu sein, die über Gender im Cyberspace und ideologische Implikationen von neuen Technologien spricht und gleichzeitig diversen Eskalationen zusieht? Wie damit umgehen, dass eine kritische Position zutiefst widersprüchlich ist?

"Wir sehen jetzt, dass der Abgrund der Geschichte Raum für alle hat. Wir fühlen, dass eine Kultur genau so hinfällig ist wie ein einzelnes Leben. Die Welt, die ihrem Hang zu unseliger Verstandesschärfe den Namen "Fortschritt" gibt, trachtet, die Güter des Lebens mit den Vorteilen des Todes zu verbinden. Sie kauft Raum und Zeit als imaginäre Werte menschlichen Kapitals und schafft damit die Vervielfältigung ihrer Eingänge", sagt Jacqueline, eine der fiktiv-realen Protagonistinnen Europas aus Eva Meyers und Eran Schaerfs bimedialem Hörspiel-Film-Projekt *Europa von weitem*. Bis zum Schluss bleibt unklar, ob Jacqueline Perserin, Jüdin, Europäerin, Christin, arabische Israeli, Schauspielerin oder eine einbalsamierte koptische Frauenleiche ist. Und Piemanta, Jacquelines Grossmutter/Schulfreundin/Doppelgängerin erwidert: Sie [die Welt] hat völlig das ökonomische Prinzip begriffen, demzufolge der Eingang das einzige ist, was zählt und sich bezahlt macht. Es geht darum, in einen Raum zu gelangen, der erst aus der Zeit entstanden sein wird. Da er nicht aufhört, sich zu vergrössern, wird er zu einer Weltausstellung, die keinen anderen Gegenstand als ihre Eingänge hat."

Tatsächlich stehen viele trotz forcierter Werbung für angebliche Eingänge vor verschlossenen Türen: "Was wäre aus meiner Anstellung in der Medienklasse eurer Hochschule geworden", fragt meine polnische Mitbewohnerin, "hätte ich nicht auch noch einen kanadischen Pass gehabt?" [5]

Das sind die paradoxen Räume und Konditionen des Posthumanismus, d.h. jener Welt, die sich, gegründet auf humanistische Ideale, in einem widersprüchlichen Prozess von deren Auflösung und gleichzeitiger Restitution befindet. Schon der Begriff des Posthumanen selbst ist so gespalten, ambivalent und vage. Als Metapher für das Nicht-Natürliche und als Indikator für das Ende humanistischer Ideale wird er sowohl von TechnodeterministInnen als auch von (Post-)Feministinnen benutzt. Ich verwende ihn einerseits, um mich in die feministische anti-essentialistische und anti-androzentristische Tradition einzuschreiben, andererseits um ein Wort ins Spiel zu bringen, das, wie und wo man es auch einsetzt, immer gleichzeitig auch an einem anderen Ort ist, das heisst immer wahr und falsch, Hype und Utopie zugleich und damit nie wirklich festgelegt ist - ein Wort also, das das Paradoxe von Orten und Zeiten und die Temporalität von Perspektiven immer wieder neu verkörpert.

In diesen posthumanen Räumen läuft, wie Saskia Sassen sagt, die Internationalisierung des Kapitals unter dem Stichwort Globalisierung, während die Internationalisierung der Arbeit unter dem diskriminierenden und veralteten Begriff der Migration geführt wird.[6] Während mit der Transnationalisierung der Wirtschaft die Gesetze der Nationalstaaten und die Rechte der darin lebenden Menschen übergangen werden können, sehen wir uns gleichzeitig mit einer Verstärkung von Rassismus, Nationalismus, Sexismus und Fundamentalismus konfrontiert. *Luna 10* zeigt - neben vielen post- und cyberfeministischen Theoretikerinnen wie Donna Haraway, Rosi Braidotti, Anne Balsamo, Carol A. Stabile, Katherine N. Hayles, dass auch auf der Ebene des Körpers trotz technikdeterministischer Schwelgereien[7] und realen Grenzverschiebungen ideologische Differenzen wie Alter, Klasse und Geschlecht nicht aufgelöst sind, sondern verstärkt und rekonstituiert werden. Es zeigt aber auch, dass es Möglichkeiten gibt, in diese Prozesse zu intervenieren, respektive aus seiner/ihrer Perspektive mitzutun. Die Wirkungen der neu gezogenen Nord-Süd-Grenzen der internationalen Arbeitsteilung auf Körper und Geschlecht ist das Thema von Ursula Biemanns Projekt *Performing the Border*. Dass es nicht einfach dieses schöne leichte Grenzüberqueren gibt, wie Berta Jottar in *Performing the Border* zu recht sagt, bringt auch der Netzkünstler Alexei Shulgin mit einer Aktion prägnant auf den Punkt. Shulgin war mit seiner Punkrockband (einem alten Computer) vom Tijuana Media Center für ein Konzert nach Mexiko eingeladen worden, erhielt aber als temporär in den USA lebender Russe kein Visum. Aus diesem Grund veranstaltete er sein Konzert direkt am Grenzzaun. Er selbst betätigte sein Keybord auf der US-Seite, der Computer spielte auf der mexikanischen Seite. "Since borders have become more permeable for products and less passable for people, Shulgin's computer is allowed to travel freely between Mexico and the USA without a visa«, schreibt Natalie Bookchin in der Presseaussendung. Shulgin benennt die diskriminierenden posthumanen Bedingungen und codiert sie zu einem Fest um. Damit schafft er die temporäre Möglichkeit, die ausschliessenden Nord-Süd und Ost-West-Verhältnisse ins Absurde zu drehen, so dass sie ohne Subordination sogar genossen werden können. Shulgin inszeniert minimale Gesten, die das individuelle Überleben-Wollen plötzlich als etwas Subversives darstellen, als systemkohärente Antworten und Re-Aktionen auf spezifische ausschliessende Bedingungen. In dieser Inszenierung von Anpassung und Fest liegt ein politisches Potential, weil die Idee einer Party an einem dafür nicht vorgesehenen Ort symbolisch auf Überschreitung eng abgezirkelter Grenzen hin angelegt ist.

Insofern möchte ich die obig gestellte Frage – was es für meine Identitäten bedeutet, wenn die Räume, in denen ich mich bewege, zynisch und paradox werden – nur vorläufig und indirekt beantworten. Nämlich damit, dass ich nach Positionen, wie denen von Shulgin und anderen, suche und Kollaborationen anstrebe, in denen das Paradoxe unserer jeweils unterschiedlichen Situierung und Perspektive als fundamentaler Ausgangspunkt für die eigenen Identitäten, Lebensentwürfe und Handlungsräume auf sich genommen wird.

Ich möchte also diese Frage über den Umweg der Diskussion von Arbeiten beantworten, in denen KünstlerInnen spezifische Ästhetiken entwickeln, welche Identitätsentwürfe für eine Existenz im posthumanen Raum kartographieren. Ich möchte konkreter betrachten, mit welchen Mitteln einige KünstlerInnen "Erscheinungsräume" (Irit Rogoff, Hannah Arendt zitierend) konstruieren. Sie alle enthüllen das Diskriminierende und die Gewalt aktueller Grenz- und Technologiediskurse, ohne in Opfer- und Larmoyanzdiskussionen stecken zu bleiben. Wie die Hoffnung und den Glauben an die Wichtigkeit ästhetischer Identitätsentwürfe aufrechterhalten, wenn an einem schönen Frühlingstag (fast) alles zunichte gemacht wird?

Es ist kein Zufall, (aber auch kein Grund essentialistisch zu werden oder zu verallgemeinern) dass die grosse Mehrheit der von mir ausgewählten KünstlerInnen Frauen sind. Erstens vertrete ich als Frau eine situiert weibliche Perspektive, und zweitens könnte das Bejahen der posthumanen paradoxen Konditionen im Begriff des Weiblichen, so wie er sich symbolisch artikuliert, bereits eingeschrieben sein. Denn wie die feministische Theorie generell und hier Teresa de Lauretis im besonderen aufzeigten, ist der "Status [der Frau] als Objekt und Zeichen gleichermassen" immer schon widersprüchlich: "Das weibliche Subjekt ist gleichermassen FRAU wie Frauen."[8] Die nach de Lauretis als "weiblich" herausdestillierte Verbindung von Objekt- und Zeichenstatus gilt allerdings für andere subalterne Gruppen und "unheile Allianzen" wie Mensch/Tier oder Mensch/Maschine und kann deshalb nachgerade als die posthumane Kondition schlechthin gelten.[9]

Zentral bleibt die Frage, welche ästhetischen Strategien entwickelt werden, damit wir als mehrfach codierte, hybride und differentielle Subjekte angesprochen werden und uns re-formulieren können? Wie kann das spezifisch situierte Wissen von Kunst- und DiskursproduzentInnen unterschiedlicher Herkunft für Identitätsdiskurse, die nicht fixiert sind und auf neue Fixierungen hinauslaufen, genutzt werden? Anhand Yvonne Rainers Film *The Man Who Envied Woman* kommt de Lauretis zu folgendem Schluss, den ich zur Voraussetzung der hier diskutierten Ansätze nehme. Mit ihren Fragen von Post-Nation, Post-Kolonialismus etc. gehen diese Künstlerinnen allerdings über de Lauretis zitierten Diskussionspunkt von A-Frau-Sein[10] hinaus: "Genau in diesem widersprüchlichen Raum, in der gespaltenen und sich hintergehenden Verkettung seiner Grammatik des Erzählens und seiner bildlichen Mehrdeutigkeit, spricht der Film mich, Zuschauerin, als a(-)woman an. Hier bemüht sich der Film um meinen (un)weiblichen Blick und schreibt meine im Geschlecht befangene Subjektivität ein in das, was ich ein "Erkennen des Verkennens" nennen könnte; in die persönlich-politischen Widersprüche meiner eigenen Geschichte von A Weiblichkeit."[11] Wichtig an dieser Aussage von Teresa de Lauretis ist für uns die paradoxe Position, in der sich das weibliche Subjekt befindet und aus der heraus es sich stets neu konstruiert. Als Frau geboren und erzogen, identifiziert sich das weibliche Subjekt immer wieder mit seinem Status als Zeichen und seiner Situierung als Frau, die sie aber gleichzeitig nicht sein kann, da es sich dabei um phantasmatische Konstruktionen handelt. Dieser Prozess des Verkennens ist gleichzeitig der Prozess ihrer multiplen Konstruktionen von Subjektivität, respektive die eigentliche Voraussetzung dazu. Aber nur dann, wenn dieser Prozess als phantasmatische Setzung dekonstruiert wird – gewissermassen in der Verneinung dieses Optionsraumes – ermöglicht er dem weiblichen (Betrachter)Subjekt eine Möglichkeit zu utopischen, temporären Identitätskonstruktion. De Lauretis sagt: "Durch die Dekonstruktion des narrativen Raumes erzeugt der Film einen kritischen Raum, in dem ich gerade als Frau und als A-Frau angesprochen bin." Nur dann also, wenn das Subjekt als total paradoxes adressiert wird, kann es sich in diesen nicht fixierten "kritischen Raum" artikulieren.

## Symptomwerdung

Ich möchte diesen Prozess erkennender Verkennung am Beispiel von Milica Tomic' Video- und Netzarbeit *Ich bin Milica Tomic* erläutern. Tomic steht in einem weissen Unterrock da, sie erscheint strahlend schön, leuchtet überirdisch. Dann beginnt sie zu sprechen: "Ich bin Milica Tomic, ich bin Deutsche." Sie wiederholt das in 65 verschiedenen Sprachen und Nationen. "Ich bin Österreicherin, ich bin Amerikanerin" und so weiter. Bei jedem Satz erscheint eine Blutspur auf ihrer Haut, so dass sie am Schluss völlig gezeichnet ist von Wunden, aus denen Blut strömt. Nach den 65 Sprechakten schliesst sich alles wieder zum vollkommenen Körper und beginnt von vorne. Nationale Identität und Muttersprache sind in unserer Noch-Zeit der Nationalstaaten wichtige identitätsbildende Faktoren und konstituieren unsere Gefühle von Heimat und In-der-Welt-Sein. Die Sehnsucht danach ist dem Körper gleichsam eingeschrieben, macht sein Wunschpotential aus, das sich im unversehrten Körper äussert. Die Realität heisst aber auch, dass das Phantasma der Nation die Körper verstümmelt, dass sich das Subjekt als kontingentes, verwundbares und verwundetes artikuliert, und zwar unabhängig davon, ob die "eigene" Nation eine besonders blutrünstige ist oder nicht. Das Subjekt, als Abspaltung eines solchen Phantasmas, befindet sich immer schon im Paradox von Körper-und-Zeichen-Sein. Tomic' unmittelbar aus den Sätzen resultierende Wunden enthüllen, dass jeder ihrer performativen Akte ihres zwanghaften Identitätssprechens ein Akt der Verkennung ist. Mir ihrer hysterische Mimetisierung des Wunsches nach nationaler Identität bei dessen gleichzeitiger Dekonstruierung durch die klaffenden Wunden verwirft sie aber den Wunsch nach (nationaler) Identität nicht einfach a priori, sondern vielmehr nimmt sie ihn ernst, sowohl bezüglich seiner subjektkonstituierenden als auch seiner traumatisierend-tödlichen Produktivkraft und treibt ihn in einem gleichsam rituellen Sprechakt erkennender Verkenntnis ad absurdum. Ihre hysterische Identifikation mit der ödipalen Position (sie ist verblendet und wird kastriert), in welcher sich die Befangenheit als Frau mit Eigennamen und als nationalstaatliches Subjekt entäussert, mithin ihre Aufführung eines symptomatisch Zu-einer-Wunde-Werdens bewirkt, dass auch wir als ZuschauerInnen aufgefordert sind, in diese mimetischen Prozesse einzusteigen und uns mit ihrer Rolle der völligen Verletzlichkeit zu identifizieren. Was bleibt, ist dieser ästhetische Raum, wo die Frau auf der Leinwand (und im Netz) als "ekstatisch Sprechende" (Haraway) perform(ier)t, und aus dem sich die Möglichkeiten eines ungleich multipleren und variableren Raumes ableiten, eines mythischen, utopischen, eines "Erscheinungsraumes", in welchem "politische Repräsentation und Partizipation ausserhalb der traditionellen Institutionen der parlamentarischen Systeme"[12] gedacht werden und stattfinden kann.

## Topographien

Milica Tomic hat ihr Video *Portrait von M.M.* Monate später trotzdem gedreht oder erst recht. Den Weg zu ihrer Mutter, die in einem sicheren Gebiet wohnte, musste sie zur Zeit der Nato-Angriffe tatsächlich jeden Abend zurücklegen, so dass sie nicht nur die vorläufige Protagonistin ihres Realität gewordenen zukünftigen Videos wurde, sondern die Realität ist auch die Simulation einer noch nicht stattgefundenen fiktionalen Passage geworden. In *Portrait meiner Mutter* kommen verschiedene Wege zusammen: Der Weg der Tochter durch Belgrad und der Lebensweg der Mutter, der nicht unabhängig vom historischen Verlauf Jugoslawiens ist: Die Mutter, im modernen Belgrad eine Schauspielerin mit Tendenz zu minimalistischer Avantgardeästhetik (gegen die vorherrschende Ästhetik des sozialen Realismus), zieht sich in den 80er Jahren, zur Zeit forcierter Nationalisierung also, von ihrem Schauspielberuf zurück. In einem Akt weiblicher Selbstkastrierung sagt sie mitten in einer Rolle, sie sei eine schlechte Schauspielerin. In der Folge wendet sie sich einer esoterisch-weltflüchtigen Form christlicher Orthodoxie zu. In der Diskussion der drei Frauen zeigt sich klar, dass der als zutiefst persönlich erlebte Lebensweg der Mutter mit ihrem fatalistischen (d.h. sich politisch fatal auswirkenden) Glauben unter der Schirmherrschaft einer staatsaffirmativen Kirche parallel zur Reterritorialisierungspolitik Serbiens verläuft. Tomic' Video wird damit zur Fortsetzung des von der Mutter abgebrochenen Wegs eines Künstlerinnenlebens voller Engagement und Kritik.

Die Geschichte der Mutter wird aber nicht bebildert oder kontinuierlich erzählt. Man hört im Off die Stimmen von Tochter, Mutter und deren bester Freundin, die über das Leben der Mutter und die aktuelle Situation reden. Erst ganz am Schluss des 63-minütigen Videos sieht man Tochter und Mutter, wie sie sich in der Wohnung treffen. Das ist der Moment, wo die Stimmen verstummen, wo sich die beiden in einem Moment unendlich erscheinender Stille in die Augen schauen und umarmen. Dazwischen die körperlos-körperhafte Passage - zu Fuss, mit Bus und Taxi - durch die Strassen eines unerwartet unversehrten Belgrads, stumme Begegnungen mit Menschen - Fremden und Verwandten - mit subjektiver

Kameraführung gedreht, die gleichsam Tomic' unsichtbaren Körper in Bewegung versetzt. In den Seh- und Hörfluss schieben sich in unregelmässigen Abständen Schwarzfilmsequenzen ein, die von undefinierbaren Störgeräuschen begleitet sind und, den diskontinuierlichen Gesprächsverlauf der Frauen unterbrechend, nicht nur nochmals alles in Frage zu stellen scheinen, sondern auch repräsentationslose Momente möglicher Eintritte in den videografischen Raum sein könnten. Es ist, als ob diese Momente uns Betrachterinnen aufforderten, ebenfalls durch diese schwarzen Löcher und undefinierbaren Geräusche hindurch zu gehen und unser eigenes Leben einzuschreiben, um das Leben als bios graphein sozusagen mental zu praktizieren. Dass uns Tomic einen Raum zur Verkörperung und Partizipation zur Verfügung stellt, macht die Installation nochmals klar. Neben dem frontalen Videoscreening plaziert sie vier Diaprojektoren, die die Längswände paarweise mit Bildern füllen. Darauf sind u.a. Aura-Bilder aus den spirituellen Büchern der Mutter, oder Gebrauchsanweisungen für Tampons aus den 60er Jahren von der Mutter, die die Vorstellungen des weiblichen Körperinneren des kleinen Mädchen Milica widerspiegeln. Topografische Verhältnisse (Stadtraum/Galerieraum/weibliches Körperinneres) werden gleichsam zur Grundbedingung personen- und ortsübergreifender biografischer Einschreibung und Partizipation.

## Orte des Überlebens

Der Ort gewinnt seine Bedeutung durch seine Funktion der Ver-Ortung von (realen und virtuellen) Körpern, mithin der Bildung von Identitäten. Anders gesagt, da wo KünstlerInnen mit der Realisierung des Begehrens nach Subjektwerdung operieren, spielen auch Orte in ihrer realen und symbolischen Bedeutung eine zentrale Rolle. Ann-Sofi Sidén z.B. untersucht die Situation von Prostituierten aus verschiedenen Ländern Osteuropas an der deutsch-tschechischen Grenze und hält sich v.a. in Dubi auf. Der spezifisch gewählte Ort ist aber lediglich ein Symptom in einer ganzen Reihe von Verkettungen. Für die Installation *Warte mal!* baute Sidén u.a. eine Reihe von Glaskabinen auf, je eine für ein Video, in die man sich, einem Peepshow-Besucher ähnlich, niederlässt und der Frau zusieht, die auf Sidéns (herausgeschnittene) Fragen anwortet. Damit simuliert Sidén einerseits eine reale Situation, in der eine Sexarbeiterin auf dem Monitor für einen männlichen Zuschauer agiert, andererseits rekonstruiert sie diese völlig künstlich und falsch (in realen Peepshows sind die Kabinen gerade nicht transparent und besteht die Handlung der Frau nicht im einfach Dasitzen und über ihr Leben reden). Diese Glaskabinen baute Sidén zweireihig auf, links werden die Interviews mit den Besitzern eines Stundenhotels und den darin lebenden Frauen gezeigt (Sidén lebte hier während ihrer einjährigen Recherche), rechts die Frauen, die in einem anderen Bordell leben. Erst mit der Zeit findet man heraus, dass gleiche Namen fallen, oder dass Leute, von denen man reden hörte, nun vor der Kamera sitzen. Die Konzentration auf den gleichen oder wenige Orte hat den Effekt, dass eine Situation vertrauter und durch mehrere Perspektiven gebrochen erscheint, so dass man als BetrachterIn eine symbolische Position einnimmt: Und zwar sowohl die des Kunden, der/die nicht viel zu sehen, dafür umso mehr zu hören kriegt, als auch die der sitzenden und sprechenden Frau, die angesehen wird. (Sidén spricht fast ausschliesslich mit Prostituierten, Interviewsituationen mit einem Freier, dem Besitzer des Stundenhotels und Polizisten bilden die Ausnahme). Die Re-Konstruktion der Sprechsituation der Frauen qua Transparentboxen führt dazu, dass ich als ZuschauerIn unmittelbar in eine Doppelrolle verfalle, in der ich virtuell zu der werde, die ich doch gleichzeitig begehren muss, aber daran gehindert werde, weil sie ihre Fetischfunktion nicht erfüllt und Unerhörtes sagt. In dieser Doppelrolle, in der man plötzlich Komplize und Opfer ist und doch nicht ist, erfährt man die Gewalt und die Verletzungen, von der jede dieser Frauen ihre eigene erschreckende Version erzählt, buchstäblich am eigenen Leib: Unfreiwillig hinein-gezogen (so wie viele dieser Frauen auch, die geraubt und verkauft wurden) besetzt man die prekäre Position erniedrigter Menschen, in der sich sogar der Unterschied von Freier und Prostituierter aufhebt, weil sie/wir alle (auch Sidén sieht man manchmal agieren) als AgentInnen in einer Reihe voneinander abhängiger Wirkungen und Ökonomien positioniert sind. Das stundenlang dauernde Anhören unterschiedlicher individueller Bedingungen enthüllt klar, dass es auch sich wiederholende Umstände gibt (Kapitalisierung, Transnationalisierung, Diskriminierung der Frau, Konstruktion der Grenze als Ort von Konsum und Überschreitung).

"Mein Interesse gilt der Gestalt einer gebrochenen und leidenden Humanität, die – ambivalent und widersprüchlich, in gestohlenem Symbolismus und unendlichen Verkettungen nichtunschuldiger Übersetzung, eine mögliche Hoffnung bezeichnet. Ebenso aber bezeichnet sie eine nichtendende Reihe mimetischer und simulatorischer Ereignisse, die mit den grossen Völkermorden und Massenvernichtungen der antiken und modernen Geschichte vermacht sind"[13] schreibt Donna Haraway. In Sidéns Arbeit kommen solche posthumanistischen Züge zum Tragen, wie sie Haraway einfordert. Hört man den endlos sich wiederholenden Geschichten zu, die die Frauen erzählen, so erscheint das wie ein zum einzelnen Gesicht gewordenes Gemurmel anderer (historischer und gegenwärtiger) Erzählungen: die Frau als Opfer, als Ware, als migrantische Glückssucherin und als um ihr Überleben Kämpfende - aktualisiert für das Zeitalter neuer Weltordnungen und globaler Kapitalströme. Und dennoch steckt in vielen Geschichten Hoffnung: Frauen, die verschleppt wurden, konnten Geld verdienen und werden zurückkehren, andere machten sich selbständig und bereiten sich auf eine neue Existenz vor, wieder andere bauten sich ein gutes soziales Netz auf oder betrügen ihre Betrüger auf ihre Weise. Aus den verschiedenen Lebenswegen der Frauen, die sich einerseits eklatant wiederholen und sich andererseits vom individuellen Erlebnishorizont her markant unterscheiden, wird klar, dass die persönlichen Strategien des Überlebens – um es mit Biemanns *Performing the Border* zu sagen "vielfältig und variabel" sind.

## Mobilität als Metapher

Obwohl *Performing the Border* auch eine Videorecherche über Frauen an einer Grenze ist und Möglichkeiten weiblichen Lebens in subalternen Verhältnissen einer Neubewertung unterzieht, ist Biemanns Interesse ein ganz anderes als das von Sidén. Sidéns Annäherung an die Frauen ist getragen von der Partizipation an ihrem Leben. Sie verwendete Monate, um ihr Vertrauen zu gewinnen und diese Interviews überhaupt durchführen zu können. Aufgrund dieser körperlichen und privaten Involvierung in die Materialrecherche ist es konsequent, dass Sidén den Verkörperungen und ihrer Voraussetzung im Ausstellungsraum soviel Gewicht gibt.

Biemann geht kapitalismuskritischer und theoriegeleiter vor. Ihr geht es explizit um die Frage, welche Rolle territoriale Grenzen und weibliche Körper, mithin Geschlechtergrenzen im Kontext der neuen internationalen Arbeitsteilung spielen. Sie zeigt, um mit Saskia Sassen zu sprechen, die Frauen als Benutzerinnen der vom internationalen Kapital geschlagenen transnationalen Brücken. Die Ästhetik des Videos suggeriert unausgesprochen, dass der Grenzort Ciuad Juarez sowohl ein Ort der Ausbeutung der Frau im Zeitalter transnationaler High-Tech-Konzerne als auch ein Raum zur Konstruktion von Körpern, Geschlechtern, Identitäten, Nationen und Kapital ist. Landkarten, Zäune, digitale Grenzlandschaften und Kontrolltechnologien visualisieren die territoriale Nord-Südkonstruktion und parallelisieren sie gewissermassen mit der von Biemann nur verbal angedeuteten Körperkontrolle und Überwachung, der die

Frauen am Arbeitsplatz ausgesetzt sind. Eine Ästhetik von Mobilität und Fluktuation, die begrifflich der Diskurs um Migration, transnationales Kapital und Industrialisierung umreissen, bestimmt den visueller Rhythmus des Videos, der nur durch die Einblendung dasitzender sprechender Theoretikerinnen und Aktivistinnen ins Stocken kommt. Mit der Kamerafahrt aus einem Auto beginnt das Video, mit tanzenden Körpern endet es. Dazwischen die Bewegungen der in die Maquiladora strömenden Frauenmassen, die morgendlichen Busfahrten, die Autos und Reiter in der Wüste, das Ausgraben der toten Leiber, die flimmernden Bilder im Fernsehen, die virtuellen Detonationen von Minenfeldern, die Fahrt entlang der 5000 Meilen langen Grenze, das treibende Schlauchboot, die Lauftexte, die von Hand Wäsche waschende Frau, das die Strasse hinuntergehende kleine Mädchen: "Sie ist immer noch ein kleines Mädchen. Findet sie einen Weg, sich durch diese kulturellen Brüche zu steuern?" fragt die weibliche Stimme im Off. Die Bewegungen der Kamera, der Filmmontagen, der Menschen können als die ästhetische Inszenierung eines Diskurses von Migration und Kapitalfluss interpretiert werden, der die verschiedensten Felder mittels dieser gemeinsamen Eigenschaft ineinander und damit strukturell gleichschaltet: der Rhythmus des Fliessbandes, der Fluss des Finanzkapitals aus dem Norden, der Menschen aus dem Süden, die stampfenden und klatschenden Mädchen beim Schönheitswettbewerb, das weibliche Begehren, wie es sich in den Liebesliedern artikuliert, die in den morgendlichen Busfahrten oder in der Disco zu hören sind, die Hiebe und Stiche, denen die Frauen zum Opfer fallen: alles ist Effekt dieser Bedingungen von Bewegung und Grenzverschiebung, die voller Widersprüche sind. "Gender spielt für das Finanzkapital eine Rolle", sagt ein Lauftext. Biemann enthüllt nicht nur das Leben an der Grenze als Set völliger Sexualisierung - wie Sidén - sie zeigt darüberhinaus auch, dass die (Re-)Stabilisierung von Geschlecht immer noch und immer wieder ein Mittel zur Kontrolle, mithin Produktion von Menschen ist. Mit anderen Worten, sie macht evident, dass die Multis durch die Arbeitsplatzbeschaffung für Frauen und deren Ermächtigung zu Konsumentinnen einer für sie aufgebauten Vergnügungsindustrie einerseits einen Prozess der Zerstörung patriarchaler Strukturen einleiten, ihn andererseits durch Reterritorialisierung unter Kontrolle bringen.

Orte der Wünsche

Viele dieser Künstlerinnen wählen ganz bestimmte Orte zum Ausgangs- und Schnittpunkt ihrer Projekte. Das hat vordergründig mit dem Recherchecharakter dieser Ansätze zu tun: Man wählt eine bestimmte Situation und schaut sich dort genauer um. Biemann etwa nimmt die Grenzstadt Ciudad Juarez, die Künstlerin Dorit Margreiter den Wohnort ihrer Tante und Cousine namens *Short Hills* oder Sidén Dubi. Das sind Strategien, um reale Kontexte herzustellen und auf der gelebten Realität verkörperter Subjekte zu bestehen. Alle diese Arbeiten zeigen diese Orte aber auch als Räume, in denen sich eine Vielheit an Wünschen versammelt, Räume also, die über ihren Authentizitätscharakter hinaus hochgradig symbolisiert, mithin konstruiert und imaginär besetzt sind.

Biemanns Titel *Performing the Border* sowie die gezeigten Landkarten, Grenzüberwachung und -situationen spielen deutlich darauf an, dass es die Natürlichkeit eines Ortes nicht gibt, dass er immer konstruiert ist, auch wenn dies seinen Realitätscharakter in keiner Weise schmälert. Milica Tomic' gefilmter und passierter Stadtkörper ist ein anderes Belgrad als das von der Nato angegriffene oder der von ihrer Mutter erzählte. Dorit Margreiters *Short Hills* betitelte Arbeit wiederum ist zwar der Name einer Vorstadt in New Jersey, in der sie ihre Tante und Cousine - eine chinesisch-amerikanische Familie - zu Hause besucht und zu ihren Lieblingssoaps befragt, dieser Name erinnert aber ebenso an Titel von Soap

Operas. Der Lebensort ist sowohl real als auch medial konstruiert - ein Aspekt, den Margreiter dadurch verstärkt, indem sie *Short Hills* wesentlich um das Nacherzählen der Inhalte der Soaps kreisen lässt sowie um den von der Tante neugebauten TV-Room. Darüberhinaus bettet sie die Apparatur ihres Videos auf ein riesiges Landschaftsmodell. Das Video-Hörspiel *Europa von weitem* spielt mit dem Phantasma des Eurozentrismus, in dem Europa plötzlich "von weitem" gesehen wird, auch wenn sich die kosmopolitischen Frauen, die Europa in dem Video spielen sollen, in Paris, im Herzen des kolonialen Europa gewissermassen, treffen: Europa ist nurmehr eine (alte) Konstruktion, die allerdings als wertvoll genug betrachtet wird, aus dem Todesschlaf gerissen und für utopische Neueinschreibungen aufgeführt zu werden. Auch in *Europa von weitem* ist die Thematik des Neukartografierens und Wiederbauens, die hybride Überlagerung von weiblichem Körper und Territorium offensichtlich: Das Video beginnt visuell mit dem Markieren eines Sportfeldes und dem Ausmessen magerer Körperteile einer älteren Frau (Elfriede Jelinek) während einer Anprobe bei einer Schneiderin.

Es scheint, als ob der Ansatz performativer Konstruiertheit von Orten und Menschen es diesen Künstlerinnen überhaupt erst ermöglichte, eine Neu-Konstruktion respektive ein Re-Mapping der territorialen und körperbezogenen Räume zu denken. Eva Meyer und Eran Schaerf tun das z.B. dadurch, dass sie dieses abgefuckte und reterriorialisierte Wort Europa sowohl in seiner patriarchal-territorialen Bedeutung als weibliche Allegorie als auch in seiner neukartografierten Schengenland-Funktion ernst nehmen und in einem Akt völlig künstlicher, vor jeder Zementierung entfliehender Sprach- und Bildrekonfigurationen für eine mögliche Umbesetzung freischlagen, in der Frauen einen Platz haben.

Auch Dorit Margreiter operiert in *Short Hills* mit dem dekonstruktiven Re-Mapping stereotyper Zuschreibungen von Frau und Territorium, respektive Frau und Stadt. Ging es in traditionell-patriarchalen Entwürfen darum, die Frau als Land zu skizzieren, damit ein (männliches) Subjekt es besetzen und unterwerfen konnte, so geht es jetzt darum, Räume zu schaffen, in denen sich posthumane, postkoloniale, weibliche Subjekte frei bewegen können. Als Beispiel sei eine Szene aus *Short Hills* erwähnt, in der sich das Gesicht der Tante in einer Fotografie hinter Glas von Hongkong spiegelt, der Stadt, aus der sie vor über 20 Jahren emigrierte, um in den USA zu studieren. Margreiter spielt hier subtil damit, dass Hongkong ihre frühere Heimat war, zu der sie, wie man im Verlaufe des Videos erfährt, immer noch eine grosse Affektion hat, die sie mittels Hongkong-Soaps stillt. Andererseits ist die Gleichsetzung von Frau und Stadt der patriarchale Mythos schlechthin. Auf diese Festschreibungsgeschichten von urbanem Weiblichen und ureigentlicher Heimat spielt nun Margreiter mit dieser Videoeinstellung an, markiert aber auch eine Differenz. Das Gesicht geht nicht auf in den Fassaden, sondern spiegelt sich abgehoben im Glas; und diese Frau spricht, sie spricht über die Stadt und dass sie sie aus guten Gründen verlassen hat. Und weil sie diese Stadt nicht visuell verkörpert, sondern gleichzeitig von ihr getrennt und ihr eng verbunden ist, öffnet sich damit ästhetisch jener virtuelle Zwischenraum, der sich gleichsam in einem Umschlagen der Zuschreibungen eröffnet und in den sie sich einschreibt. Da die Frau nicht direkt von der Kamera aufgenommen ist, ist die Intensivierung dieses Moments, als das Zur-Erscheinung-Kommen eines Möglichkeitsraumes, nur strukturell, eine Spiegelung und vielleicht sogar nur eine Täuschung. Die Verkörperung der Frau im Spiegelglas ist eine Reflektion, respektive eine Reflexion auf die Möglichkeiten ästhetischer Subjektkonstruktion.

Einer von Ursula Biemanns virtuellen Orten des In-Erscheinung-Tretens ist die nächtliche Disco. Von ihrem Erscheinungsbild in der ruralen Stadtlandschaft der Grenzzone her wirkt die Disco zuerst einmal ebenso wie ein implantierter Fremdkörper wie die technoide Maquiladora. Zeigt Biemann die Vergnügungsstätte zuerst in all ihrer herkömmlich-brachialen Lärmigkeit, geht der Ton abrupt in einen elektronischen Ambientsound über, dessen strömende Durchlässigkeit so gar nichts mit den zu einer folkloristischen Musik tanzenden Frauen zu tun hat. Die in Blaulicht getauchte Atmosphäre und die Kluft, die sich aufreisst zwischen den sich bewegenden und exhibitionierenden Körpern und der Schönheit und Ruhe der Musik lässt plötzlich etwas anderes erahnen, das noch gar nicht da ist, sich aber hoffnungsvoll blau über die Szene legt. Der Raum der anderen Möglichkeiten tut sich auf inmitten jener Orte, deren Marktwert sich auf dem leeren Versprechen gründet, Überschreitung und intensive Begegnung zu ermöglichen. Im Zentrum simulierter, aber nichtsdestrotz erlebter Transgressionen wechselt der Ton und zieht uns Zuschauerinnen nochmals ganz anders hinein in ein nächtliches Treiben verkörperter "Ekstasen".

### Wege, Passagen

Kunstmachen im Zeitalter des Posthumanismus heisst also auch, in einer offensiven Weiterführung dekonstruktiver Praktiken auf ihr Suffix hin, aber im Bewusstsein um die Negativität und die Paradoxie aktueller Konditionen, die spezifische Situiertheit eigener Perspektiven in den Vordergrund zu stellen. Anerkennt man diese primäre und universale Relativität und Temporalität eigener und anderer Positionen, dann braucht man sich auch nicht mehr vor Stereotypen oder Essentialismen zu scheuen, wie das engagierte künstlerische Praktiken der letzten Jahre oft taten, sondern kann sie imitierend durchqueren und ad absurdum treibend für die eigene Widersprüchlichkeit umzucodieren versuchen. Skepsis ist angebracht gegenüber simplen Identitätsmodellen und heilbringenden Rekonstruktionsversuchen. Skepsis aber auch gegenüber allzugrosser Abarbeitung an territorialisierten Zonen. Strategien der Infiltration, Invasion und des auf Überleben hin konditionierten Dennoch sind angesagt. Strategien der Simulation und Konstruktion, die jede Naturalisierung von vornherein zertrümmern.

Es erscheint mir bezeichnend, dass eines der für mich hoffnungsvollsten Bilder überhaupt, die ich in letzter Zeit wahrnahm, eine von der Videokamera sehr lange festgehaltene Szene auf einem Flughafen aus *Europa von weitem* ist. Man sieht eine alte muslimisch gekleidete Frau, die auf einem Gepäckwagen sitzt und wartet. Sie passt auf ein Baby und ein grösseres Kind auf, das spielerisch den Wagen hin und herschiebt. Da ist immer nur diese Bewegung des Hin und Her und dieses Zusammenkommen des alten und der ganz jungen Menschen, die orientalisch gekleidet sind in dieser panwestlichen Flughafenästhetik. Ein Bild, das sich in seiner Zusammenstückelung des Heterogenen einprägt, ein alltägliches Bild, das gleichzeitig als widersprüchliches herausfällt und eine Art Stillstand in der Bewegung produziert.

**1** Diese Wortverdichtung prägte die Schriftstellerin Ginka Steinwachs mit Bezug auf George Sands Überschreitung weiblicher Grenzen. Es setzt sich zusammen aus lat. explorari: erforschen, lat. terra: Erde und Terrorismus.
**2** Donna Haraway: *Ecce Homo. Bin ich nicht eine Frau und un/an/geeignet anders: Das Humane in einer posthu*

*manistischen Landschaft.* In: Monströse Versprechen. Coyote-Geschichten zu Feminismus und Technowissenschaft. Hamburg/Berlin 1995, S.118

[3] Marina Grzinic/Aina Smid: *Luna 10. The Butterfly Effect of Geography*, Ljubliana 1994

[4] Ausstellungskatalog Milica Tomic. Galerie im Taxispalais, Innsbruck, Dezember 1999

[5] Aus: *Europa von weitem*. ein bimediales Hörspiel-Film-Projekt. Realisation: Eva Meyer/Eran Schaerf. Komposition: Inge Morgenroth. BR 1999

[6] Saskia Sassen: *Die Immigration überdenken: Eine internationale Perspektive*. In: Inklusion: Exklusion. Probleme des Postkolonialismus und der globalen Migration. Hg. Peter Weibel/Slavoj Zizek. S. 107-116

[7] Der Katalog zur Ausstellung *Post Human*, kuratiert von Jeffrey Deitch, ist ein Beispiel für die Fantasmen totaler Machbarkeit. Wichtig ist diese Ausstellung auch deshalb, weil sie das Wort Post Human populär werden liess.

[8] Theresa de Lauretis: *Strategien des Verkettens. Narratives Kino, feministische Poetik und Yvonne Rainer*. In: Yvonne Rainer. Talking Pictures. Filme, Feminismus, Psychoanalyse, Avantgarde. Herausgegeben von Kunstverein München, Wien 1994, S. 48

[9] An anderer Stelle führte ich zudem das Symtomatischwerden des Weiblichen mit seinen Metaphoriken des Fliessens und der Entkörperlichung als Zeichen des Posthumanismus näher aus. Yvonne Volkart: Kunst; Medien, Geschlecht. Gender in der Kunst- und Medientheorie. In: Gender Studies Reader, herausgegeben vom Frauenrat der Universität Konstanz, Konstanz 2000.

[10] Teresa de Lauretis zitiert dieses Wort aus Yvonne Rainers Filmscript *The Man Who Envied Women*: "Ich kann nicht ohne Männer leben, aber ich kann ohne einen Mann leben. [...] Aber ich weiss auch, dass jetzt etwas anders ist. Etwas in Richtung einer Unweiblichkeit. Nicht eine neue Frau, nicht eine Nicht-Frau oder Frauenhasserin oder Antifrau, und keine platonische Lesbe. Wahrscheinlich ist Unfrau auch der falsche Begriff. A-Frau ist besser. A-fraulich. A-Weiblichkeit." In einer Fussnote fügt de Lauretis jedoch an: "Aber das Gefühl, dass 'es die Richtung der Unweiblichkeit' ist, in die einen der 'Feminismus in Höchstform' führt, ist mein ganz persönliches und klarerweise nicht Yvonne Rainers Gefühl - jedenfalls noch nicht." S.59 und S.63

[11] Teresa de Lauretis, S.59/60

[12] Irit Rogoff: *Wegschauen. Partizipation in der visuellen Kultur*. In: Texte zur Kunst, Dezember 1999, Köln, S. 111

[13] Donna Haraway: *Ecce Homo*, S. 119

# Border Project

# _FREE ZONE PLAN

**When the U.S.A. closed the Bracero Program in 1964, over 200,000 Mexicans who were working on American fruit and cotton plantations in the southern states were sent back to the border. Some of them took the risk of crossing the Rio Grande illegally and became "wetbacks," but most of them remained in the border towns, unemployed. The sudden and massive rise in unemployment soon created political frictions. The Mexican government found itself in a vulnerable position, making it willing to agree to the plan of a free zone on Mexican territory along the border, a zone where foreign firms could set up assembly plants, pay the Mexican workers a fragment of corresponding U.S. salaries, not bother with social security, and curb the taxes or customs levied by either government, a zone where national and labor laws had been largely suspended.**

Following these incentives on the part of both administrations, the U.S. electronic industry moved swiftly into the border area. Many closed their factories in the North and outsourced production south of the border. For those who already had assembly operations in the Far East, this was an opportunity to move them closer to their markets. Thus were born the maquiladoras (the Golden Mills), a program of twin plants one on either side of the border. Labor-intensive processes were located in Mexico, capital-intensive ones in the U.S.

From the Mexican perspective, the initial plan to create jobs for unemployed men failed. The corporations hired a different segment of the population for the electronic and later the digital industry. From the beginning, the maquiladoras were powered by young, single women between the ages of 16 and 23. The reason given is that they are considered non-organized, cheap, dexterous, and highly productive workers. This major shift from the reproductive to productive functions of women on the border and the resulting social transformation of gender roles in the family, at work, and in the public sphere is the subject of the *Border Project*.

# _FREE ZONE PLAN

Als die USA 1964 das Bracero-Programm strich, setzte sie damit mehr als 200'000 mexikanische Landarbeiter, die durch dieses Abkommen in den Frucht- und Baumwollplantagen in den Südstaaten arbeiten konnten, schlagartig an die Grenze. Einige riskierten, den Rio Grande als "wetbacks" illegal wieder zu überqueren, also mit "nassem Rücken" in die USA einzuwandern. Die meisten aber blieben in den Grenzstädten, arbeitslos. Die plötzlich massive Anzahl Arbeitsloser führte bald zu politischen Reibungen. In dieser geschwächten Position war die mexikanische Regierung bereit, dem Plan für eine zollfreie Zone auf mexikanischem Territorium beizustimmen; eine Zone, in der ausländische Firmen ihre Montagefabriken einrichten konnten, den mexikanischen Arbeitskräften nur einen Bruchteil der US-amerikanischen Löhne zu bezahlen brauchen, wo sie sich nicht um Sozialleistungen kümmern müssen und an die mexikanische Regierung weder Taxen noch Zollgebühren abzugeben

haben – eine Zone, in der nationale Regelungen und Arbeitsgesetze vorwiegend ausser Betrieb gesetzt sind. Mit diesem Anreiz von Seiten beider Regierungen zog die US-Elektronikindustrie eilig ins Grenzgebiet. Viele schlossen ihre Betriebe im Norden und lagerten ihre Produktion an die Grenze aus. Für jene Firmen, die schon Montagestätten im Fernen Osten besassen, war dies eine Gelegenheit, näher an ihre Märkte zu rücken. So wurden die Maquiladoras geboren, die goldenen Mühlen, ein Programm von Zwillingsfabriken, eine auf jeder Seite der Grenze. Arbeitsintensive Operationen finden in Mexiko statt, kapitalintensive Operationen bleiben in den USA.

Aus mexikanischer Perspektive schlug der ursprüngliche Plan fehl, Jobs für die arbeitslosen Männer zu schaffen. Die Firmen stellten ein ganz anderes Segment der Bevölkerung für die elektronische und später digitale Industrie ein. Die Arbeitskräfte der Maquiladoras waren von Anfang an junge, unverheiratete Frauen zwischen 16 und 23 Jahren, denn diese gelten als nicht gewerkschaftlich organisiert, billig, geschickt und hochproduktiv. Diese radikale Verschiebung von einer reproduktiven zu einer produktiven Funktion der Grenzfrauen und die daraus entstehenden gesellschaftlichen Veränderungen der Geschlechterbeziehungen in der Familie, an der Arbeit und in der Öffentlichkeit sind Inhalt des *Border Projects*.

UTA
HONEYWELL BULL
PHILIPS
CHRYSLER
AMERICAN SAFETY
STACKPOLE COMPONENTS
RCA
THOMSON
GENERAL INSTRUMENTS
CHLORIDE POWER ELECTRONICS
GENERAL MOTORS
NIELSEN CLEARING HOUSE
TYLER SCIENCE TECHNOLOGY
RECON
ACSA
ELECTRO MECH COMPANY
PACKARD ELECTRIC
SIEMENS-ALBIS
ELECTRO-WIRE PRODUCTS
MARSH
TED
TOSHIBA
ITT
EDMONT COOPER
POTTER BLUMFIELD
FORD

## If you're trying to cut your production costs, Mexico beats the Far East by 10,000 miles.

You don't have to go overseas to get off-shore savings. Assembly labor in Juarez, Mexico, is less than $1.00 per hour including fringe benefits. And with full factory burden, including customs brokerage, the assembly labor rate is about $3.00 per hour. Electronic technicians, quality assurance inspectors, production engineers, and other skilled support personnel are even more economical.

Elamex, Mexico's leader in custom contract assembly, cuts start up costs, lead time, and red tape to a fraction of what they would be with your own plant. We function as if we were your subsidiary, providing the plant facilities, assembly operators, indirect support, management personnel, and corporate shelter to begin production quickly and economically and with productivity and quality that will exceed your present standards.

Plus, we're close to your U.S. offices and markets. So your inventory is low, turnaround fast, delivery convenient by truck or rail, communication direct dial, and travel schedule easy. Also, no advance payments or letters of credit are necessary.

So whether you manufacture components, subassemblies, or computers in volumes that require 25 (or 225) direct labor personnel, call Elamex. Then look us over. We're 15 minutes from the El Paso Airport. Take a day to see for yourself how Elamex can cut your production costs in half.

**For a visit or a free seminar on manufacturing in Mexico tailored to your needs, contact Fred Mitchell, our U.S. representative:**

Maquila Communications, Inc.
Box 10015, El Paso, Texas 79991
Phone: 915 593-5066

## ELAMEX S.A.
The Contract Manufacturing Company.

Sunday morning
Earth streets earth houses
un nuevo barrio
a new neighborhood
she wore a sweat suit
on her way to buy milk
somehow pleasant
not so made up
I stopped the car
asked if I could interview her

Sonntagmorgen
Erdstrassen Erdhäuser
un nuevo barrio
ein neues Wohnviertel
sie war im Trainingsanzug unterwegs
Milch einkaufen
irgendwie sympathisch
nicht so aufgemacht
Ich halte den Wagen an
frage, ob ich sie interviewen könne

She agreed  
We drove to her house  
beyond the wall  
Honeywell Bull  
that's where she works  
She disappeared in the dark  
I installed the camera  
in front of the rose bush  
in the court  
waited  
Finally she came  
made up  
slick  
in tight jeans

Sie war einverstanden  
Wir fuhren zu ihrem Haus  
hinter der Mauer  
Honeywell Bull  
dort arbeitet sie  
Sie verschwand im Dunkeln  
ich stellte die Filmkamera  
vor den Rosenbusch im Garten  
wartete  
Schliesslich kam sie  
geschminkt  
gelackt  
in engen Jeans

¿Para la televisión?

At sixteen
she moved to the north
had relatives
in the border town Juarez
found work
in one of the countless plants
what was left over from the pay
she sent to her parents
in the arid back country

Mit sechszehn
zog sie in den Norden
hatte Verwandte
in der Grenzstadt Ciudad Juarez
fand Arbeit
in einer der unzähligen Fabriken
was vom Lohn übrig blieb
schickte sie den Eltern
im kargen Hinterland

Later she was followed by
her younger sister
who found work
in the same company
With two salaries
they support the entire family
Then came her parents
and brothers
no work for them
only for young nimble female
fingers

Später kam ihre kleine
Schwester nach
auch sie fand Arbeit in der
gleichen Firma
mit zwei Einkommen
unterhalten sie die ganze Familie
dann zogen Eltern und Brüder nach
für sie gibt es keine Arbeit
nur für junge, geschmeidige, flinke
Frauenhände

They all moved to the North
in the seventies
into the maquiladoras
the Golden Mills in the
borderland
between the first
and the third world
over two million
female Mexican hands
soldering semi-conductors
for global electronics

Alle zogen sie in den Norden
in den 70er Jahren
über zwei Millionen Mexikanerinnen
zu den maquiladoras
den Goldmühlen
im Grenzland
zwischen der ersten
und der dritten Welt
löten Leiterplatten
für die globale Elektronik

What does
cultural identity
have to do
with optimizing production
in the monetary West?
What does
cultural identity
have to do
with red and green
ribbons in the hair?

Was hat
kulturelle Identität
mit der Optimierung
der Produktion
im monetären Westen
zu tun?
Was hat
kulturelle Identität
mit roten und grünen Bändern
im Haar
zu tun?

**What meaning
Can cultural identity have
in the globalisation of
production
of new technologies
electronic communications media
hyper mobility
computer animation
artificial intelligence
cyber entertainment?**

Welchen Sinn hat
kulturelle Identität noch
in der Globalisierung
der Produktion
neuer Technologien
electronic media communications
hyper mobility
computer animation
artificial intelligence
cyber entertainment?

The woman on the left is photographed by surprise
The woman at her side is photographed against her will
The woman in the center knows she is being photographed
The woman on the right charges for being photographed

**La mujer de la izquierda es fotografiada por sorpresa**
**La mujer de al lado es fotografiada en contra de su voluntad**
**La mujer del centro sabe que esta siendo fotografiada**
**La mujer de la derecha cobra por ser fotografiada**

# _PERFORMING THE BORDER

video script 43 min. 1999

TIJUANA, YUMA, NOGALES, SANTA CRUZ, AGUA PIETA, CIUDAD JUAREZ, PIEDRAS NEGRAS, NUEVO LAREDO, MATAMOROS. AND THEN THE GULF.

**Bertha**  In a way the border is always represented as this wound that has to be healed, that has to be closed, that has to be protected, from contamination and from disease. Because where is AIDS coming from? From the border. Where is all this desease, poverty, and contamination coming from? From the border. So we have to heal this wound through various systems of militarization, purification, cleansing. It's like a surgical place.

**Angela**  It's a world of labor, there is no way to draw anything from the soil because there is no water, there is no way to get anything from nature, no way to get anything from your environment, here you have TO MAKE.

**Bertha**  In a way you do need the crossings for the border to become real otherwise you just have this discursive construction and that's what should really be clear about the border, there is nothing natural about it, in fact it's a constructed place that gets reproduced through the crossings of people, because without the crossing there is no border, right? It's just an imaginary line, it's a river or it's just a wall. So you need the crossings of bodies to produce the discursive space of the nation state and also to produce a type of real place as a border. The border is a highly performative place.

**Angela** I have known Concha for about five years. I knew her when her house was here, made from what was left over from the maquiladora. At some point she found herself abandoned by her husband and she found out that in Juarez there was no work for pregnant women, there was no way to be six months pregnant and find work. So Concha found herself in this situation - I don't know if it was good or bad for her - where she met someone who told her that she could sell cigarettes to the U.S., when I say U.S., I mean El Paso. What Concha did was she would cross to the other side where she would sell her cigarettes cheaper because she didn't pay taxes, then she would buy her merchandise over there, bring it back here, take off the taxes and put it back into circulation there.

Later on, based on her facility to cross and avoid the U.S. immigration officers Concha passed "wetbacks." Her strategies have been multiple and varied in all her trajectories of crossing to the U.S. She was also confronted with the militarization of the border in 1994. When Sylvestre Reyes closed the border to the U.S., the aggressivity towards people who crossed was getting to be too much. Concha had always managed to pass the border undercover and at a given moment in her life - without thinking about it - she started to lead people across.

**shifting paradigms, sliding spaces, soft monies, hard realities, circulating goods passing people**

Angela Escajeda

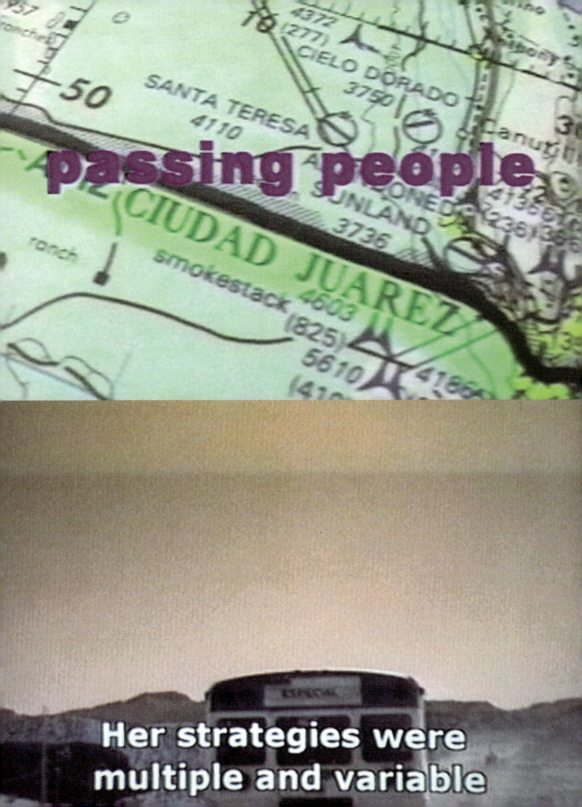

**Angela**  One thing Concha does on a regular basis is to help pregnant women cross the border so they can give birth in the U.S. These women want their children to have American citizenship in the hope that they at some point will be able to help their parents obtain papers thus allowing them to benefit from services provided in the U.S. Concha runs a "service for pregnant women." She leaves her charges at the public hospital where there are professionals to take care of them.

**Bertha**  How are you crossing? Are you crossing in English, in Spanish, in Spanglish, with a U.S. passport, jumping, as a tourist, as a migrant, as a middle-class woman, as a doméstica? There are all these different ways of crossing and that's the way the border gets rearticulated through the power relationships that the crossing produces. Because it's not just this happy crossing.

Over twenty years ago, the U.S. industry started to install their cheap-labor assembly plants called maquiladoras, the Golden Mills, south of the border. In a matter of a few years, they attracted thousands of new workers into the zone, making the borderline into a borderland, a cultural corridor, an uncharted territory, inhabited by millions of people who vacillate between rural and urban, between a world of street vendors and streets of sand and the production of high-tech equipment for the information industry. Within a short time, a new technological culture of repetition, registration, and control has been introduced in the desert city.

EXPORT PROCESSING ZONE

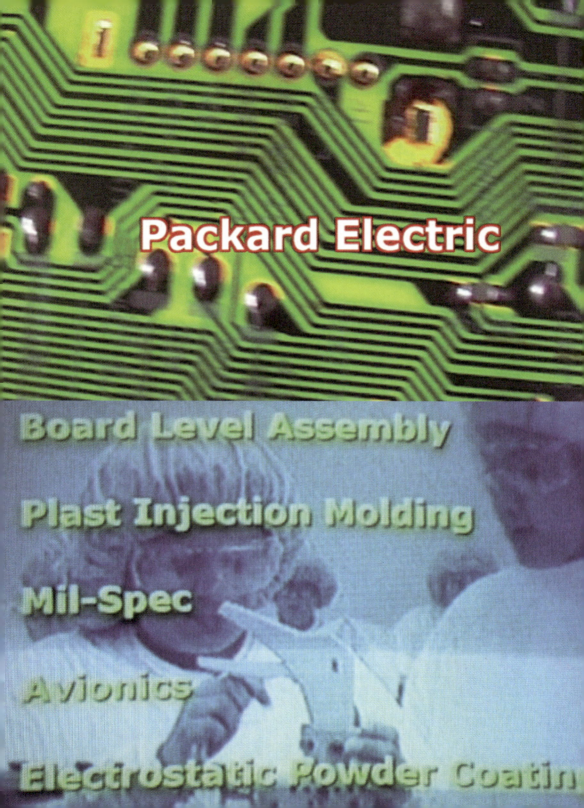

**Under the local logic lies the great map of transnational operations: leanness, efficiency, competition.**

**Cipriana** So we arrived here to work at the maquiladoras. In the beginning there were only women working at the factory. That led to some changes in the cultural pattern that we have as Mexican women. Because the tradition in Mexico was that the woman stays at home to do the domestic work and the man – brothers, uncles, whatever man there was in the family – sustains the household.

## MAQUILADORAS HAVE SERVED AS A LABORATORY FOR DEREGULATION

A zone from which life emerges, nevertheless, an alien way of life: corporate culture in the morning, kneading el maíz at night. The rhythms of the barren highland giving way to optimized production modes. Life on the border teaches you to cope with contradictions, to shift out of habitual formations on a daily basis, to operate in a pluralistic mode, because flexibility is a matter of survival when you are among the extras on the set of corporate culture. New members subscribing to transnational citizenship that will afford mobility and the freedom to consume, not for themselves, but for millions of others in the North.

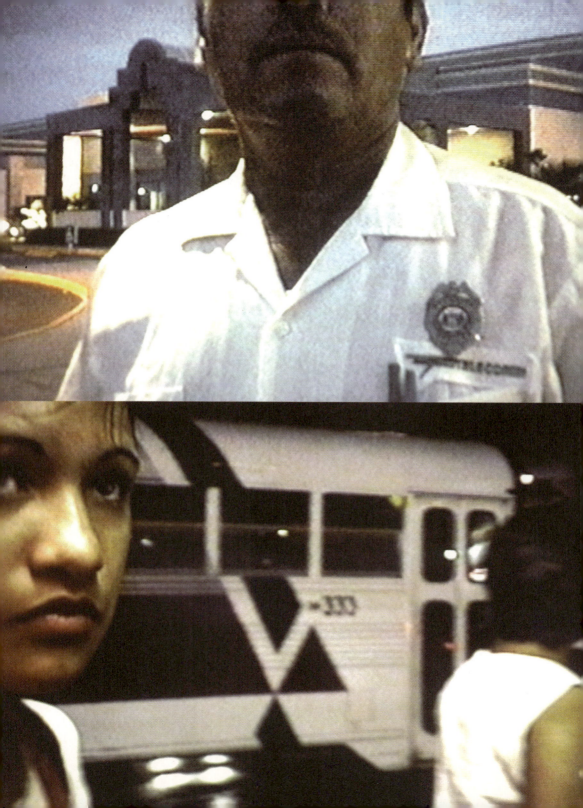

**Isabel** The social customs have changed and the economy has changed but for poor women it has not necessarily translated into a lot of advancement. We believe there is a price for modernization but the price has to be shared. Working women don't have to pay that price. If you are producing progress you should also share in that progress. It's an empowerment that comes with a very high price.

Juarez is a city that produces some of the most sophisticated things on the market: computer chips, televisions, airplane components. In the automotive industry we have one of the most important design centers worldwide, some of the biggest companies in the world produce here. And every year the city produces millions and millions of dollars of value-added goods, but the city doesn't have a shelter for battered women, neither public nor private.

**Cipriana** In standing up for our rights in the maquiladora, we encountered serious problems such as repression because even though we have the right to form an independent union, the maquiladora is strategically important to Mexico's economy and the Mexican government is careful about looking after the maquilas' interests.

**Cipriana** I was head of the line in the first factory that pushed me off. To be nominated for this kind of post you need to be very docile. It wasn't a movement to form a union, we just needed a cafeteria. We had no cafeteria for three years and the plant was located outside an industrial park.

A blacklist is often used in the maquiladora, a list with names of persons who did things in the maquiladora. With the modern use of computers, the whole system is interconnected with other maquiladoras. Now it's more difficult to enter a maquila without being detected. Well, this list isn't permitted by law.

**Capital has fled from Canada and the United States to Mexico, where it is still legal to place gender specific advertisements. The maquila program management has shown a strong preference for women, especially young, single women workers.**

# GENDER MATTERS TO CAPITAL

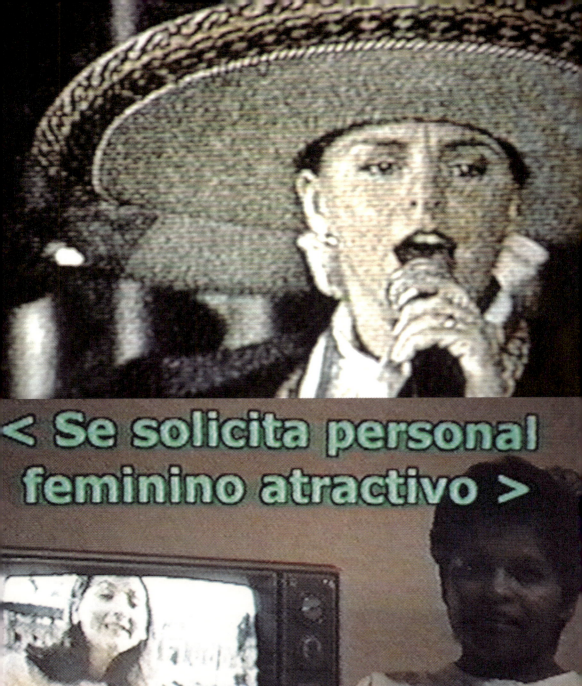

**A struggle against being violated by stringent regulations, offended in one's sexual integrity, manipulated in one's cultural identity. At times the borders between the personal formations within and the large-scale social reality out there get blurred.**

`Isabel` Take a lingerie maquiladora. A woman in Germany, Switzerland or the U.S. who buys some negligee has no idea that the women who made it had to get up at 4:30 in the morning and had no fresh water to bathe themselves before going to work. Everything should be shared, there is a social price that's not being shared and there is a wealth that's not being shared. It's not enough to pay minimum wage, it's not enough to give breakfast to your workers. It's not enough. It's also an issue of time, because you sell your time to your company, you sell your life and you should get something back.

**In the corporate language any activity and any person can be thought of in terms of disassembly and reassembly. The body of the worker gets technologized and fragmented in a posthuman terminology. Assembly lines, the ultimate fragmentation of labor into its smallest possible particles, located geographically on the line between capital-intensive production in the North and female labor-intensive production in the South.**

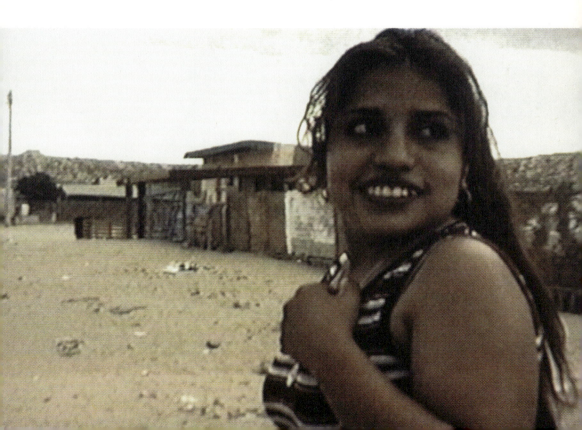

**Judith** The fact that women earn money has indeed produced independence. The liberation which has been going on since the seventies, i.e. five years after the industry arrived, has brought us some freedom having led to the integration of a majority of married, divorced, or single women into the labor force. Yet a very disturbing phenomenon is that there are hundreds of girls who left school at the age of thirteen, fourteen, fifteen, to work in the maquiladora. You cannot tell a girl, a woman, who earns her own money that she cannot go and enjoy herself. The only forms of entertainment here are the nocturnal dance centers and drinking places, where they go dancing since the work at the factory is a very tiring routine. Most of these women are assemblers. These activities don't produce any knowledge, on the contrary, they produce major stress and tiredness. So when the girls leave the factory, what they need is to either relax or have fun. And many have opted for the latter.

The border is a highly gendered region. Economic power relations along the line of gender difference are spelled out in sexual terms. Relationship patterns are being re-mapped quite drastically. There is a certain reversal of income pattern that empowers women. In the dance halls, the shift of buying power to young women is obvious. Entertainment mainly caters to female customers, i.e. shows of male strippers where women cheer and rate their sex appeal. Even in the lyrics of the music we often find explicit reference to satisfying female sexual desires.

**Bertha** We have to understand that the border is highly constructed by the power relationship that exists between the two nations, and that this power relationship gets materialized in the maquiladoras, in the bars that are there for the U.S. tourists and for the migrant workers on their way to the North. So the place has been constituted through the crossings and through the economic relationships of the two places, and that has to be clear, otherwise the border gets naturalized as a place of excess, a place of prostitution and corruption.

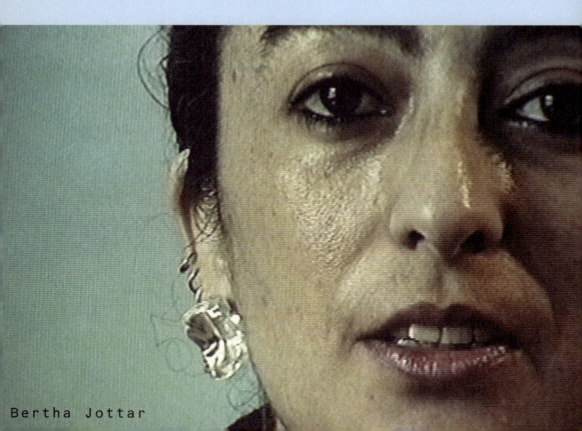

Bertha Jottar

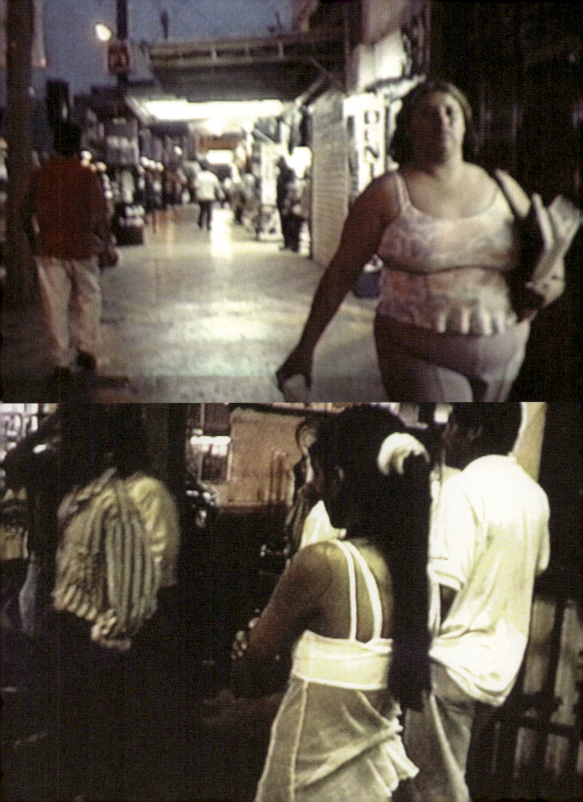

**Angela** It's called invasion because it's a group of people who take private land and position themselves. They settle down and look for a way to provide for themselves for the time being and later obtain more formal papers for their houses. It's an irregular form of obtaining housing but the city doesn't provide for the necessities of housing because there are too many people coming and all of the infrastructure goes to the transnational companies and not to the people who work for them.

**Angela** It's considered forgotten area, urban development doesn't get here. They end up building the houses themselves mostly from waste material of the maquiladoras, such as pallets. They are made of wood and paper. There is no running water, they have to keep it in containers which are also from the maquiladoras, chemical containers at one point.

# FOR MANY, LIVING IN THE CITY STILL MEANS A RURAL LIFESTYLE

onja Aguiano

She leaves her family and travels long distances to work on the border. She leaves behind the towns of Zacatecas, Durango, Torreon on the arid central plateau just above the Tropic of Cancer to move up to the Rio Grande, the stretch that's called Rio Bravo del Norte. She is the hope of those she leaves behind.

THERE SEEMS TO BE LITTLE DEMARCATION BETWEEN THE SIERRA AND THE AREA THEY CALL URBAN

Here she faces transnational employers, white factory bosses, a new social system, different family values, gender relations at work, competition with her co-workers, economic imbalances in the family, power relations with her father and brothers and later with her husband. She is still a girl. Can she find a way to steer through these cultural ruptures?

**Bertha** We, at least for people of my generation, can think about the border in terms of before NAFTA and after NAFTA. In the post NAFTA situation we have a good-neighbor-type attitude in which the free trade agreement wants to produce a border that is a place where goods travel happily and the access to goods is absolutely egalitarian. On the other hand, we maintain a situation where the crossing of people is forbidden. So goods cross, but the people who produce the goods don't cross.

## AS TEENAGERS THEY COME AND START A LIFE BY BUILDING A SHACK RIGHT INTO THE DESERT SAND

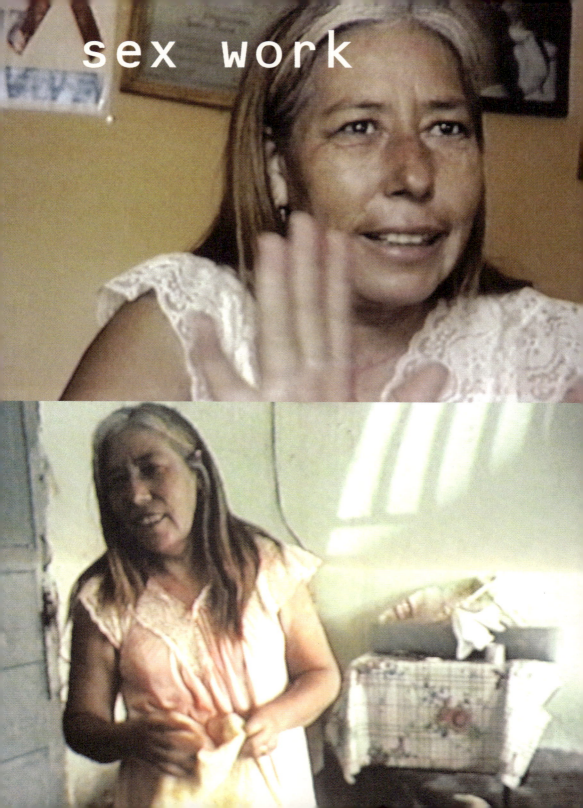

**Juana** I actually came to Ciudad Juarez to prostitute myself. I didn't want to in Torreon because during all this time I kept it a secret from my family. They still don't know that I prostitute. I did it out of necessity. One of my brothers had an accident, before that I had good work. I started what I do now at age 31, I didn't prostitute myself young. So my brother had this accident he was the father of seven children. I began prostituting myself to continue his treatment at the hospital and to help him a bit with the children. The money I made I took with me and spent it over there.

I wouldn't say it was much, but it was still much more than a salary. Let's say that I made three, four times more than a salary. Say, if in three days I made 300 pesos, well, I would take home 1,500, 1,200. Before, there was money, work and money, not anymore. Because you see there used to be a lot of passage of Americans and people who worked on the other side. They brought their money and spent it over here. Not so anymore. Now with the war they led against wetbacks, well, money has dried up here in Juarez.

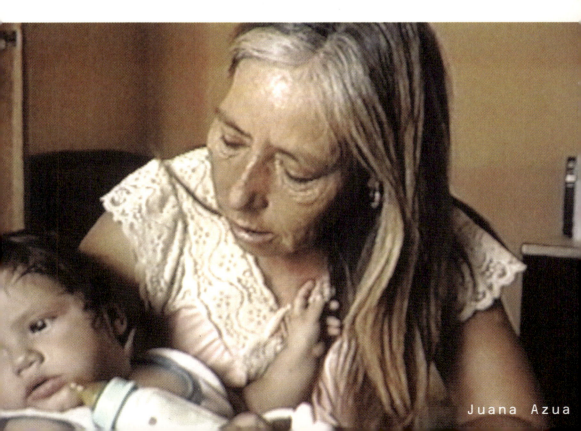

Juana Azua

**Sonia** Sex workers come and tell us their experiences, why they came from the South, why they were in the sex trade. As the woman from the South comes with very little education, she is not always accepted at the maquiladoras. In this case she also has the option of working as a maid in a private house. But here she will be asked for references of recommendation, otherwise she won't be trusted with domestic work. And if the woman doesn't find work at the maquila or in a private house, she is left with only one path, that of prostitution. If a woman is not accepted at the maquila nor in a house, well, she goes into prostitution.

# HOW DO YOU FEEL ABOUT THE THREE OPTIONS?

**Juana** I would sometimes come out of the room vomiting I would be so nauseated. But it was work that I chose because I needed money. Let's just say you end up getting used to it, it's not exactly that you like it. You get used to going to bed with young people, with old people, with drunk people. I hardly worked with people with vices, very crazy ones. Since I worked during the day, people usually weren't very drunk. Sure it is very dangerous. Yes, one gets scared to even move in the milieu, of course one gets incredibly frightened.

There are a lot of young prostitutes from other places but also from Juarez, a lot of girls from the maquila too. They come on weekends to prostitute themselves, the ones from the maquila and the migrants. Some stay here; others come and go. But a lot of them are very young, girls of thirteen, fourteen, fifteen years. They come here to prostitute themselves, and they falsify their papers so they get into bars, because minors are not allowed, and of course they always do get in. That's why there is very little money for adults like me because there is a lot of competition from young people. If I am fourty-three years old and ask for 50 pesos and another girl is seventeen and charges 50 pesos too, the man will take the young girl.

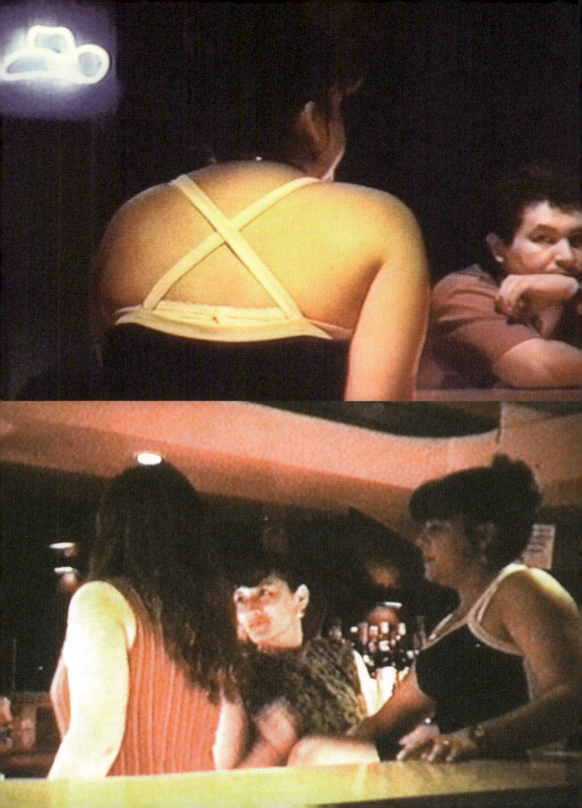

**Juana** These girls don't work every day because many of them do sex work and join the maquila. There are many at the maquila who move over here and the other way around in search of a secure salary, as minimal as it might be.

The baby is mine, I got it as a present. A girl in the sex trade who doesn't take care of it, gave it to me. She is HIV positive, she cannot take care of her baby because she is a heroin addict.

Now I'm handing out 12,000 to 18,000 condoms per month, I distribute them among the prostitutes, the women, and the hotels.

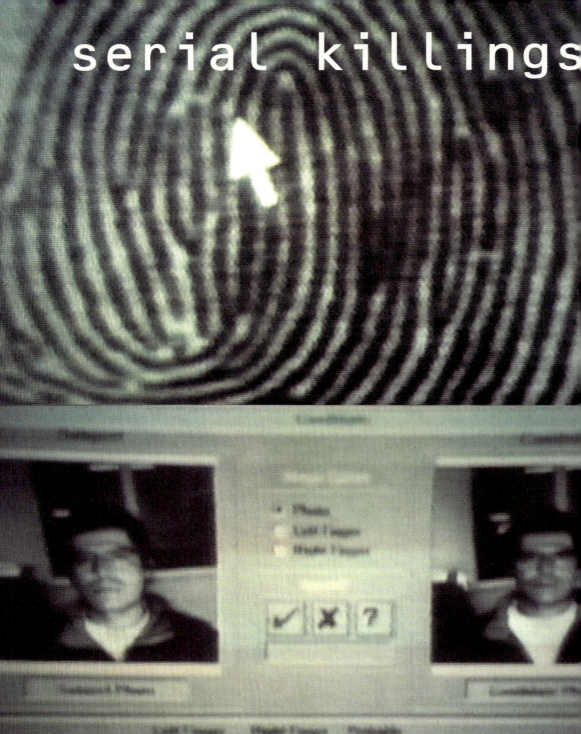

There is a connection between repetitive sexual violence and the forms of production of a high-tech culture, between the technologies of identification, reduplication, simulation, and the psychological disposition of a serial killer. In this pathological mind, there is a closed circuit between individual desire and collective information, between intimacy and technology.

Esther   We are very preoccupied. We have had 124 women registered dead since 1993. We recognize that not all of them are the victims of serial killings. But all of them represent violence against women. Someone has taken advantage of the killer's pattern and simply discards these women in the same manner: My wife or my girlfriend doesn't suit me, let's get rid of her. I rape her, strangle or stab her, and throw her away.

The serial killer experiences identity – his own and others' – as a matter of numbers, of simulation and likeness. He is a type of non-person, he fails to distinguish himself from others and this lack of self-difference, of self-distinction, is immediately translated into violence along the line of sexual difference, the one fundamental difference he recognizes.

**Sylvia's mother** When they found a girl at Zaragoza near the canal, they said it was my daughter. I got frightened, they asked me to come and see the body, but it wasn't her, it was a girl from Honduras. This upset me a lot, I was scared, what if it had been my daughter. Thank god it wasn't her. But then they found the other body of Argelia and I went to the morgue because I thought it was my daughter, but they didn't let me see her. Listen, wasn't your daughter wearing a red sweater? I told them a red blouse and white sneakers. Oh, then it can't be her. But the part about the red sweater stayed in my mind, and I asked the inspector if they would let me see the dead body, but they wouldn't because they said it would upset me. We are going to show you all the photographs of the unidentified ones, the ones who haven't been claimed yet. So I looked at them but none was her. It stayed in my mind how they asked whether my daughter was wearing a red sweater. I was left with that.

**By border culture we mean the robotic, repetitive process of assembly work, the intimate implication of the body with technology and the association of this process with the gendered, racialized body. Her body gets fragmented, dehumanized and turned into a disposable, exchangeable, and marketable component.**

Sylvia's Mother

**Sylvia's mother** The problem is that they always find a body in that way, maybe they find only one shoe, one sock, part of a dress but none of the rest of her clothes. There is a girl who disappeared in '95, her clothes were found but not her body. Sometimes they find the clothes and the body is never found. We don't know what happens to the bodies of these girls.

Losing the boundaries between the self and others, he is perpetually in search of a border. He is attracted by the border of his country precisely because it signifies the boundary of a larger entity of belonging, the nation. Going to the border becomes the physical expression of his mental extremity, merging his physical body with the national body, confusing the inside and outside, the private and public.

# LETHAL SPACES

There is little distinction between habitat and environment. In the early morning hours, a great number of women cross through these widely undefined spaces on their way to the maquiladoras, in transit between private and work space, between desert and urban space. There is a basic non-differentiation, a merging back into milieu or ground, a crucial failure of distinction between subject and space, an assimilation of the subject into the space.

Judith  The characteristics of the murders are similar: rape, in many cases the clothes are placed elsewhere. There are several cases where the victims are wearing clothes that don't even belong to them – they belong to other women who have disappeared.

The border is a metaphor for the artificial division between the productive and the reproductive, between the machine and the organic body, between the natural and the collective body, between the sexual and the economic, between concepts of masculinity and femininity. But the border is also the site where the blurring of these distinctions takes violent forms.

## MERGING THE NATURAL BODY WITH THE NATIONAL BODY

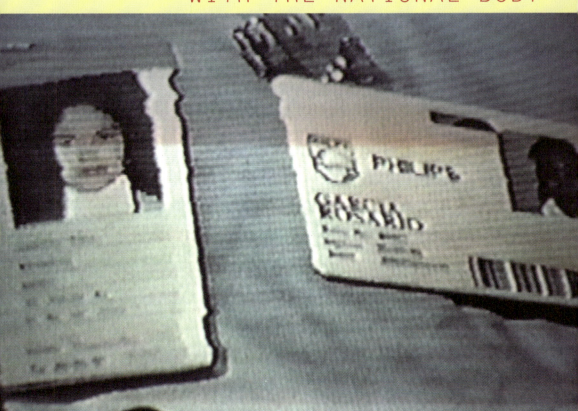

**Case 108**  January 3, 1998
13-year-old girl murdered. Bite marks on her arm, one nipple is missing.

**Case 109**  January 25, 1998
Young woman raped and murdered. Worked for Philips. 21 wounds on back, throat, and torso.

**Case 110**  January 26, 1998
20-year-old woman, crushed ribs and a large orifice in her breast.

**Case 111**  January 27, 1998
16-year-old female raped and killed, lower part of chest smashed. Black and white striped sweatshirt and bra were lifted above her breasts.

**Case 112**  February 3, 1998
Woman died of 40 stab wounds, she was found half decapitated.

**Case 113–15**  February 16, 1998
Female bones and skull containing a platinum tooth with an engraved letter R.

**Case 116**  February 19, 1998
Another female victim, head was smashed with a big stone.

**Case 117**  February 21, 1998
Woman was found, the left half of her body is burnt.

**Case 118**  March 18, 1998
Woman with 30 stab wounds in chest and throat. She suffered four infarcts probably caused by terror during rape and torture.

**Case 119**  April 17, 1998
Victim found in desert area, naked except for a black blouse and a white bra lifted above her breasts. One nipple was bitten off.

**Case 121**  April 30, 1998
Woman's body found in the desert near Loma Blanca. Five stab wounds: three in the chest, two in the back.

**Case 122**  May 5, 1998
15-year-old girl was attacked by several men and died last night of a 3-inch deep wound in her ear.

**Case 123**  May 24, 1998
Woman in male clothes was strangled, apparently with a belt.

Serial killing is a form of public violence proper to a machine culture. The Industrial Revolution has produced famous serial killers. Our era of the Second Industrial Revolution, also called "the information society," has outsourced production to the U.S.-Mexican border, exporting, at the same time, this urban pathology.

**Isabel**  It is horrible. The form in which these women and girls are treated is cruel and horrible. But what it's saying is that as a society we have allowed this to happen. We haven't mobilized, we haven't protected our young women, and it's well known that all of these women are poor. A lot of them were workers, others were students but all of them were poor, that's their common denominator.

It's as if the victims have no rights, they're dead so they have no rights, they are a number. If the women were workers, the name of the plant is seldom used in the newspapers, because the company doesn't want to be associated. But the name of the victim is used, it's speculated that she was a drug user or promiscuous or that she was wearing a miniskirt. The families' names are used and the children's pictures are used, she has no rights. And that's very offensive. If you're watching the evening news, it's not uncommon to see the corpse of a girl right there. Even if she is dead she should have her rights. Her image is her right, even if she's no longer there.

**Bertha** It's an issue of representation, but at the moment of performance, the reality is that we have to build a wall, we have to put up lights and we have to double the personnel of INS officers in addition to drug inforcement officers and the military. You have this discursive representational space and you have this material space which again is constituted through the crossing of people and the halting of these people.

It is an issue of representation, but at the moment of performance, the reality is that it's young Mexican women who assemble the digital technology, that their time and their bodies, down to the monthly cycle, are strictly controlled by the white male management; that in this economy, prostitution is a necessity for many; and that sexual violence is characterizing the public sphere.

You have this discursive representational space and you have this material space which again is constituted through the performance of gender and the management of these gender relations.

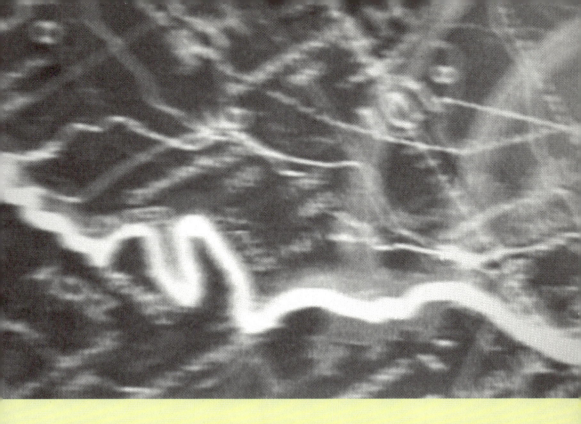

Angela Escajeda, CISO – Centro de investigación y solidaridad, cisoorg@infolink
Cipriana Jurado Herrera, labor activist, CISO
Bertha Jottar, artist, former member of Border Workshop, Tijuana
Juana Azua, health promoter for AIDS prevention program Sadec, femap@mail.infolnk.net
Esther Chavez, 8 de Marzo, feminist activist group, echavez@infolnk.net
Judith Galarza, CICH – Derechos humanos, cich@infolnk.net
Sonja Auguiano, maquiladora worker at UTA
Sylvia's mother

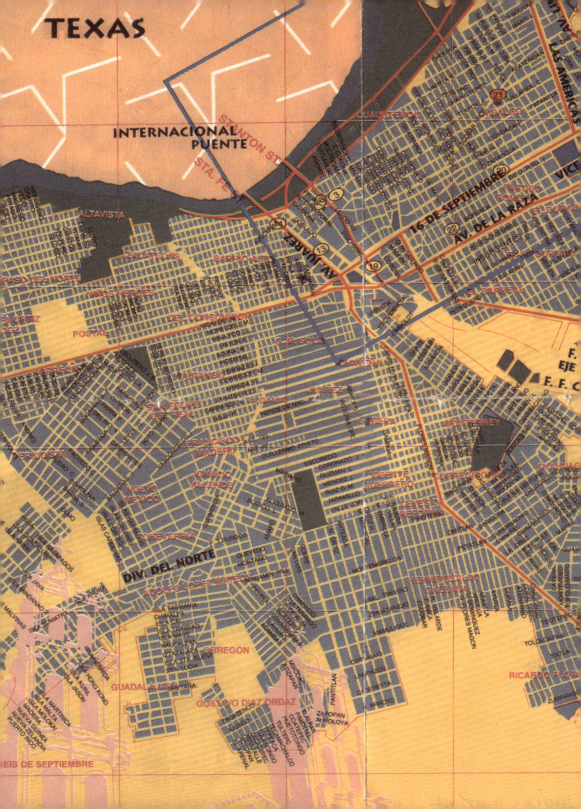

# _PERFORMING THE BORDER
## On gender, transnational bodies, and technology
Ursula Biemann

My video *Performing the Border* opens with a shot from inside a car moving through the Mexican desert near Ciudad Juarez. In the off, Bertha Jottar comments: "You need the crossing of bodies for the border to become real, otherwise you just have this discursive construction. There is nothing natural about the border; it's a highly constructed place that gets reproduced through the crossing of people, because without the crossing there is no border, right? It's just an imaginary line, a river or it's just a wall..."[1] In this shot I was filming the woman driving the car and thus I myself inevitably became a part of the road narrative unfolding as Bertha Jottar spoke about the U.S.-Mexican border being a highly performative place. It is a place that is constituted discursively through the representation of the two nations and materially through the installation of a transnational, corporate space in which different national discourses are both materialized and transcended. It is an ambivalent space at the fringe of two societies, remote-controlled by their core powers.

## Export processing zone
In artificial post-urban industrial parks that stretch over large desert areas, U.S. corporations assemble their electronic equipment for the communications industry. Whereas the capital-intensive operations remain in the North, the labor-intensive operations are located south of the border. Within a short time the maquiladoras – the Golden Mills – introduced a new technological culture of repetition, registration, and control into the desert cities. This is where microelectronic components are being produced for information processing, medical instruments, cyber technologies, satellite systems, identification and simulation technologies, and optical instruments for the aeronautic and military industry. There is nothing natural about the transnational zone, and, looking at postmodern theory, it may even be that there's nothing real about it either. It is an entirely simulated place with simulated politics, a zone from which the idea of public has been thoroughly eradicated. Housing, water, transportation, telephone wires, power supply, street lighting, sewage system, health care, childcare, and schooling become the responsibility of the individual and consequently the site of spontaneous community initiatives. These ad hoc formations struggle to provide the most rudimentary social services. It's like starting all over again. Any humanist claim is out of order in this sort of place. The post-human age expressed in futuristic imagery, computer-generated for us by the hottest designer tanks in the North, is living out its dark side here on the border.

I don't mean to demonize technology, the way my own existence has been transformed by the new media into a more connected, mobile, and accelerated lifestyle is certainly one of the reasons why I decided to go to this high-tech production site and make it, if only temporarily, into my own production site of digital visualization. Throughout this essay it will become clear, however, that the kinds of subjectivities this new transnationalism brings forth in the North are radically different from the ones it produces in the South. The representations of transnational subjects produced by global capitalism differ greatly. While discourses about residents of technology-consuming societies tend to efface specificities related to identity in favor of transnationally mobile consumers, those on the producing end become even more over-determined and restricted by gendered, sexualized, racialized, and nationalized representations. I recognize a growing need in cultural practice to locate questions of gender and other categories of identity, such as ethnicity and nationality, within the context of the wider transformations of the public sphere, particularly of urban reality. The question that interests me here is how prevailing representations relate to the material reality of a specific site, i.e. how the border as a metaphor for various kinds of marginalizations becomes materialized not only in architectural and structural measures but also in corporate and social regulations of gender. I will focus, therefore, on the circulation of female bodies in the transnational zone and on the regulation of gender relations in representation, in the public sphere, the entertainment and sex industry, and in the reproductive politics of the maquila.

A vital resource for this research comes from the rich cyber-feminist theoretical debate and art practice that has recently begun exploring the entanglement of the female body with technology and image production. I will draw on these contemporary feminist discussions to examine border identities and their multifaceted subversive potential. Further, I propose a reading of the serial killings in Ciudad Juarez, for here we are given a glimpse of how urban politics, serial sexual violence, and technology converge in a dramatic way to reveal deeper layers of the psycho-social meaning of the border.

For a number of reasons the assembly plants here draw mainly young women into their labor force. Every day hundreds of women arrive in Ciudad Juarez, which is located across the Rio Grande from El Paso, Texas. These women make up the majority of the population of the border town. They have created new living spaces and consume their own entertainment culture. They have changed social structures and gender relations and in doing so they are rewriting the texts of their bodies and their society. These women are the ones who produce the instruments that enable the kind of cyberspace that affords mobility and the freedom to consume, a freedom not enjoyed by themselves but by millions of others north of the border. Their own mobility remains confined to the limits of the "free zone" of post-Fordist manufacturing. They are the new members of transnationalism, but their type of transnational citizenship functions on very different terms than that of the transnational consumer.

## Communicating borders

Within the language of corporate offshore operations the designations for the U.S.-Mexican border zone are very explicit. Any facility and person can be thought of in terms of dis-assembly and re-assembly. Companies either set up or close down shop wherever the conditions are optimal. The terms used for the assembly work process have been transferred onto the person doing the work. The female worker, in particular, gets "technologized" by a post-human terminology that fragments and dehumanizes her body and turns it into a disposable, exchangeable, an marketable component. The latent violence in this kind of language has been perhaps most clearly expressed in the recent serial killings of maquiladora workers. I will return to this parallel later.

The science critic Donna Haraway has examined the role of the linguistic reformulation of new forms of domination in the information system in which everything is communicated in terms of rates, cost cuts, speed, proximity, degrees of freedom.[2] It is the language of leanness, efficiency, and competition that any corporation understands, the universal translation of terms on which to operate worldwide. Let us look at an advertisement for Elamex Communications – a maquila broker in El Paso, Texas – to see how this kind of imagery tends to reinforce certain borders of identity in reaction to the breakdown of national borders in the information society.

This particular Elamex advertisement targets U.S. corporations that are considering transferring their labor-intensive electronic assemblies to an offshore subcontractor.[3] Predictably, the ad addresses the customer in the language he understands, i.e. it communicates the desire to cut labor costs to a fraction, it communicates a certain quality assurance, tax shelter, speedy start-up, proximity to the HQ and U.S. markets, fast turnaround, low transportation costs, direct dial communication, airport proximity, etc. In these terms, labor is only a figure: $1 per hour, but it is also represented as a depersonalized, quantifiable unit like any other incentive offered to entice manufacturers to fold their activities in the national space and set them up in the free zone. By contrast the image, I would argue, speaks an entirely different language. It communicates a web of psychological, social, and historical relations that are being suppressed by rational arguments for efficiency.

In the border zone, everyone is being transformed into transnational subjects, and ethnic peoples in particular articulate this discourse. Only bodies that allow themselves to be marked, to be exchanged, to be turned into a commodity, and to be recycled will be granted the entry visa that allows certain mobility in the transnational space. The ad operates, first of all, as a technology of surveillance in that it positions the two women it showcases within the confines of racial and sexual criteria. On the left we have what we are expected to recognize as an Aztec profile with red, white, and green silk ribbons woven into the braids, and on the right we have a generic Asian profile with a pageboy hairstyle and eyeliner that simulates slanted eyes. Both women wear some sort of national folkloric outfit, so that in addition to a racialized discourse the image clearly links the women to a generic exotic/erotic national entity. This reduces them further to a geo-body, a body that is turned into an allegory for a gendered, racialized, and nationalized body of people whose national virtues are tightly linked with corporate interests. While this procedure nationalizes the female body, it also feminizes the offshore national spaces of Mexico and the Philippines, which is the other country this ad supposedly refers to.

Historically, women's bodies have encapsulated the desire for conquest. In Anne McClintock text *The pornotropics of the European Imagination*, the female figure is mapped as the boundary marker of the empire, as the mediating figure on the threshold to the feminized space of the terra incognita. McClintock explains this formation with the profound, if not pathological, sense of male anxiety and boundary loss at the event of leaving the known world to explore the unfamiliar. From the outset, the feminizing of the land has been a strategy of violent containment, one belonging in the realm of both psychoanalysis and political economy.[4] The production of these historically cultivated desires in the Elamex advertisement foregrounds the role these desires play in the hiring of female labor by placing the bodies of women within the fantasy narratives of colonial conquest. "Mexico beats the Far East by 10,000 miles," the headline reads. In this all too familiar scenario the two women are pitted against each other, set up to use their sexuality and femininity to compete for the favor of the male corporate employer. Their racialized, gendered figures become the articulators of the border, that fragile line marking the fringe of the national body. It is here, according to national(ist) discourse, that all disease, illegality, contamination, and poverty come from. This is the most vulnerable, penetrable site, the place where anxieties tend to concentrate. What better site to localize the panic of national identity. Above all, U.S. customers need to be assured that the offshore female bodies are not out of control. The ad makes a point of assuring a domesticated, docile, dependable, and disciplined female workforce. Her manicured hands meet corporate standards; her face expresses seriousness, concentration, and precision, her demeanor betrays no emotions. In short, she represents the replica, the instrument itself. Holding the semiconductor in her hand, she and it become one, her body becomes inscribed in a robotic function; the chip becomes the extension of her hand and takes the place of her upper torso. Her body has become completely technologized.

A cyber-feminist view interprets the image of organic/mechanic borderline fusion as potentially empowering in that it shatters at least the attempts at creating the representation of a fixed, sovereign subject. Even though I have reservations about assigning empowering qualities to this particular Elamex image because of the gender and race clichés it cements, I recognize that it is only rarely that the low end subjects of the high-tech complex are represented at all in the commercial context. Commercial representations ordinarily feature only designers and high-end users who then benefit from the dazzling images associated with the futuristic technologies that enhance their social image and their value in the labor market, while other contributors to the industry – e.g. secretarial staff and maintenance personnel in the office sector or technicians and assembly workers in the manufacturing sector – are systematically excluded from these representations. More often, maquila women find themselves in rather dull representations associated with poverty and exploitation discourses in sociological and development contexts. Why do I have to pay the young male technician $120 an hour to repair my computer, whereas the young female worker who assembled it only receives $1 an hour? What we have here is also a question of representation and its performative force.

The Elamex ad (see page 72) operates through a double discourse by which the apparently directly opposed registers of naturalized and technologized bodies are coordinated and managed. Here, the normative link between "the female" and "the natural" is replaced not by another clear equation but rather by the disturbing identification of the feminine with an uncertain mixture of the natural and the technological. In this entanglement of mechanism and gender, the natural female body is disarticulated, inscribed onto the machine, and individually reembodied as the "hand" or the "eye" of a new corporate whole. These happen to be the body parts for which a maquila woman gets hired – her eyes and her fingers – because digital and microelectronic manufacturing demands both great optical precision and tactile nimbleness. But her biological components also make her fragile and vulnerable. Her eyesight is sharp enough for about eight years, but then she will have to be replaced by a fresh young worker. Her organic vision is consumed in the making of the visualization technologies our society relies on. She belongs to the process of periodic replacement by other bodies; she needs to be continuously recycled.

The compulsive desire to see and to make visible is one of the defining features of industrial society, as Mark Seltzer analyses with great accuracy in respect to the body-machine complex at the end of the last century.[5] This desire has driven scientists and engineers to develop an arsenal of apparatuses and instruments to multiply the potencies of the human eye. In the 1990's, Rosi Braidotti has observed, the biotechnological gaze penetrated into the very intimate structure of living matter, seeing the invisible, restructuring that which has no shape yet.[6] The desire to make everything visible is also an imperative of making things legible and governable; it expresses at once a fantasy of surveillance and a need for embodiment.[7] The predominantly optical technologies manufactured on the border convey the great importance artificial vision holds for power, now and in the future. Medical and cyber optics, surveillance, x-ray satellite technologies, micro- and telescoping, AV media and virtual technologies, identification, scanning, digitizing, controlling and simulating electronics; they all engineer the relation between seeing and the exercising of power, between vision and supervision. Haraway tries to rescue the faculty of seeing from a disembodied technological cyclopean vision of the phallogocentric kind and to re-possess it for feminist discourse. In *Situated Knowledges* she pleads for an embodied objectivity and suggests that we learn to see in compound, multiple ways, in partial perspectives that shatter the idea of passive vision in favor of the notion of the eye as an active perceptual system, continuously translating, always accountable.[8]

In the present situation of what seems like a global inevitability it might be more important than ever to scrutinize what Haraway suggests are the possibilities of living and of lived femininity in a cyborg world and to reinstall notions of singularity and subjectivity within a discourse that functionalizes the female body to the extreme. Concha's story, later in the text, is an example of an unexploitative, unspectacularized case history. Many accounts have already related the mechanisms of containment that affect women's lives on the border. I chose not to focus on the instruments of repression in my video *Performing the Border* because I assume change is not a matter of information. But I want to describe the conditions in more detail here as they exemplify the relations between gender, body, and technology in explicit terms.

## Technologies of control

The technologies of border and labor control installed in Juarez make the relations between vision, vigilance, power, and bodies violently obvious. Labor organization is strictly prohibited in Juarez, and one of the major reasons why maquiladoras prefer female workers is that they are supposed to be more docile and less likely to organize into unions. Also, since adolescent female workers are often the only ones in the family with an income, there is much pressure from male family members on women to acquiesce to existing working conditions in order to save their jobs. The maquila program relies strongly on prevailing patriarchal family relations. At any rate, in recent years the entire industrial zone has become interconnected via a computer network, and plants have established blacklists with the names of undesirable persons, starting with assassins, delinquents, and "enemies" of the maquila, i.e. people trying to alter the conditions in the maquiladoras. Blacklists of this sort are prohibited by law because if someone is let go by a factory, there is no chance of finding work anywhere else in the zone. Labor activist Ciprianana J. Herrera told me that she got fired, together with two other "compañeras", for requesting a cafeteria.[9] Their plant was located outside the industrial park, and for several hundred workers there was no place to have lunch. We weren't even talking about forming a union, about wage policies, health hazards, or human rights. Women are afraid of losing their jobs for the slightest disobedience, of never being able to find another one again, and of imposing the consequences on their families.

For the Mexican government the maquiladora program is strategically important to the economy, ranking well above any other national income from oil or tourism. The government keeps a close eye on the maquilas' interests. And we can assume that the purpose of the strong U.S. military presence is not merely to keep "illegals" from crossing the border but also to protect the gigantic U.S. industrial investment on Mexican territory. Guillermina Villalva Valdez, a leading labor activist and academic who was extremely supportive during my first visit to Juarez in 1988, died in a plane crash on her way to Texas in 1991. In the small plane, which exploded in mid air presumably because of a bomb, were also four other key figures of the labor movement. Labor activities are watched closely by the networked corporate system.[10]

Time management is another efficient means of control. For practical reasons, the industrial parks are located on the outskirts of the city. Regular public transportation doesn't go there so at the changing of the shifts private companies shuttle the workers back and forth between the city center and the plants at exorbitant fairs that can swallow up to a third of one's monthly salary. Before dawn, the worker leaves the settlement at the periphery, walks to the bus station in the center of town, and takes a one-hour bus ride out to the maquila to make the morning shift at six o'clock. She spends nine hours at the plant and goes back home the same way. That leaves no time to live, no time to think, no time to organize. The workers' excruciating time investment enables the further development of technology that accelerates our lives. In his essay *Going at Different Speeds* Andrew Ross identifies speed differentials and relative time scarcity as the basic principles for uneven development in the world economy "Beyond a critical speed," he quotes Ivan Illich, "no one can save time without forcing another to lose it."[1]

In the electronically networked maquila system every individual is identified and profiled. Time, productivity, and the body of the female worker are strictly controlled oftentimes by white male managers The body control goes as far as to require a monthly cycle check to ensure the worker is not pregnant Forced birth control and pregnancy tests are the order of the day and, needless to say, pregnancy means immediate dismissal. Reproduction of these bodies becomes strictly controlled from the moment they are determined to be productive. The speedy industrialization has imposed rather violent transformations between contradictory registers of public and private spaces, between work and plant on the one hand, and home and family, on the other, or more generally between the economic and the sexual. In Mexico, like everywhere else, these registers have traditionally been divided along the lines of sexual difference. Women took care of the domestic sphere whereas the men in the family – father uncles, brothers – sustained the family financially. What Juarez has seen over a short period of time is the conflation of the separate spheres of the private, female, domestic space of reproduction and consumption and the public, male space of production. With the hiring of predominantly young women these traditional patters are being forcefully transformed and, of course, not without conflict. Not surprisingly, the female worker emerges as the central figure in this conflict as she embodies the two functions of production and reproduction. She is the embodied problem that needs to be contained and managed.

Since NAFTA, the border has materialized this conflict on an ever more impressive scale in that the agreement assures the free flow of goods but prevents the free passing of people who produce the goods. The crossing of merchandise stands for good neighborly relations whereas the crossing of people is criminalized and policed. The border becomes a metaphor as well as an actual material institution that capitalizes on the differences between the economic and the sexual.

## Sexualizing the territory

One of the most striking, and maybe most disturbing, insights I gained on the border is that international labor in the South is not only feminized but also sexualized. The female workers are literally interpellated in their sexuality. Structurally speaking, a young woman in Juarez has three options: Either she becomes an assembly worker; if she is not accepted at the factory because of insufficient education, she can become a doméstica and work as a maid in a private house; but if she can't produce a recommendation for such a position, her only option is prostitution. Yet securing a factory job is not always the end of the story. Low salaries force many women to seek supplementary income from prostitution on weekends. Sexual and labor markets interpenetrate within this economic order. The figure of $1 per hour I cited earlier in my discussion of the Elamex ad is also responsible for sexualizing the offshore labor market because it pushes women to the verge of being reducible to sex. The figure also means that pimping takes place on a corporate level. Not that transnationals are creaming off the profits from prostitution, but they do benefit from getting labor for pocket money by making women dependent on commodifying their bodies. Prostitution is not just part and parcel of a tax-free consumer binge; it is a structural part of global capitalism. Since the closing down of the border fence and its military enforcement in the 1990's competition has become more fierce between professional prostitutes and a growing number of young, often adolescent maquila workers who prostitute themselves on weekends. The dynamics on the border clearly show that even though customers who spend their U.S. dollars in Juarez are getting scarcer, prostitution is growing. In other words, prostitution is not generated by customer demand, as is usually thought, but by the women's need to generate income. Initially these women offered sexual services to anyone who could pay for them. Gradually, however, this situation has given rise to an entertainment industry, and it is not insignificant to note that here in Juarez where prostitution emerged from a maquila economy the sex districts are pimp free.

In the official media discourse, the border is always represented as a place of delinquency, debauchery, and prostitution, a magnet for all subjects who don't meet the moral standards of society. The media rarely wastes a word on the fact that these conditions are engineered by the maquila industry which implements the free zone plan that was designed and signed by both national administrations and the Dow Jones people. The media, it seems, has mistaken the effect for the cause. It's not that I'm particularly interested in tracing simple causality. In an overwhelmingly complex site like the border it can be more fruitful to record the synchronicity of events and to point out correspondences without necessarily building an overarching theoretical framework. Also, it seems inadequate to offer hasty interpretations for formations that are quite malleable and changeable. On the border, identities are constantly forming and collapsing, conforming and transgressing. And the last thing I want to propose is easy categories for the new types of subjectivities that are currently evolving. And one thing we must not forget is that there is much ambivalence within synchronicity caused by conflicting interests and competing desires.

It just so happens, however, that sexuality has become a site where desires for self-expression and control mechanisms converge violently. Thousands of assembly jobs have been created in the desert city of Juarez and women are the ones who get them. As gender relations are greatly determined by economics, the reversal of income patterns has had an immediate impact on the way women relate to men. For one thing, women have gained greater autonomy over their sexuality. On Friday at 4 p.m., when the assemblers leave the morning shift, hundreds of bars and dance saloons are already open for business in downtown Juarez. Ten years ago on my first shoot in Juarez the contests organized in the nightclubs were modeled on traditional gender roles. Women sucking lollipops competed on stage for male attention by performing with the most desirable body language they could muster. The winner wasn't the woman who danced erotically and assertively, but a girl who slowly stepped back and forth between two stage corners in aimless anticipation. It didn't seem like much, but the audience reacted with great enthusiasm to her nervous passivity that let their gaze take possession of her. She embodied all the visual pleasures Laura Mulvey spoke about in the seventies in regard to cinema.[12] Today, in the dance halls the shift of buying power to young women is obvious. Entertainment mainly caters to female customers with male strip shows and male dance contests where women cheer in appreciation of men's sex appeal. Songs are dedicated to the girls from Torreon or from Durango, who make up the majority of maquila workers, the song lyrics often refer to female sexual desires, and the entire entertainment machine is aligned to their pleasure. The shift in the income pattern empowers women in their personal relationships. It has enabled their overt expression of sexual desires and affords the satisfaction of these desires by economic means rather than by the more traditional ones, i.e. in the domestic setting through emotional or reproductive pathways.

### Technologies of survival

The continuing diasporic movement of women in transnational space attests to their flexibility, resilience, and endurance. They are often still very young - 13-, 14-, 15-year-olds – when they leave their families and travel long distances to work on the border. They come from towns like Zacatecas, Durango, Torreon, on the arid central plateau and move to the Rio Grande. They are the hope of those left behind. Often they come in small groups: three or four girls of the same age and from the same town. Upon their arrival they won't find accommodations because municipal investments are only made for the transnationals, not for the people who work for them. So they go to the edge of the settlements, which spread far out into the Sierra, choose a vacant spot, and build a shack right into the desert sand. To do this they use leftovers from the maquiladoras. Pallets will serve as walls, chemical containers become water tanks, and so forth. Some people call this procedure "invasion" because the migrants take a piece of land and settle down and wait for official papers for their houses. It may be an irregular way, but it is inevitably the only way to obtain housing. Here are vast stretches of land where mainly women live, streets of sand, no streetlights, no public transportation, and no security. It is not unusual to see young maquila women moving through their desert neighborhoods wearing the little flesh-tone prostheses that protect them from the excessive electromagnetic charges that run through their bodies during assembly and testing. They are electromagnetic discharge needles, and the workers wear them strapped to their wrists. Attached to them are pink curled cables that link the female body to the workbench. The maquila women keep the devices around their arms on weekends for fear of forgetting them on Monday morning.

It is an alien way of life: corporate culture in the morning, kneading "Maiz" at night. The rhythm of the barren highland gives way to optimized production modes. Life on the border teaches its inhabitants to cope with contradictions, to shift out of habitual formation on a daily basis, and to operate in a pluralistic mode because flexibility is a matter of survival. It is a life in transition and survival is a good place to start. The courage to endure the situation is a desire that exceeds power; it doesn't pretend to overcome oppression or to master it but to survive it, says Homi K. Bhabha. He proposes a philosophy of survival rather than subversion, and this seems to me to be an appropriate model at the close of this century, when postindustrial systems of production and information seem to have made oppositional mass politics utterly redundant.[13] But we should keep in mind that survival can be motivated by different situations. While intellectuals like Bhabha and cultural producers like me may choose strategies of transgressions because these seem to be of particular cultural interest at this point in time, Concha is forced into transgression by the oppressive situation she finds herself in, even if she actually prefers a different kind of life.

### Transgressive identities

Even the most sophisticated technologies of surveillance have fissures and leaks, and there are holes in the border fence and trails that lead through the desert valley. It is here at night that other women help pregnant women across the border. The former know how to avoid snakebites and dehydration and charge little to bring the latter safely to a U.S. hospital. In the new transnational space we will be looking for these road narratives. Transgressive trajectories express alternative desires. And even though in number and agency these nomadic transgressive subjectivities are modest, I believe, philosophically speaking, it is important to theorize them.

"I have known Concha for about five years," says Angela Escajeda while we drive out to the settlement on the periphery, "from when she used to live here in a house made from leftover materials from the maquiladora. At some point she found herself abandoned by her husband and realized that there was no chance for a pregnant woman to find work in Juarez. So Concha met someone, I don't know whether it was good or bad for her, who told her that she could sell cigarettes in the U.S. What Concha did was she would cross to the other side where she would sell her cigarettes cheaper because she didn't pay taxes, then she would buy her merchandise over there, bring it back here, take off the taxes and put it back into circulation there. Later on, based on her facility to cross and avoid the U.S. immigration officers Concha passed as a wetback. Her strategies have been multiple and variable in all her trajectories of crossing to the U.S. Concha was also confronted with the Mexican militarization of the border in 1994, when Sylvestre Reyes closed the border to the U.S., and the attitude towards people crossing was getting more and more aggressive. Concha managed to pass undercover, and at one moment in her life, without thinking about it, she started to lead people across. Her fame grew to the point where people from Central America, all the way down to Nicaragua, came to find her. She would bring them into the U.S. and charge only a small amount compared to others. Concha also often helps pregnant women who want to give birth across the border because they want to have American children. Their thinking is that they can use them one day to obtain papers and benefit from the services over there. Concha runs a 'service for pregnant women' that leaves them at the public hospital in El Paso."

Concha's narrative of transgression is a radical contradiction to the docile, knowable, manageable kind of bodies presented in the Elamex ad. Tracing new paths that blur with the first winds, she crosses the border, moving in and out of legality. Hers is not a one-time crossing with the aim of becoming some one else on the other side. Rather, she is a subject in transit, moving through the transnational zone while finding ever-new strategies to get around the prevailing power structures on her clandestine trajectory. The figure of the "coyote" – someone who smuggles people across the border – expresses in a number of ways the sort of "new subjects" feminists and poststructuralists may be imaging. As the passer between cultural locations the new subject is the mediator and constant translator of different sedimentations, registers of speech, and cultural codes. When I passed by what used to be Concha's house, she had already packed up and gone. She left no forwarding address. She is not addressable in the ordinary sense by the system of citizen control. She is profoundly subversive through the fleeting utterly mobile and transitory nature of her activity and through the dis-identification with and disloyalty to any national program. With Concha's help the pregnant, maternal body, which is ordinarily the object of great biotechnological interest and reproductive control, becomes the site of transgression. She transfers these bodies from the transnational zone, where social services are denied to them by U.S. corporate employers, to a new national space, which is ironically dominated by the same corporation but where they can still collect the benefits due to them.

In *Nomadic Subject*, Rosi Braidotti reads desire as that which evades us in the very act of propelling us forward, leaving as the only indicator of who we are, the traces of where we have already been. In her terms, the nomad's identity is a map of where s/he has already been; it stands for movable diversity, an inventory of traces of what we have already ceased to be. Braidotti sees identity as a retrospective notion and nomadic cartographies as something that needs to be re-mapped constantly.[14] Perhaps we have come to such images of subjectivity because many people, including cultural critics and cultural producers, live diasporic, transient existences even if we admit that this type of diasporic lifestyle typical of an intellectual in the North is not equal to the one evolving in resistance to corporate politics in the South. Yet life on the border is of a permanently transitory nature, the female diasporic subject emerges as the transgressive identity. She keeps moving back and forth between rural and urban, between rudimentary survival strategies and high technology for cyber culture, between traditional folk lore and robotics. She crosses the boundaries between production and reproduction and she circulates in these multi-layered spaces, making connections with local coalitions and international feminist networks on labor rights, environmental issues, human rights. Braidotti's nomadism does not mean fluidity without borders but rather an acute awareness of the nonfixity of boundaries. It is the intense desire to go on trespassing, transgressing.[15]

## Serial killings

There is another, more violent aspect to the clash between bodies, sexuality, and technology in the U.S.-Mexican border zone that I want to turn to now. Since 1995, close to 200 women have been killed in Juarez and all according to a similar pattern: Poor, slender women with long dark hair, mainly workers, rarely students, have been raped, tortured, stabbed, or strangled, and tossed into the desert. Many of them had just moved to the city, nobody knew them or claimed their bodies. Fifty women are still lying in the morgue, unidentified.[16]

Women's organizations have been formed in reaction to the acute violence in the public space.[17] Most of them interpret it as violence against women, as revenge taken by men on women who have stolen their jobs, who have started to talk back to them, to go to dance halls, and generally challenge gender roles. The fact that the police haven't bothered to investigate the crimes is just another sign of male consent to this scenario. So feminists and human rights advocates took it upon themselves to investigate the cases and establish a list of missing women to prove that the cases bear too many similarities to possibly be individual crimes of passion. These groups recognize, however, that some cases are ordinary domestic violence disguised as one of the serial killings. They also understand that extreme poverty, lack of education, and economic subjugation are all conditions that prepare the ground for a criminal to come to the city and commit crimes. U.S. criminologist Robert K. Ressler, who was invited to analyze the case in Juarez, which now constitutes the largest case of serial killings known just about anywhere in the world, also points to drug traffic, gangs, migration, quick money, and prostitution as further conditions that might have led to these crimes, conditions no different than those in any major metropolis in the States. But apart from the widely scattered migration settlements, Juarez is a small border town, and serial killing is not an ordinary crime of passion. In view of the very particular constellation of economic, sexual, social, and technological factors on site generic explanations simply don't suffice.

In his recent cultural study on serial killers, Mark Seltzer draws a number of intriguing connections between sexual violence and mass technologies proper to a machine culture. Even though he never mentions this unresolved case, the relevance of his analysis to the events in Juarez is undeniable. He traces connections between this form of repetitive and compulsive violence to the styles of production and reproduction that make up machine culture and particularly relates technologies of identification, registration, and simulation to the psychological disposition of serial killers.[18]

Seltzer assigns serial killers an identity problem. "He" (with one known exception serial killers have been male) lacks boundaries. He fails to distinguish himself from others, and this lack of self-distinction, of self-difference is immediately translated into violence along the line of sexual difference which is the one fundamental difference he recognizes, writes Seltzer in his introduction *Serial Killing for Beginners*. With this logic the gendered other is undistinguishable, exchangeable, and reduced to a number in a body count. Exchangeability appears to be a determining factor in the murders reported in Juarez. Not only do the victims have a similar physical profile but also the bodies are often found in locations different from where their clothes were found, which makes identification more difficult after a certain time. Perversely, many bodies are found wearing clothes that belonged to other missing women. The confusion of their belongings that might serve as identification emphasizes in literal terms the exchangeability of the bodies. Conversely, there are new distinguishing markings, marks of violence left by the killer on the body through branding and cutting.

According to Seltzer's extensive research on serial sexual violence, a common psychological denominator of the killers lies in the undoing of identity to the point of becoming a non-person, the desire to blend into the social and physical environment. There is a strange permeability of bodies and the urban environment in Juarez, where the habitat blends into the natural surroundings and the built reality blurs with the unpaved roads. The crime often happens at dawn, when the distinction between night and day is unclear and the boundaries between the private houses, the unpaved streets, and the desert aroun[d] it are undistinguishable. There are large areas like this where the nominal division between public an[d] private is blurred, in part because the public is nothing more than private improvisation. In the ear[ly] morning hours, a great number of women cross through these widely undefined spaces on their way t[o] the maquiladoras, in transit between private and work space, between desert and urban. The assimila[-]tion of the subject to the milieu becomes nowhere better realized than in this terrain where contour[s] are virtually absent. In Seltzer's accounts we find a rich collection of wild analogies similar to this on[e] where for the serial killer, persons and landscapes, bodies and technologies, public and private merg[e] literally.

As I have argued, the border is a gigantic metaphor for the artificial division between these divergin[g] concepts, as well as a site where the blurring of distinctions takes on violent forms. On the represen[-]tational level, the image used by Elamex exemplifies how the act of technologizing the female bod[y] simultaneously sets identity markers of nature, gender, ethnicity, and nationality. On the material leve[l] this process is paralleled by the robotic, repetitive process of assembly work, the intimate implicatio[n] of the body with these technological functions and the association of this process with the gendere[d] racialized body. The serial killer, in turn, translates the violence of this entanglement into urban patho[-]logy, publicly reproducing the repetitive, disassembling, disidentifying performance on the body. Wha[t] the industry constructs as consumable, disposable bodies is literally tossed into the desert nearby in[-] formal "garbage disposals." In his own morbid way, the serial killer does nothing more than to make li[t-]eral and visible the prevailing discourse. The serial killer's identitary transparency makes him the pe[r-]fect mediator between discourse and institution. He is THE performer.

Sexual offense and eroticized violence crosses the boundaries between the natural and the collectiv[e] body, turning private desire into public spectacle. This transgression, so characteristic of the psycholo[-]gical configuration of the serial killer, is performed on a gendered and racialized body, and the borde[r] becomes the perfect stage for it. Losing the boundaries between the self and other, the serial killer i[s] perpetually in search of a border. He is attracted to the border of his country, precisely because it sig[-]nifies the boundary of a larger entity of belonging, the nation. Going to the border becomes the phys[i-]cal expression of his mental extremity, merging his physical body with the national body, confusing th[e] inside and outside.[19]

There is a limit to my fascination with his pathological mind because, after all, he is killing women in ra[w] numbers, for Christ's sake. But a discursive reflection on the killings allows us to understand them a[s] an urban pathology brought by a highly accelerated industrialization and modernization. Then we star[t] to recognize how deeply the post-industrial world is implicated in the disturbing changes taking plac[e] on the border and the impact they have on the lives of Mexican women.

To look at the border involves examining issues of representation, but the performative realisatio[n] weighs on young Mexican women. They assemble the digital technology; their time and their bodie[s] down to their monthly cycles, are strictly controlled by the white male management; prostitution is [a] necessity for many in this economy, which is characterized by sexual violence. Feminists in Juarez hav[e] the courage to survive – and beyond that to struggle – under repressive conditions, to say no to indi[-] ference and exploitation. I acknowledge every effort they make to support other women in finding better and alternative ways of living on the border, for in doing so they are rewriting the text of their subjectivity and society as it changes and as they change it.

[1] Bertha Jottar, Mexican artist, introduces the video essay *performing the border* (43 min. 1999).

[2] Donna J. Haraway, *A Cyborg Manifesto,* in *Simians, Cyborgs, and Women – The Reinventions of Nature* (NY: Routledge 1991).

[3] Elamex is the largest contract manufacturer in Mexico with annual sales of 129 million U.S. dollars (in 1998) and 17 manufacturing plants with operations in electronic and electro-mechanical assembly for the automotive, telecommunications, computer peripheral, military, and medical industries. This ad circulated in industrial trade magazines in the mid-eighties. (www.elamex.com)

[4] Anne McClintock, *Imperial Leather Race, Gender and Sexuality in the Colonial Context* (NY: Routledge 1995), pp. 23-24.

[5] Mark Seltzer, *Bodies and Machines* (NY: Routledge 1992) p. 95.

[6] Rosi Braidotti, *Nomadic Subjects, Embodiment and Sexual Difference in Contemporary Feminist Theory*, (NY: Colombia University Press 1994) p. 43.

[7] Mark Seltzer, *Bodies and Machines* (NY: Routledge 1992) p. 96.

[8] Donna J. Haraway, *Situated Knowledge,* in *Simians, Cyborgs, and Women – The Reinventions of Nature* (NY: Routledge 1991).

[9] Cipriana Herrera works for CISO, Centro de investigación y solidaridad.

[10] Guillermina Villalva Valdez was founder of COMO, centro de organisation para mujeres obreras where women workers were educated and politicized.

[11] Andrew Ross, *Going at Different Speeds*, in *Readme! Filtered by nettime*, (NY: Audonomedia, 1999) p. 174.

[12] Laura Mulvey, *Visual Pleasures and Narrative Cinema, Art After Modernism, Rethinking Representation*, ed. Brian Wallis (The New Museum of Contemporary Art, New York, 1984) reprinted from Screen 16, no. 3 (autumn 1975).

[13] Homi K. Bhabha recently gave a lecture in Zurich in the context of an exhibition and symposium on cultural practice in South Africa.

[14] Rosi Braidotti, *Nomadic Subjects*, p. 35.

[15] Idem. p. 36.

[16] From conversations with Judith Galaza, of CISO, human rights organization.

[17] March 8, CISO, a circle of 9 journalists, CICH.

[18] Mark Seltzer, *Serial Killers – Death and Life in America's Wound Culture* (NY: Routledge 1998).

[19] Mark Seltzer quotes in his introduction, Anne Rule, *Serial Murders: Hearing on Patterns of Murders Committed by One Person, in Large Numbers with No Apparent Rhyme, Reason, or Motivation* (Washington D.C.: U.S. Government Printing Office 1984).

# _PERFORMING THE BORDER

## Geschlecht, transnationale Körper und Technologi[e]

Ursula Biemann

Über den Videobildern einer durch die Wüste fahrenden Frau hört man im Off die Stimme der mexika[ni]schen Künstlerin Bertha Jottar: "Es gibt nichts natürliches an der Grenze, sie ist ein höchst konstrui[er]ter Ort, der durch überschreitende Leute reproduziert wird, denn ohne das Überschreiten haben wir k[ei]ne Grenze. Dann ist sie nur eine imaginäre Linie, ein Fluss oder einfach eine Wand."[1] Ich habe die Fra[u] am Steuer gefilmt und wurde unweigerlich Teil dieser Reise-Erzählung, die von der US-mexikanische[n] Grenze als einem performativen Ort spricht; einem Ort, der sich diskursiv über die Repräsentation d[er] beiden Nationen konstituiert und der materiell wird durch die Einrichtung einer transnationalen, korp[o]rativen Zone, in der die nationalen Diskurse sowohl materialisiert als auch übergangen werden. Es i[st] ein ambivalenter Raum am Rande der beiden Gesellschaften, ferngesteuert von ihren Machtzentrale[n].

### Export-Fertigungszone

In künstlichen posturbanen Industrieparks, die sich über gro[s]se Wüstengebiete hinstrecken, montieren US-Firmen ihr elektronisches Equipment für die Kommu[ni]kationsindustrie. Die kapitalintensiven Operationen bleiben im Norden, die arbeitsintensiven Operati[o]nen sind südlich der Grenze angelegt. Innerhalb kurzer Zeit führten die Maquiladoras – die goldene[n] Mühlen – eine technologische Kultur der Repetition, der Registratur und der Kontrolle in die Wüste[n]stadt Ciudad Juarez ein. Hier werden die mikroelektronischen Komponenten hergestellt für die Date[n]verarbeitung, für medizinische Instrumente, für Cybertechnologien, Satellitensysteme, Identifizierung[s]- und Simulationstechnologien und die optischen Instrumente für die Luftfahrt- und Militärindustrie.

Da ist nichts natürliches an dieser transnationalen Zone, und möglicherweise ist auch nichts Reales da[r]an. Es ist ein total simulierter Ort mit simulierter Politik – eine Zone, aus der jeder Begriff von Öffe[nt]lichkeit entfernt wurde. Jede Art von Versorgung, von der Unterkunft bis zur Wasser-, Gesundheits- u[nd] Kinderversorgung, ist der Verantwortung des Einzelnen überlassen bzw. spontaner BürgerInne[n]Initiativen, die jahrelang für die Beschaffung der rudimentärsten Sozialleistungen kämpfen. Es is[t w]ie nochmals von vorne beginnen zu müssen. Aller humanistischer Konsens ist hier ausser Betrieb. D[ie] posthumane Ära, die sich in den nördlichen Industriestaaten in den digitalen, futuristischen Bildern v[on] gehypten Designern ausdrückt, lebt hier an der Grenze ihre dunkle Seite aus. Dabei soll Technolog[ie] nicht dämonisiert werden, die Art, wie meine eigene Existenz durch die neuen Medien in Richtung a[uf] einen verbundenen, mobilen und beschleunigten Lebensstil verändert worden ist, ist einer der Gründ[e] weshalb ich beschlossen habe, Ciudad Juarez als einen Ort für eine Hightech-Produktion aufzusuchen und ihn wenigstens zeitweise zum Ort meiner eigenen visuellen elektronischen Produktion zu machen. Es wird deutlich werden, dass die Art von Subjektivität, die Transnationalismus nördlich der Grenze hervorbringt, sich radikal von der Subjektivität unterscheidet, die im Süden produziert wird. Die Repräsentationen von transnationalen Subjekten, die vom globalen Kapitalismus produziert werden, unterscheiden sich hier deutlich. Während die identitären Eigenschaften der mobilen KonsumentInnen von Technologie verwischt werden, werden die Subjekte am produzierenden Ende immer mehr überdeterminiert und reduziert auf geschlechtliche, sexualisierte, ethnifizierte und nationalisierte Repräsentationen.

In meiner künstlerischen Arbeit versuche ich auch der wachsenden Notwendigkeit zu begegnen, Gender-Fragen und andere Kategorien von Identität wie Ethnizität und Nationalität innerhalb grösserer Transformationen der öffentlichen Sphäre zu verorten, speziell der Realität der Städte. Dabei interessiert mich insbesondere die Frage, welche Beziehungen vorherrschende Repräsentationen zur materiellen Wirklichkeit an einem bestimmten Ort eingehen, d. h. wie sich die Grenze als Metapher für verschiedene Arten von Marginalisierung materialisiert, in baulichen und strukturellen Massnahmen, aber auch im sozialen und industriellen Management von Geschlecht. Ich werde mich deshalb in meiner Arbeit darauf konzentrieren, wie weibliche Körper in der transnationalen Zone zirkulieren, wie Geschlechterbeziehung reguliert werden in der Repräsentation, im öffentlichen Raum, in der Unterhaltungs- und Sexindustrie, in der Maquila-Politik der Reproduktion. Eine wichtige Quelle für diese Untersuchung kommt aus der theoretischen Debatte und künstlerischen Praxis des Cyber-Feminismus, der sich in den letzen Jahren mit dem Beziehungsgeflecht zwischen dem weiblichen Körper und der Technologie und der Produktion von Images beschäftigt hat. Ich benütze diese aktuelle feministische Diskussion, um über Grenze und Identitäten sowie über deren Mobilität und subversive Potenziale nachzudenken. Zudem interpretiere ich die Serienmorde in Ciudad Juarez, so dass Städtepolitik, serielle sexuelle Gewalt und Technologie auf dramatische Weise zusammentreffen und die tieferen Schichten der psychosozialen Bedeutung von Grenze blosslegen.

Aus verschiedenen Gründen stellen die Montagefabriken hauptsächlich junge Frauen als Arbeitskräfte an. Jeden Tag treffen Hunderte von Frauen in Ciudad Juarez ein, einer Stadt, die direkt am Rio Grande gegenüber von El Paso, Texas, liegt. Diese Frauen machen den Grossteil der Bevölkerung der Grenzstadt aus. Sie haben sich einen neuen Lebensraum geschaffen und gehen ihrer eigenen Vergnügungskultur nach. Sie haben Sozialverhältnisse und Geschlecherbeziehungen verändert und schreiben so die Texte ihrer Körper und ihrer Gesellschaft um. Sie sind die Hardware-Produzentinnen des Cyberspaces, welcher Mobilität und Konsumfreiheit schafft – nicht für sich, sondern für Millionen anderer nördlich der Grenze. Sie gehören zwar zu den neuen Mitgliedern einer transnationalen Bürgerinnenschicht, aber zu ganz anderen Bedingungen.

## Grenzen kommunizieren

In der Sprache der Konzerne werden die Bedingungen dieser Zone ausdrücklich klar. In der Sprache der Konzerne kann jede Einrichtung und jede Person in Begriffen von Demontage und Remontage gedacht werden. Sie stellen ihre Stätten auf und bauen sie wieder ab, je nachdem wo die Bedingungen am günstigsten sind. Die für die Fertigungsarbeit entwickelte Technologie ist schon lange auf die Personen übertragen worden, welche die Arbeit verrichten. Die Arbeiterin wird in einer post-humanen Terminologie technologisiert, in der ihr Körper fragmentiert, dehuman[isiert] siert und zu einer verfügbaren, austauschbaren und marktfähigen Komponente gemacht wird. Es ist au[f]fällig, wie die Serienmorde in Juarez diesem Prozess entsprechen oder ihn sprichwörtlich kopieren, wo[rauf] auf ich noch zurückkommen werde.

Die Wissenschaftskritikerin Donna Haraway untersucht die linguistischen Umformulierungen neue[r] Herrschaftsformen im Informationssystem, in dem alles in Begriffe von Quoten und Raten, Preisa[b]schlägen, Geschwindigkeit, Nähe und Freizügigkeit kommuniziert wird.[2] Es ist die Sprache der Optimi[e]rung, der Effizienz und Konkurrenz, die jedes Unternehmen versteht: Es ist die universelle Übersetzun[g] der Bedingungen, nach denen weltweit Geschäfte gemacht werden.

Eine Werbeanzeige von Elamex Communications, einem Maquila-Unterhändler in El Paso, Texas, vera[n]schaulicht die Kommunikation von Grenze, die in Reaktion auf die Auflösung anderer Grenzen der I[n]formationsgesellschaft mit allem Nachdruck aufgerichtet werden. Die Werbung von Elamex richtet sic[h] an US-Konzerne, die eine Verlagerung ihrer arbeitsintensiven Elektronik-Montagen erwägen.[3] Der Te[xt] setzt den Schwerpunkt auf Arbeitskosten, die auf einen Bruchteil gekürzt werden, auf Qualitätskontro[l]le, Steuerparadies, beschleunigte Inbetriebnahme, Nähe zum Hauptsitz und zum US-amerikanische[n] Markt, auf schnellen Umsatz, tiefe Transportkosten, Direktwahl, Flughafennähe. In ihren Begriffen i[st] Arbeit eine Ziffer: $1.00 die Stunde. Sie ist eine entkörperte, bezifferbare Einheit wie jeder andere A[n]reiz, der den Industriellen geboten wird, um ihre Tätigkeiten im nationalen Raum zu beenden und in de[r] Freizone einzurichten. Das Bild der Anzeige spricht hingegen eine ganze andere Sprache. Es kommu[ni]ziert ein Zusammenwirken von psychologischen, sozialen und historischen Beziehungen, die im rati[o]nalen Argument für Effizienz unterdrückt werden.

In dieser Zone wird jede und jeder in ein transnationales Subjekt verwandelt, und ethnisierte Leute sin[d] die Artikulatoren dieses Diskurses. Nur jenen Körpern wird ein Visum für Mobilität im transnationale[n] Raum zugesprochen, die es zulassen, markiert, ausgetauscht, kommodifiziert und wiederverwertet z[u] werden. Die Anzeige funktioniert insofern als eine Technologie der Überwachung, als es die beiden a[b]gebildeten Frauen innerhalb von sexuellen und ethnischen Kriterien einkapselt. Auf der linken Seite ei[n] aztekisch gemeintes Profil mit rot-weiss-grünen, in die Zöpfe geflochtenen Seidenbändern und auf de[r] rechten Seite ein asiatisches Profil mit Pagenschnitt und Lidstrich, der schräg gestellte Augen simuli[e]ren soll. Beide tragen eine Art folkloristische Kleidung. Über den ethnozentrischen Diskurs hinaus bi[n]det das Bild die Frauen an eine allgemein exotisch/erotische nationale Einheit. Dies reduziert sie we[i]ter auf einen Geo-Körper, einen Körper, der in eine Allegorie für einen geschlechtlich, ethnisch un[d] national gezeichneten Kollektivkörper verwandelt ist, wobei die nationalen Tugenden eng mit den I[n]teressen des Konzerns verknüpft sind. Während dieser Vorgang den weiblichen Körper nationalisier[t] feminisiert er gleichzeitig die Offshore-Nationen Mexiko und die Philippinen, das südostasiatische Lan[d] auf das sich diese Werbung vermutlich bezieht.

Der weibliche Körper schliesst immer schon das Begehren nach Eroberung in sich ein. In Anne McCli[n]tocks *Pornotropen der europäischen Imagination* zeichnet sie die weibliche Figur als die Grenzmarke de[s] Imperiums nach, als die Vermittlerfigur an der Schwelle zum feminisierten Raum der terra incognita[.] Sie erklärt dies durch ein tiefes, wenn nicht pathologisches Gefühl männlicher Angst, einem Abgre[nzen] zungsverlust beim Verlassen der bekannten Welt und dem Erforschen des Unbekannten. Von Anfang an war die Feminisierung des Landes eine Strategie der gewaltsamen Bändigung und Eindämmung, die sowohl in den Bereich der Psychoanalyse als auch in den der politischen Ökonomie gehört. Die Erzeugung dieses historisch kultivierten Begehrens in der Elamex-Anzeige verdeutlicht die Rolle, welche dieses Begehren auch beim Einstellen der weiblichen Arbeitskraft spielt. Es stellt die Körper der Frauen in die Fantasiegeschichte der kolonialen Eroberung hinein. "Mexico schlägt den Fernen Osten um 10'000 Meilen", heisst es in der Schlagzeile. In diesem allzu bekannten Szenario werden die zwei Frauen gegeneinander ausgespielt und mit ihrer Sexualität und Weiblichkeit in Wettbewerb zueinander gebracht.

Die geschlechtlich und ethnisch gezeichnete Figur wird zur Artikulatorin der Grenze, dieser fragilen Linie, die den Rand des nationalen Körpers markiert. Im nationalen Diskurs ist die Grenze der Ort, von dem alle Krankheit, Illegalität, Verschmutzung und Armut kommt. Sie ist der verletzlichste, durchdringbarste Ort, an dem sich Ängste stauen. Wo würde sich die Panik um die nationale Identität besser verorten lassen? US-amerikanische Kunden müssen vor allem davon überzeugt werden, dass diese weiblichen Offshore-Körper kontrolliert sind. Die Anzeige macht es sich zur Priorität, eine gezähmte, fügsame, verlässliche und disziplinierte weibliche Arbeitskraft zu versichern. Ihre manikürten Hände entsprechen dem Firmenstandard; ihr Gesicht drückt Ernsthaftigkeit, Konzentration und Präzision aus. Gefühllosigkeit. Kurz, sie stellt ein Replikat dar, das eigentliche Instrument. Mit dem Chip in der Hand ist ihr Körper in eine robotische Funktion eingeschrieben, er wird zur Verlängerung der Hand und nimmt den Platz des Oberkörpers ein. Ihr Körper wird vollständig technologisiert.

Eine cyberfeministische Sichtweise interpretiert das Bild der organisch-mechanischen Grenzgängerin als potenziell insofern ermächtigend, indem es jeden Wunsch nach einem fixierten, souveränen Subjektes zunichte macht. Ich habe meine Vorbehalte, dieser Elamex-Bildkonstruktion beispielsweise ermächtigende Qualitäten zuzuschreiben, da sie Geschlechter- und Rassenklischees zementiert. Dennoch ist es selten genug der Fall, dass Subjekte vom unteren Ende des Hochtechnologie-Komplexes im kommerziellen Kontext überhaupt repräsentiert werden. Kommerzielle Repräsentationen stellen gewöhnlich nur die Designer und die high-end-Benutzer dar, die von diesen aufregenden, futuristischen Technologiebildern wieder profitieren. Sie verbessern ihr Gesellschaftsimage und ihren Wert im Arbeitsmarkt, während andere Beteiligte der Industrie – z. B. das Verkaufs- und Verwaltungspersonal im Bürosektor oder die TechnikerInnen und MontagearbeiterInnen im industriellen Sektor – systematisch von der Repräsentation ausgeschlossen sind. Meist finden sich Maquila-Frauen in ganz faden Darstellungen, in Verbindung mit Armut und Ausbeutungsdiskursen im soziologischen und Entwicklungs-Kontext wieder. Warum muss ich einem jungen männlichen Techniker $120 die Stunde bezahlen, um meinen Computer zu reparieren, und der jungen weiblichen Arbeiterin $1 die Stunde, damit sie ihn zusammenbaut? Es ist eben auch eine Frage der Repräsentation und ihrer performativen Kraft. Die Repräsentation transnationaler Subjekte, die der globale Kapitalismus hervorbringt, sind unterschiedlich in einer Technologie konsumierenden Gesellschaft, in der die Identitätsmerkmale ausgelöscht werden, und einer Technologie produzierenden Gesellschaft, deren Repräsentation durch geschlechtliche, ethnische, sexualisierende und nationale Zuschreibungen überdeterminiert wird.

Die Elamex-Anzeige (siehe Seite 78) wirkt durch einen doppelten Diskurs, durch den die offenbar gegensätzlichen Register des naturalisierten und technologisierten Körpers koordiniert werden. Die gängige Verbindung von "weiblich" und "natürlich" wird nicht durch eine andere klare Gleichsetzung e[r] setzt, sondern durch die beunruhigende Identifizierung des Weiblichen mit der unbestimmten Mischur[g] von natürlich und technologisch. In dieser Verwicklung von Mechanik und Geschlecht wird der natürli[ch] weibliche Körper abgekoppelt, auf die Maschine zugeschrieben und individuell neu verkörpert als "d[ie] Hand" oder "das Auge" eines neuen korporellen Ganzen. Dies sind übrigens jene Körperteile, für d[ie] eine Maquila-Frau eingestellt wird: ihre Augen und ihre Finger, denn digitale und mikroelektronisch[e] Herstellung erfordert ebenso grosse optische Genauigkeit wie Fingerfertigkeit. Doch ihre biologisch[e] Komponente macht sie anfällig und verletzlich. Ihre Sehkraft ist scharf genug für gerade acht Jahr[e,] dann muss sie ersetzt werden durch eine frische Arbeitskraft. Somit wird ihre organische Sicht bei d[er] Herstellung der Visualisierungstechnologien, auf die unsere Gesellschaft baut, konsumiert. Das zwan[g]hafte Begehren nach Sehen und Sichtbarkeit ist ein bestimmendes Merkmal unserer Informationsg[e]sellschaft, wie Mark Seltzers Analyse des Körper-Maschinen-Komplexes Ende des letzten Jahrhunder[ts] mit grosser Genauigkeit feststellte.[5] Es hat dazu geführt, dass Wissenschafter und Ingenieure ein ga[n]zes Arsenal an Apparaten und Instrumenten entwickelten, um das Potenzial des menschlichen Auge[s] zu vervielfachen. In den 90ern, beobachtet Rosi Braidotti, dringt der biotechnologische Blick in die i[n]timste Lebensstrukturen ein und macht das Unsichtbare sichtbar, restrukturiert das noch Ungeformte[.] Der Wunsch, alles sichtbar zu machen, ist auch eine Forderung, Dinge verständlich und regierbar zu m[a]chen. Es drückt gleichzeitig eine Fantasie der Überwachung und die Notwendigkeit der Verkörperu[ng] aus.[7]

Die an der Grenze gefertigte überwiegend optische Technologie veranschaulicht die Bedeutung küns[t]licher Sicht für den Machtapparat, jetzt und in der Zukunft. Medizinische Optik und Cyberoptik, Übe[r]wachungssysteme, Technologien für Röntgensatelliten, Mikro- und Teleskoping, audiovisuelle Medie[n] und virtuelle Technologien, elektronische Apparate zur Identifizierung, Scanning, Digitalisierung, Ko[n]trolle und Simulation, sie alle arbeiten für die Beziehung von Vision und Supervision. Haraway versuch[t] die Sehfähigkeit aus der phallogozentrischen entkörperten, technologischen Zyklopensicht zu rette[n] und für einen feministische zu besetzen. In Situated Knowledge plädiert sie für eine verkörperte Obje[k]tivität das Erlernen eines zusammengesetzten, vielteiligen Sehens; partielle Perspektiven, welche d[ie] Idee der passiven Sicht zerschmettern zugunsten einer Auffassung des Auges als eines aktiven Wah[r]nehmungssystems, ständig übersetzend und verantwortungstragend.[8]

Heute könnte es wichtiger denn je sein, die Möglichkeiten von Leben und von gelebter Weiblichkeit i[n] einer Cyborg-Welt zu untersuchen und Begriffe von Singularität und Subjektivität in einem Diskurs [zu] reinstallieren, der den weiblichen Körper so ungebrochen funktionalisiert. Die im Video erzählte G[e]schichte über Concha, später im Text, ist so ein Versuch eines nicht-ausbeuterischen, nicht-spektaku[l]lären Fallbeispiels. Natürlich beziehen sich viele Berichte, die ich vor Ort gehört habe, direkt auf die Ko[n]trollmechanismen, die das Leben der Grenzfrauen beeinträchtigen. Obwohl ich mich im Video nicht a[uf] die Instrumente der Unterdrückung konzentriert habe, weil ich denke, dass Veränderung nicht durc[h] Information passiert (weil sie sonst schon stattgefunden hätte), will ich hier die Kontrollumstände d[e]taillierter beschreiben, denn sie verdeutlichen die Beziehung zwischen Geschlecht, Körper und Techno[o]logie.

## Technologien der Kontrolle

Die in Juarez installierten Technologien der Grenz- und Arbeitskontrolle machen die gewaltsame Beziehungen zwischen Vision, Überwachung, Macht und Körper offensichtlich. Gewerkschaftliche Organisation ist in den Maquiladoras strikt verboten. Einer der Hauptgründe weshalb die Maquiladoras weibliche Arbeitskräfte bevorzugen ist, dass Arbeiterinnen angeblich fügsamer sind und nicht gleich darangehen, sich gewerkschaftlich zu organisieren. Da die jugendlichen Arbeiterinnen oft das einzige Familieneinkommen nach Hause bringen, üben die männlichen Familienmitglieder erheblichen Druck aus, den Job zu halten und sich den Arbeitsbedingungen zu fügen. Das Maquila-Programm verlässt sich auf die vorherrschenden patriarchalen Familienbeziehungen. Auch hat sich in den letzten Jahren die ganze Industriezone elektronisch vernetzt, und die Fabriken stellen Schwarze Listen auf mit Namen unerwünschter Subjekte, angefangen mit Mördern, Straffälligen aber auch "Feinden" der Maquila; gemeint sind Leute, die versuchen, die Bedingungen in den Maquiladoras in irgendeiner Weise zu verändern. Schwarze Listen sind eigentlich gesetzlich verboten, denn wenn man von einer Fabrik entlassen wird, gibt es keine Chance, irgendwo in der Zone noch Arbeit zu finden. Die Aktivistin Cipriana J. Herrera erzählte mir, dass sie zusammen mit zwei "compañeras" gefeuert wurde, weil sie eine Cafeteria verlangt hatten.[9] Ihre Fabrik lag ausserhalb des Industrieparks und es gab für mehrere Hundert ArbeiterInnen keinen Platz zum Essen. Wir sprechen nicht einmal davon, eine Gewerkschaft zu bilden, nicht von Lohnpolitik, Gesundheitsrisiken oder Menschenrechten. Frauen haben Angst davor, wegen des geringsten Ungehorsams ihren Job zu verlieren, niemals mehr einen anderen finden zu können und ihren Familien die Konsequenzen aufzubürden.

Das Maquila-Programm ist ein strategisch wichtiger Punkt in der Ökonomie der mexikanischen Regierung. Das Einkommen aus der Export-Fertigungszone übersteigt bei weitem jenes der Wirtschaftszweige Öl oder Tourismus. Die Regierung kümmert sich intensiv um die Interessen der Maquilas. Und wir können davon ausgehen, dass die US-Militarisierung der Grenze nicht nur dazu da ist, Illegale davon abzuhalten, die Grenze zu überqueren, sondern auch um die gigantischen Investitionen der US-Industrie auf mexikanischem Boden zu schützen. Guillermina Villalva Valdez, eine führende ArbeiterInnenbewegungs-Aktivistin und Akademikerin, die mich während meines ersten Besuches in Juarez sehr unterstützt hat, starb vor wenigen Jahren in einem Flugzeugabsturz auf dem Weg nach Texas, zusammen mit 4 anderen Schlüsselfiguren der Arbeiterbewegung.[10] Die kleine Maschine explodierte in der Luft; wahrscheinlich durch eine Bombe. Gewerkschaftliche Aktivitäten werden von dem vernetzten korporativen System aufs genaueste verfolgt.

Zeitmanagement ist ein anderes wirksames Kontrollmittel. Aus praktischen Gründen sind die Industrieparks am Stadtrand angesiedelt. Sie sind durch öffentliche Verkehrsmittel nicht zu erreichen, also fahren private Busgesellschaften die ArbeiterInnen bei Schichtwechsel zwischen dem Stadtzentrum und den Fabriken hin und her, oft zu horrenden Tarifen, die bis zu einem Drittel des Monatslohns ausmachen können. Vor Tagesanbruch verlassen die ArbeiterInnen ihren Wohnort an der Peripherie, marschieren den langen Weg ins Zentrum, fahren von dort mit dem Bus eine weitere Stunde zu den Maquilas hinaus und treten um 6 Uhr die Frühschicht an. Sie verbringen dann 9 Stunden in der Fabrik und nehmen den gleichen Weg zurück. Da bleibt keine Zeit zu leben, keine Zeit zu denken, keine Zeit zu organisieren. Ihre ungeheure Zeitinvestition kommt der Technologie zugute, die unser Leben im Norden beschleunigt. In seinem Essay *Going at Different Speeds* bespricht Andrew Ross Geschwindigkeitsunterschiede und relativen Zeitmangel als Grundprinzip für ungleiche Entwicklung in der Weltökonomie. "Bei einer kritischen Geschwindigkeit", zitiert er Ivan Illich, "kann niemand Zeit gewinnen, ohne jemand anderen dazu zu zwingen, Zeit zu verlieren."[11]

Im elektronisch vernetzten Maquila-System wird jede einzelne Person identifiziert und profiliert. Zeit, Produktivität und der weibliche Körper werden vom weissen, männlichen Management streng überwacht. Die Körperkontrolle reicht bis zum Überprüfen des Monatszyklus, um sicherzustellen, dass die Arbeiterin nicht schwanger ist. Zwangsverhütung und Schwangerschaftstests sind an der Tagesordnung, und selbstverständlich bedeutet Schwangerschaft sofortige Entlassung. Die Reproduktion dieser Körper ist streng kontrolliert, von dem Moment an, in dem sie als produktiv bestimmt wurden. Die beschleunigte Industrialisierung hat heftige Veränderungen bewirkt zwischen den gegensätzlichen Registern von öffentlich und privat, von Arbeit und Fabrik einerseits und Heim und Familien andererseits, oder generell gesagt: zwischen dem Ökonomischen und dem Sexuellen. Wie überall waren in Mexiko diese Register traditionell geschlechtlich getrennt. Frauen kümmerten sich um die häusliche Sphäre, während die Männer, Väter, Onkel, Brüder die Familie finanziell versorgten. Was Juarez in kurzer Zeitspanne erlebte, ist die Verschmelzung der getrennten Bereiche des privaten, weiblichen, häuslichen Raums der Reproduktion und des Verbrauchs mit dem des öffentlichen, männlichen Raums der Produktion. Mit der Einstellung von vorwiegend jungen Frauen ist dieses traditionelle Muster stark verändert worden – natürlich nicht konfliktlos. Es überrascht nicht, dass die Arbeiterin als die zentrale Figur des Konfliktes hervorgeht, denn sie verkörpert die beiden Funktionen der Produktion und der Reproduktion. Sie verkörpert gewissermassen das Problem, das es zu kontrollieren gilt.

Seit NAFTA materialisiert die Grenze diesen Konflikt eindrücklich. Das Abkommen garantiert den freien Fluss von Gütern, verhindert aber den Durchlass von denjenigen Personen, die diese Güter herstellen. Das Überqueren der Ware steht für gute nachbarschaftliche Beziehungen, während das Überqueren von Personen kriminalisiert und polizeilich überwacht wird. Die Grenze wird zur Metapher und zur eigentlichen materiellen Institution, die aus der Differenz zwischen dem Ökonomischen und dem Sexuellen Kapital schlägt.

### Die Sexualisierung des Territoriums

Eine der deutlichsten und vielleicht auch bedenklichsten Einsichten, die ich an der Grenze gewonnen habe, ist dass die Arbeiterschaft im Süden nicht nur feminisiert, sondern auch sexualisiert worden ist, dass die Arbeiterinnen im wahrsten Sinne des Wortes in ihrer Sexualität adressiert werden. Strukturell gesehen haben junge Frauen in Juarez drei Optionen, ihren Lebensunterhalt zu verdienen: Sie können in der Maquila arbeiten. Wenn sie in der Fabrik wegen mangelnder Ausbildung nicht genommen werden, können sie domestica werden und privat als Hausmädchen arbeiten. Wenn eine Frau keine Empfehlung für eine solche Stelle aufbringen kann, bleibt ihr noch eine Option: die Prostitution. Doch auch die Sicherung eines Fabrikjobs ist oft nicht die letzte Lösung. Die ungenügenden Löhne zwingen viele Frauen dazu, zusätzlich Geld durch Wochenend-Prostitution zu verdienen. Seit der Schliessung der Grenze und ihrer militärischen Durchsetzung gibt es jedoch sehr viel weniger US-Kunden und weniger in den USA lebende Mexikaner, die die Grenze überqueren, um ihre Dollars in Juarez auszugeben. Darin zeigt sich schon die gegenseitige Durchdringung von Arbeitsmarkt und Sexualmarkt innerhalb dieser Wirtschaftsordnung. Diese eine Ziffer, 1 pro Stunde, bedeutet die Sexualisierung des ausgelagerten Arbeitsmarkts, der die Frauen an den Rand der Obszönität treibt und sie auf Sex reduziert. Diese eine Ziffer impliziert Zuhälterei durch Grosskonzerne. Nicht dass sie direkt am Profit aus der Prostitution partizipieren, aber sie profitieren davon, Arbeitskräften nur ein Taschengeld geben zu müssen und die Frauen abhängig zu machen, ihren Körper zu kommodifizieren. Prostitution ist nicht nur Bestandteil von Exzess in der zollfreien Zone. Sie ist ein struktureller Teil des globalen Kapitalismus. Seit die Grenze in den 90er-Jahren dichtgemacht und militärisch verstärkt wurde, hat sich die Konkurrenz zwischen den professionellen Prostituierten und den jüngeren, oft heranwachsenden Maquila-Arbeiterinnen, die am Wochenende auf den Strich gehen, verschärft. Die Dynamik an der Grenze zeigt wie auch der Kundenschwund die Prostitution nicht abnehmen, sondern zunehmen lässt. Bezeichnenderweise ist in Juarez, wo Prostitution aus der Maquila-Ökonomie hervorgeht, frei von Zuhältern.

Im offiziellen Mediendiskurs wird die Grenze immer als ein Ort der Straffälligkeit, der Verderbtheit und Prostitution dargestellt, als Magnet für alle Subjekte, die dem moralischen Standard der Gesellschaft nicht gerecht werden. Die Medien verlieren selten ein Wort darüber, dass es tatsächlich die Maquila-Industrie ist, die diese Verhältnisse produziert, indem sie den Freizonenplan durchsetzt, der von beiden nationalen Regierungen und den Dow-Jones-Leuten entworfen und umgesetzt wurde. Die Medien verwechseln Wirkung mit Ursache. Ich bin nicht daran interessiert, einfache Kausalitäten nachzuzeichnen. In einem überaus komplexen Ort wie der Grenze kann es nützlicher sein, die Gleichzeitigkeiten zu registrieren und auf ihre Entsprechungen hinzuweisen, ohne gleich ein allumfassendes theoretisches Gebäude zu errichten. Es scheint auch unangebracht, hastige Interpretationen für Formationen zu liefern, die recht formbar und veränderlich sind. An der Grenze bilden sich Identitäten und kollabieren wieder, passen sich an, um dann erneut zu übertreten. Und das Letzte, was ich hier vorschlagen möchte, ist das Etablieren von leichtfertigen Kategorien für neue Subjektivitätstypen.

Sexualität ist ein Ort, wo der Wunsch nach Selbstausdruck und Kontrollmechanismen heftig aufeinanderprallen. Tausende von Fliessbandjobs wurden in dieser Wüstenstadt geschaffen, und die Frauen sind diejenigen, die sie bekommen. Da Geschlechterbeziehungen stark ökonomisch bestimmt sind, hatte die Umkehrung der Einkommensstrukturen eine sofortige Wirkung darauf, wie sich Frauen auf Männer beziehen. Frauen haben grössere Autonomie über ihr Leben gewonnen, auch über ihre Sexualität.

Mit der Maquila-Industrie sind mehrere Hundert Bars und Tanzclubs in Juarez entstanden. Freitags und samstags um 16 Uhr, wenn die Frauen von der Frühschicht zurückkehren, sind diese Bars und Tanzclubs in Downtown Juarez geöffnet. Vor zehn Jahren, während meiner ersten Drehzeit in Juarez, waren die Tanzwettbewerbe nach ganz traditionellen Geschlechtervorbildern gestaltet. Frauen konkurrierten mit Schleckstängeln auf der Bühne und führten die begehrlichste Körpersprache auf, die sie für den männlichen Blick zustande brachten. Die Gewinnerin war nicht etwa eine Frau, die erotisch konfrontativ tanzte, sondern eine, die langsam und in zielloser Erwartungshaltung auf der Bühne auf- und abschritt. Es sah nicht nach viel aus, aber das Publikum reagierte mit grossem Enthusiasmus auf ihre nervöse Passivität, mit der sie erlaubte, dass die Blicke Besitz über sie nahmen. Sie verkörperte alle visuellen Genüsse, von denen Laura Mulvey in den 70ern in Bezug auf den Film sprach.[12] Heute ist die Verschiebung der Kaufkraft auf die jungen Frauen in den Tanzclubs offensichtlich. Die Unterhaltung richtet sich mit Shows männlicher Stripper und Tanzwettbewerben für Männer vornehmlich an weibliche Kunden. Hier sind es Frauen, die den Sex-Appeal von Männern bewerten. Die Songs sind den Mädchen von Torreon oder von Durango gewidmet, den Geburtsorten eines Grossteils der Maquila-Arbeiterinnen. Oftmals drücken die Musiktexte explizit sexuelles Begehren von Frauen aus; die ganze Unterhaltungsmaschine ist auf ihr Vergnügen ausgerichtet. Die Verschiebung der Einkommensmuster ermächtigt die Frauen in ihren persönlichen Beziehungen. Sie ermöglicht ihnen den öffentlichen Ausdruck von sexuellem Begehren und leistet die Befriedigung dieser Wünsche mit ökonomischen Mitteln anstelle von anderen traditionellen Dienstleistungen im Bereich von Heim oder emotionaler Reproduktion.

### Technologien des Überlebens

Die anhaltende Migrationsbewegung von Frauen in transnationale Räume bezeugt ihre Flexibilität, ihre Widerstandsfähigkeit und ihre Ausdauer. Sie sind oft jung, und ich meine 13-, 14-, 15-jährig, wenn sie ihre Familien verlassen und den langen Weg zurücklegen, um an der Grenze zu arbeiten. Sie lassen die Städte Zacatecas, Durango, Torreon auf der dürren Zentralebene hinter sich, um an den Rio Grande zu ziehen, und werden zur Hoffnung derer, die sie zurücklassen. Oft kommen sie in kleinen Gruppen von drei oder vier Mädchen gleichen Alters und aus dem gleichen Ort. Wenn sie ankommen, haben sie keine Bleibe, da die Stadt keine zur Verfügung stellt. Städtische Gelder werden nur in die Konzerne investiert, nicht in die Leute, die für sie arbeiten. Also gehen die Frauen an den Rand der Stadt, die sich weit in die Sierra ausdehnt, suchen sich einen freien Fleck und bauen aus den Abfällen der Maquiladoras eine Hütte direkt in den Wüstensand. Paletten dienen als Wände, Chemiekanister werden zu Wassertanks umfunktioniert etc. Einige nennen diesen Vorgang "Invasion", weil die MigrantInnen ein Stück Land besetzen und sich niederlassen, während sie noch auf offizielle Unterlagen für ihre Häuser warten. Das ist zwar irregulär, aber unumgänglich. Es gibt grosse Gebiete, in denen hauptsächlich Frauen wohnen, in denen es nur Sandstrassen gibt, keine Beleuchtung, keine Sicherheit oder öffentliche Verkehrsmittel. Es ist nichts Ungewöhnliches, junge Maquila-Frauen in diesen Wüstenviertel umherkreuzen zu sehen, die eine kleine fleischfarbene Prothese am Handgelenk tragen. Diese soll sie vor übermässiger elektromagnetischer Auflading während der Montage- und Testoperationen schützen. Es ist eine Entladungsnadel, die der Arbeiterin mit einem rosa Drehkabel um das Handgelenk befestigt ist und ihren Körper mit der Arbeitsbank verbindet. Sie behalten dieses Ding auch am Wochenende um den Arm, aus Angst, es am Montagmorgen zu vergessen.

Es ist eine eigenartige Form des Lebens: Morgens Unternehmenskultur, abends wird "maiz" geknetet. Der Rhythmus des kargen Hochlandes weicht der optimierten Produktionsweise. Das Leben an der Grenze lehrt, mit Widersprüchen klarzukommen, pluralistisch zu agieren, denn Flexibilität ist eine Überlebensfrage, wenn man zu den Statisten der Konzernkultur zählt. Es ist ein Leben des Übergangs und mit Überleben fängt es an. Es geht um den Mut, die Situation zu überstehen und um den Wunsch, die Macht zu überdauern, meint Homi K. Bhabha, ohne vorzugeben, die Unterdrückung überwinden zu können.[13] Er schlägt vor, ein Philosophie des Umsturzes durch eine Philosophie des Überlebens zu ersetzen, und dies scheint mir am Ende dieses Jahrhunderts, wo post-industrielle Systeme der Produktion und Information eine oppositionelle Massenpolitik müssig gemacht haben, ein angebrachtes Modell zu sein. Es gibt jedoch Überlebensarten, die subversive Formen annehmen, auch wenn dies nicht von vornherein die Intention war.

# Transgressive Identitäten

Die raffiniertesten Technologien der Überwachung haben Risse und Lecke, und es gibt Löcher im Grenzzaun und Pfade, die durch die Wüstentäler führen, auf denen Frauen bei Nacht Schwangere über die Grenze bringen. Diese Frauen wissen, wie sie Schlangenbisse und Dehydration vermeiden können, und verlangen wenig Geld dafür, die Schwangeren sicher in einem US-amerikanischen Spital abzuliefern. In der transnationalen Zone habe ich nach solchen Erzählungen Ausschau gehalten, alternativen Wünsche, die sich in transgressiven Bahnen ausdrücken. Wir sollten jedoch bedenken, dass Strategien der Überschreitung aus unterschiedlichen Motivationen hervorgehen können. Während Intellektuelle wie Bhabha oder kulturelle Produzentinnen wie ich subversive Strategien wählen, weil sie zu einem bestimmten Zeitpunkt von kulturellem Interesse sind, wurde Concha, die ein gewöhnliches Leben bevorzugen würde, durch eine Notlage in transgressive Lebensformen hineingedrängt.

Wir müssen zugeben, dass Transgression, wie im Falle Conchas, nicht von einer aus kulturellen Gründen interessant scheinenden Strategie motiviert ist, sondern im Gegenteil als Reaktion auf eine missliche, durch oppressive Kräfte verursachten Lage entwickelt wird. Und wenn diese nomadischen, grenzüberschreitenden Subjektivitäten in Zahl und Wirkungskraft auch eher bescheiden sind, so ist es dennoch wichtig und philosophisch bedeutsam, sie zu theoretisieren.

"Ich kenne Concha seit etwa fünf Jahren", sagt Angela Escajeda, während wir zu den Ansiedlungen an der Peripherie rausfahren, "seit sie hier in diesem Haus lebte, das sie aus den Materialabfällen der Maquiladoras baute. Sie sah sich auf einmal von ihrem Mann verlassen und realisierte, dass sie als schwangere Frau keine Arbeit finden würde in Juarez. So traf Concha jemanden – ich weiss nicht, ob das gut oder schlecht war für sie –, der ihr sagte, wie sie in den USA Zigaretten verkaufen könne. Concha fing also an, über die Grenze zu gehen, dort Zigaretten billiger einzukaufen, sie hinüberzubringen, die Steuern abzuziehen und sie dann billiger auf der anderen Seite wieder in Zirkulation zu bringen. Später, dank ihren Fähigkeiten die Grenze zu passieren und die US-amerikanischen Migrationsbeamten zu umgehen, fing Concha an, Leute illegal hinüberzubringen. Ihre Strategien waren vielseitig und variabel. In 1994 war sie mit der Militarisierung der Grenze konfrontiert, als Sylvester Reyes die Grenze zu den USA dicht machte und sich die Aggression gegen Passanten verstärkte. Concha gelang es, die 'Undokumentierten' geheim hinüberzubringen und plötzlich, ohne dass sie sich dessen so richtig bewusst war, begann sie Leute zu schleppen. Sie wurde so berühmt, dass Leute von Zentralamerika, bis hinunter nach Nicaragua sie aufsuchten. Sie brachte sie hinüber und verlangte nur kleine Summen dafür, verglichen mit anderen Schleppern. Concha half oft schwangeren Frauen, die im Norden gebären wollen, um US-amerikanische Kinder zu haben, in der Überlegung, dass diese ihnen eines Tages zu Papieren verhelfen und sie von den Leistungen dort drüben profitieren lassen. Concha hatte eine Art 'Service für schwangere Frauen', die sie im öffentlichen Spital in El Paso ablieferte."

Die Erzählung von Conchas überschreitenden Praktiken steht in radikalem Widerspruch zu den zahmen, fügsamen, leitbaren Körpern der Elamex Anzeige. Concha passiert die Grenze auf neuen Pfaden, welche sich mit dem ersten Wind verwischen, und geht in der Illegalität ein und aus. Es ist nicht ein einmaliges Überschreiten mit der Aussicht, auf der anderen Seite jemand anderes zu werden. Concha ist ein Subjekt des vorübergehenden Transits, das durch die transnationale Zone kreuzt und immer neue

Strategien findet, um die vorherrschenden Machtstrukturen auf ihren Geheimgängen zu umfahren. Die Figur des coyote, der Schlepperin, die Leute über die Grenze schmuggelt, drückt diese Art von "neuem Subjekt" aus, wie es sich Feministinnen und andere PoststrukturalistInnen vorstellen. Als Passantin zwischen kulturellen Orten ist sie die Vermittlerin und ständige Übersetzerin von unterschiedlichen Ablagerungen und registriert dabei Sprache und kulturelle Codes. Als ich in Conchas Haus ankam, war sie bereits nicht mehr da, ohne Nachsendeadresse zu hinterlassen. Sie ist in diesem Sinn durch das System der BürgerInnenkontrolle nicht adressierbar. Sie ist zutiefst subversiv in ihrer Flüchtigkeit, in der mobilen und vergänglichen Natur ihrer Tätigkeit und durch die Desidentifikation und Untreue dem nationalen Programm gegenüber. Hier wird der schwangere, mütterliche Körper, der gewöhnlich das Objekt grossen biotechnologischen Interesses und reproduktiver Kontrolle ist, zum Ort der Überschreitung Concha trägt diese Körper von der transnationalen Zone, in der ihnen die Sozialleistungen von den US-Arbeitsgebern abgesprochen werden, in den nationalen Raum, in dem sie die Leistungen, die ihnen zustehen, in Empfang nehmen können.

In *Nomadic Subject* liest Rosi Braidotti Begehren als das, was uns im eigentlichen Akt des Vorwärtsstrebens entgeht. In ihren Begriffen ist die nomadische Identität eine Karte, auf der sie schon gewesen ist; sie steht für eine bewegliche Diversität, ein Inventar von Spuren dessen, was wir bereits nicht mehr sind. Braidotti sieht Identität als einen retrospektiven Begriff und nomadische Kartografien als etwas was ständig neu zu erfassen ist.[14] Wenn wir es zu solchen Bildern von Subjektivität gebracht haben dann deshalb, weil viele Leute, TheoretikerInnen und KulturproduzentInnen inbegriffen, diasporadische vorübergehende Existenzen leben, auch wenn wir zugeben müssen, dass der diasporadische Lebensstil eines Intellektuellen im Norden nicht dem gleichkommt, der sich im Widerstand gegen Konzernpolitiken im Süden bildet. Doch ist das Leben an der Grenze von einer permanent vorübergehenden Natur und das weibliche Diaspora-Subjekt geht als die transgressive Identität hervor. Sie bewegt sich fortwährend zwischen rural und urban, zwischen rudimentären Überlebensstrategien und Hightech für die Cyberkultur, zwischen traditioneller Folklore und Robotik. Sie übertritt die Grenzen zwischen Produktion und Reproduktion, sie zirkuliert in diesen vielschichtigen Orten, geht Verbindungen mit lokalen Koalitionen und internationalen feministischen Netzwerken zu Fragen von Arbeitsrecht, Umweltanliegen, Menschenrechte ein. Braidotti's Nomadismus ist nicht Flüssigkeit ohne Grenzen, sondern eine akute Gewahr um die Nicht-Fixiertheit von Abgrenzungen. Es ist der intensive Wunsch danach, immer weiter zu überqueren und zu übertreten.[15]

## Serienmorde

Es gibt einen gewaltsamer Aspekt des Aufpralls von Körper, Sexualität und Technologie an der Grenze. Seit 1995 sind nahezu 200 Frauen in Juarez ermordet worden, und alle Morde folgen einem bestimmten Muster: Arme, schlanke Frauen mit langem, dunklem Haar, vorwiegend Arbeiterinnen, selten Studentinnen, wurden vergewaltigt, gefoltert, erstochen oder erdrosselt und in die Wüste geworfen. Viele von ihnen sind erst vor kurzem in die Stadt gezogen, keiner kennt sie, keiner fragt nach ihnen. Fünfzig Frauen liegen unidentifiziert im Leichenschauhaus.[16]

Als Reaktion auf diese akute Gewalt im öffentlichen Raum bildeten sich einige kleine Frauenorganisationen.[17] Hier werden die Morde meist als Gewalt gegen Frauen interpretiert, als Rache von Männern an Frauen, die ihnen ihre Jobs weggenommen haben und die sich verbal wehren, in Tanzclubs gehen und die traditionellen Rollen herausfordern – kurz: sie interpretieren die Morde als Bestrafung. Die Polizei kümmerte sich lange nicht um die Aufklärung der Fälle – ein weiterer Hinweis auf den patriarchalen Konsens dieses Szenarios. Deshalb übernahmen Feministinnen und MenschenrechtsvertreterInnen selbst die Untersuchungen der Fälle und erstellten eine Liste aller verschwundener Frauen, um zu beweisen, dass sich die Fälle zu ähnlich sind, als dass sie als einzelne, aus Leidenschaft begangene Verbrechen betrachtet werden könnten. Den Gruppen ist klar, dass es sich bei einigen Fällen um "normale" häusliche Gewalt handelt, die sich als serial killings tarnen. Die Ursachen dafür liegen in extremer Armut, fehlender Ausbildung und wirtschaftlicher Unterwerfung. Der US-Kriminologe Robert K. Ressler, der während meines Besuches eingeladen war, die Fälle in Juarez zu analysieren, sieht auch im Drogenhandel, Gangs, Migration, schnellem Geld und Prostitution weitere Gründe für die Morde – analog zu jeder Metropole in den USA. Aber Juarez ist – abgesehen von der ausgedehnten Migrationsansiedlung – eine kleine Grenzstadt und serial killing ist kein "gewöhnliches" Leidenschaftsverbrechen. Angesichts der besonderen Konstellation von ökonomischen, sexuellen, sozialen und technologischen Faktoren vor Ort sind allgemeine Erklärungen unzureichend.

In seiner kürzlich erschienen Studie über Serienmörder stellt Mark Seltzer eine Reihe verblüffender Verbindungen her zwischen sexueller Gewalt und Massentechnologien, die der Maschinenkultur eigen sind. Obgleich er die unaufgeklärten Fälle von Juarez nicht erwähnt, sind seine Analysen durchaus auf Juarez übertragbar – insbesondere Verbindungen zwischen repetitiver, zwanghafter Gewalt und der Produktion und Reproduktion einer Maschinenkultur, das heisst zwischen Technologien der Identifikation, Registrierung und Simulation und der besonderen psychologischen Disposition der Serientäter.[18]

Seltzer schreibt dem Serienmörder ein Identitätsproblem zu. "Ihm" (mit nur einer Ausnahme sind überführte Serienmörder männlich) fehlt die Abgrenzung, "es gelingt ihm nicht, sich vom anderen zu unterscheiden. Diesen Mangel an Selbstunterscheidung, an Selbstdifferenz, übersetzt er sofort in Gewalt entlang der Linie der sexuellen Differenz, der einzigen fundamentalen Differenz, die er erkennt", schreibt Seltzer in seiner Einleitung *Serienmörder für Anfänger*. In dieser Logik wird das geschlechtlich Andere ununterscheidbar, austauschbar und auf eine Zahl reduziert. Austauschbarkeit scheint in den Fällen, über die in Juarez Bericht erstattet wurde, ein bestimmender Faktor zu sein. Die Opfer haben nicht nur ähnliche Profile, auch wurden die Kleider oft an anderen Orten als die Körper gefunden, was die Identifizierung noch erschwerte. Perverserweise sind verschiedene Leichen gefunden worden, die Kleider von anderen verschwundenen Frauen trugen. Die Verwechslung ihrer identifizierenden Habseligkeiten deudet diese sprichwörtlichen Austauschbarkeit der Körper an. Umgekehrt hinterlässt der Täter auf den Körpern Schnitt- und Brandzeichen.

Seltzers ausgedehnten Recherchen über serielle sexuelle Gewalt legten eine Auflösung von Identität als einen gemeinsamen psychologischen Nenner nahe. Dies kann beim Täter so weit gehen, sich als Nichtperson zu fühlen, und ein Begehren zu entwickeln, sich mit der sozialen und physischen Umgebung vermischen zu wollen, mit der Masse zu verschmelzen. Es gibt eine eigenartige Durchlässigkeit von Körper und dem urbanen Umfeld in Juarez, wo die Behausungen in die natürliche Umgebung eintauchen und sich die gebaute Realität mit den belaglosen Strassen verwischen. Die Morde passieren oft bei Tagesanbruch, wenn die Unterscheidung zwischen Tag und Nacht unklar ist und die Grenzen zwischen den privaten Häusern, den Sandstrassen und der Wüste nicht zu unterscheiden sind. Es gibt ausgestreckte

Gebiete, wo die nominale Unterteilung zwischen öffentlich und privat verwischt ist, wo das Öffentliche nichts weiter als private Improvisationen sind. In den frühen Morgenstunden durchqueren viele Frauen diese undefinierten Orte auf dem Weg zu den Maquiladoras, im Transit zwischen Privatsphäre und Arbeitsort, zwischen Wüste und Stadt. In Seltzers Berichten finden wir eine reiche Sammlung wilder Analogien dieser Art, wo für den Serienmörder Personen und Landschaften, Körper und Technologien, Öffentliches und Privates buchstäblich verschmelzen.

Ich versuche zu zeigen, dass die Grenze eine gigantische Metapher für die künstliche Aufrechterhaltung dieser unterschiedlichen Konzepte ist und gleichzeitig der Ort, wo die Verwischung von Differenz gewaltsame Formen annimmt. Auf der repräsentationellen Ebene ist das Bild von Elamex beispielhaft dafür, wie die Technologisierung des weiblichen Körpers gleichzeitig Identitätsmarker setzt für Natur, Geschlecht, Ethnizität und Nationalität. Auf der materiellen Ebene entspricht dieser Vorgang dem robotischen, repetitiven Arbeitsprozess der Montagearbeit, der intimen Verbindung von Körper mit technologischen Funktionen und der Verknüpfung dieses Vorgangs mit dem ausgelagerten weiblichen, farbigen Körper. Der Serientäter übersetzt die Gewalt dieser Verbindung in eine urbane Pathologie und reproduziert so auf der öffentlichen Ebene die repetitive, demontierende, desidentifizierende Performanz am geschlechtlichen Körper. Jene Körper, welche die Industrie als konsumierbare Wegwerfkörper definiert, werden buchstäblich in informellen Abfalldeponien aufgefunden. Auf seine morbide Art macht der Serientäter nichts weiter, als den bestehenden Diskurs sichtbar zu machen. Seine identitäre Transparenz macht ihn zum perfekten Mediator zwischen Diskurs und Institution. Er ist DER Performer.

Sexuelle Verstösse und erotisierte Gewalt übertreten die Grenzen zwischen dem biologischen und dem kollektiven Körper, sie tragen privates Begehren in den öffentlichen Raum. Diese für den Serienmord typische Überschreitung wird am weiblichen, farbigen Körper ausgeführt, die Grenze wird zur perfekten Bühne. Die Grenze zwischen Selbst und Anderen verlierend, sucht der Täter beständig nach einer Grenze. Er begibt sich zur eigentlichen Grenze seines Landes, denn dies ist die Abgrenzung einer grösseren Entität des Dazugehörens, der Nation. Zur Grenze zu gehen wird für ihn zum physischen Ausdruck seiner mentalen Extremität, indem er seinen natürlichen Körper mit dem nationalen vermischt, Innen und Aussen ebenso wie das Öffentliche und das Private durcheinander bringt.[19]

Die Faszination, die diese pathologische Psyche auf mich ausübt, stösst selbst an Grenzen, denn schliesslich werden Frauen in grosser Zahl ermordet. Aber eine diskursive Betrachtung der Morde lässt sie als eine urbane Pathologie verstehen, die von der beschleunigten Industrialisierung und Modernisierung herbeigeführt wurde. So zeigt sich wie tief die post-industrielle Welt in diesen beunruhigenden Veränderungen an der Grenze und deren Auswirkungen auf das Leben von mexikanischen Frauen verwickelt ist.

Die Grenze ist also eine Frage der Repräsentation, aber performative Realisierung lastet im Endeffekt auf jungen mexikanischen Frauen. Sie setzen die digitalen Technologien zusammen, ihre Zeit und ihre Körper werden bis hin zum Monatszyklus durch das weisse männliche Management strikt kontrolliert und Prostitution wird für viele von ihnen eine Notwendigkeit in dieser Ökonomie, in der sexuelle Gewalt die öffentliche Sphäre charakterisiert. Die Frauen in Juarez haben den Mut zu überleben und darüber hinaus, unter repressiven Bedingungen nein zu sagen zur Gleichgültigkeit und Ausbeutung. Ich anerkenne jede Anstrengung, die sie unternehmen, andere Frauen darin zu unterstützen, bessere und alternative Lebensformen an der Grenze zu finden und so den Text ihrer Subjektivität und Sozietät immer wieder aufs Neue schreiben und beschreiben.

[1] Bertha Jottar, mexikanische Künstlerin, leitet mein Video-Essay *Performing the Border* ein (43 Minuten, 1999).
[2] Donna J. Haraway, *A Cyborg Manifesto*, in: *Simians, Cyborgs, and Women – The Reinventions of Nature* (NY: Routledge 1991).
[3] Elamex ist der grösste Produktions-Unterhändler in Mexiko mit Jahresverkäufen von US$ 129 Millionen in 1998 und 17 Fabriken mit Operationen in Elektronik und Elektromechanik für die automotive, Telekommunikations-, Computer-, Militär- und Medizin-Industrie. Diese Anzeige zirkulierte in Industrie-Fachzeitschriften Mitte der 80er-Jahre. (www.elamex.com)
[4] Anne McClintock *Imperial Leather Race, Gender and Sexuality in the colonial context* (NY: Routledge 1995), S. 23-24.
[5] Mark Seltzer, *Bodies and Machines* (NY: Routledge 1992), S. 95.
[6] Rosi Braidotti, *Nomadic Subjects, embodiment and sexual difference in contemporary feminist theory* (NY: Colombia University Press 1994), S. 43.
[7] Mark Seltzer, *Bodies and Machines* (NY: Routledge 1992), S. 96.
[8] Donna J. Haraway, *Situated Knowledge*, in: *Simians, Cyborgs, and Women – The Reinventions of Nature* (NY: Routledge 1991).
[9] Cipriana Herrera, works for CISO, Centro de investigación y solidaridad.
[10] Guillermina Villalva Valdez war Gründerin von COMO, Centro de organisación para mujeres obreras, einem Zentrum für die Weiterbildung und Politisierung von Arbeiterinnen.
[11] Andrew Ross, *Going at different Speeds*, in: *Readme! Filtered by nettime* (NY: Audonomedia 1999), S. 174.
[12] Laura Mulvey, *Visual Pleasures and Narrative Cinema, Art After Modernism, Rethinking Representation*, hrg. Brian Wallis (The New Museum of Contemporary Art, New York 1984), erstmals abgedruckt in: Screen 16, Nr. 3 (Herbst 1975).
[13] Homi K. Bhabha gab kürzlich einen Vortrag in Zürich im Kontext einer Ausstellung und einem Symposium zu kultureller Praxis in Südafrika.
[14] Rosi Braidotti, *Nomadic Subjects*, S. 35.
[15] Idem, S. 36.
[16] Aus einem Gespräch mit Judith Galarza von der Menschenrechtsorganisation CICH
[17] 8 march, CISO, eine Gruppe von 9 Journalistinnen, CICH.
[18] Mark Seltzer, *Serial Killers – Death and Life in America's Wound Culture* (NY: Routledge 1998).
[19] Mark Seltzer zitiert in seiner Einführung Anne Rules *Serial Murders: Hearing on Patterns of Murders Committed by One Person, in Large Numbers with No Apparent Rhyme, Reason, or Motivation* (Washington, D.C.: U.S. Government Printing Office 1984).

**Next page:** border fence Tijuana/San Diego, photography by Bertha Jottar

# _INTERVIEW WITH BERTHA JOTTAR
Ursula Biemann

**How do you conceive of the border? It's both an abstract concept and yet it has strong impact on the trajectories of many people who want to cross it and on those who live in the area.**

Yes, we can think about the border in two ways. Either as a place of limitation and boundary – this is always the case when the border is produced by the nation state, it has to be a place of limitation to prevent trespassing – or as a place of crossing in relation to a populated geographical location. But either way, you need the crossing for the border to become real otherwise you just have this discursive construction. There is nothing natural about it; it's a highly constructed place that gets reproduced through the crossing of people because without the crossing there is no border, right? It's just an imaginary line, a river or just a wall. In the case of the U.S.-Mexican border you need the repetitive crossing of bodies to produce the discursive space of the nation state and also to produce a real type of place: a border. The border is a highly performative place.

But the border is very heterogeneous and in our artwork it has always been very important to point out the many different ways of crossing in the Tijuana/San Diego region. Are you crossing in English, in Spanish, in Spanglish, with a U.S. passport, with a visa, jumping, swimming, as a tourist, as a migrant, a middle-class woman, a domestic worker? There are all these different ways of crossing. And it's through the power relationships produced through the crossing that the border gets constantly rearticulated. It's not just a happy crossing. For local people who have been living in the region for generations the crossing becomes a cultural experience. People in the border region have a life. If we believe that practices in relation to a space reconfigure that space, the U.S.-Mexican border is certainly a good example. Tijuana is the border with the most human traffic in the world. Its crossings are not just a matter of prohibitions or allowances of the State; they also stand in relation to the cultural and political practices which develop at the moment of crossing and which claim the space towards the production of new rights. The border is a construction of State convenience but it is highly contested by the diversity of its crossings and the culture of resistance against its prohibitions.

In Ciudad Juarez you have to cross over a bridge. That is a very different experience from passing a building or going from one side of a wall to the other, like in Tijuana, where doors open or close depending on the crosser's legal status. The way you cross, or the knowledge of "how to cross" produces very different psychological effects. It's import to think about the border as an extremely heterogeneous but artificial place with real consequences.

**Can you think of an example of the culture of resistance?**

In the worst case, you can think about the U.S.-Mexican border as a site of crisis. It is a place between life and death, regeneration and repression, a site where the body disappears through the border crossing, something that itself is already a performative act. So this performance – this repetition and reiteration of crossing – can be considered an act of resistance to this real and discursive disappearance of the body. The "undocumented" body is also a highly narrated one because it is constantly represented through various State and mass media discourses; it is pathologized, racialized, etc. If the border is a site of national containment materialized through this "undocumented" body, illegal crossing produces a crisis, but the crossing body becomes a politicized body, liminal, barely perceptible to the law.

That's why artists and activists pay very close attention to the crossing body, the migrant who may or may not reach the other side and whose chances of succeeding depend on luck and knowledge. You need knowledge too, that's a fact. Many people get ripped off because they don't know how to find the right person to get them across. Before the wall was erected, people crossed by themselves out of experience, they didn't need anybody. Maybe it was just that you knew to look in the eyes of the INS officer if you were crossing in a car, but it was still a particular knowledge you acquired after crossing many times. This is one of the conventions of "how to cross." The multiple physical and discursive disappearance of the crossing body has been one of the major motivating themes in border art and activism. Border art is a site-specific practice, and in dealing with the disappearance of the migrating crossing body it becomes consciously political and committed. This type of resistance has its history in Latin America's struggle against various and continuous forms of colonialism, which have created a context for the production of a tactical aesthetic of resistance.

I can give you the example of *A Border of Mirrors*. In 1990, a local coalition of artists and activists from various organizations produced a counter-demonstration to the xenophobic movement and call to battle: *Light Up The Border*. This event, organized by San Diego's ex-mayor Roger Hedghcock, and the Latina widow of an ex-INS officer consisted of a line of parked cars near the San Diego border where the flux of undocumented workers is high. Given the flat and dry landscape, cars were able to line up on a long stretch, pointing their headlights south to illuminate and halt the "illegal aliens" crossing to the North. The performance/counter-demonstration consisted in the installation of hundreds of cardboard reflectors that demonstrators on foot on the South side used to bounce back the hateful light coming from the line of cars. As the car owners turned on their blinding lights, they became invisible and the artists/activists held up the reflectors like shields against the glare. The performance was framed by dogs owned by skinheads and police as well as other floodlights used by the law enforcement patrols. The whole thing became a very violent and tense set of relations, a series of unwanted and unreciprocated gazes, a long and moving line of reflections and refractions.

Through this spatial intervention of tactically casting and bouncing light back and forth, the undifferentiated, natural landscape became an artificially constructed site, not only a site of crisis but also one a contestation to that crisis. Performance can serve as an arena for representing ideological conflict mimetically, but it is also a "real" arena in which that conflict can be fought out with real consequence

The people who brought the portable reflectors eventually recycled them. Once the *Light Up the Border* activists found themselves pointing their lights toward an empty landscape, their own presence publicly vanished as their lights faded into the darkness of the night. The crossing body never materialized what remained was the memory of a future, the crossing of the body undocumented.

**You lived in Tijuana just around the time of the North American Free Trade Agreement, how did it affect life on the border?**

I arrived in Tijuana in 1985, in a period when the Free Trade Agreement was being written. I experienced Tijuana and San Diego during that political transition. The FTA has been a training ground to learn what it means to merge countries and become a part of an irrevocable global world with free consumer borders, to learn what it means for a country to be traded according to a supply-and-demand logic and terms of net value of production costs. Cost of labor in Mexico is still among the lowest in the world. The FTA wants to produce a border that is a place where goods travel happily and it pretends the access to goods is egalitarian. On the other hand it prevents the crossing of people. Goods cross, but the people who produce the goods aren't allowed to.

The pre-NAFTA period saw a very different kind of representation of the border, not only from the point of view of the U.S. – after all it's a double-sided discourse. In Mexico City the discourse of the border was one of corruption, prostitution, and drug dealing. On the other side, the U.S. representation of the border was either of a war zone or a no-man's-land.

**Has the U.S. discourse changed a lot since NAFTA?**

The U.S. representation of the border and of its southern neighbors is consistent in the way it narrates a tale of reproduction and consumption while denying the productive aspect. The migrant worker, described as an illegal alien, is portrayed as reproductive in numbers but not in profit. All you ever hear is how many illegal aliens were captured per week. The other day I heard in the news that before the steel wall, 50% of the crossers passed through Tijuana. Now, in January 2000, only 18 people were caught. The point of this message was that the surveillance mechanisms are working well now and that the area is no longer a chaos.

The presence of the migrant is understood as consuming and taking from U.S. resources and jobs. This representation of the migrant's reproductivity doesn't take into consideration the national economic growth due to profits and tax incomes generated by the immigrants. The migrant is considered a reproductive body rather than a productive subject, and this discursively places the male migrant in feminized position. What is very ironic about this logic is the selectivity through which citizenship is on ganized. The Protestant ethic of "you are what you produce" does not apply to "illegal aliens" who, in fact, not only produce considerably but also take better care of their jobs because they are more susceptible to be fired or deported. According to Protestant logic, one should protect the undocumented more than any documented worker. Undocumented workers are never represented for what they produce but for what they consume.

These dominant narratives also imply a particular understanding of the Latino family. As much as extended families have been fundamental in the survival and culture retention of the Latino/a communities in the U.S., this notion has to be revised due to its various layers of erasures. First, it assumes that all Latino families in the U.S. are immigrants and that all working class immigrants are males whose common motivation is to sustain their families back in Mexico or elsewhere. This traditional crossing narrative assumes two types of males: those who cross to work, the pollos, and those who facilitate the crossing, the coyotes. This scenario of who crosses and who stays erases the crossing of women workers and their participation in the active labor and economic force. The female workers disappear, the wives who migrate along with their husband disappear, and the women who migrate to the maquiladora cities Ciudad Juarez or Tijuana but don't cross to the U.S. also disappear. Female workers at the maquiladoras (sweatshops) are not even part of the narrative of border crossing. Not only their labor is effaced, their bodies too. So in this unequal economy of crossing, the female body disappears more than once. In the official discourse, if females enter the U.S. arena of border representations, they don't enter it as productive workers but as surrogate charges of the State, "to give birth" and "to take prenatal care and health care from the welfare system." The position of women is complicated because they don't exist as individuals just like the males don't exist as citizens. They are thoroughly kept outside the State apparatus and enter the legal and civil structure only when they get deported. The male migrant population is feminized and the female subjects, who are the most fragile ones in this crossing economy, are entirely effaced. The border is a highly gendered region.

**Is it this concern with disappearance that motivated you to make *Border Swings*?**

Exactly. Every time I crossed the border north I always wondered how many layers of invisibility women bear. In *Border Swings/Vaivenes Fronterizos (BS/VF)* I took this a few steps, or "leaps," further. I used the discursively disappearing, crossing female body to imply alternative discourses which not only considered the discursive disappearing of female crossers but their physical, material as well as their artistic production too. It is just a trailer, an introduction, but it is very ambitious in the questions it brings up. I was interested in the border art movement current at that time and how women, like men, used public space and popular culture in their artistic production. Border art is vibrant and self critical because to live on the border doesn't mean to relate to the U.S. but also to Mexico City's dysfunction and corruption. It's not only who gets to cross north, but also whose work and what type of art does or does not enter into the U.S. representational space of border art. Interestingly, after the establishment of the binational biennial INSITE, this question has still remained relevant. Another leap I intended to make with *BS/VF* was to reclaim and recycle the savviness of Mexican popular culture, particularly wrestling films. *El Santo en la Frontera del Horror* is a film in which El Santo arrives in Ciudad Juarez for a wrestling match and gets caught in the investigation of undocumented males who keep disappearing. Through the wrestling plot he discovers that the migrants ended up in the hands of a gringo scientist who kidnapped them in order to sell them to U.S. surgical companies for their body parts! This horr[ible] story of literal body parts and capitalist exchange is not only metaphorical but unfortunately a[nd] frighteningly real, too. Probably the most shocking story I've heard about females crossing is one rel[a]ted by Reverend Flor Rigoni, director of the Casa del Inmigrante in Tijuana. In 1986 he told me about [a] case where a breast was discovered in Canyon Zapata, a place known as the Soccer Field, you kno[w] Mexican humor. It is a semi-vacant hilly stretch of land, located in a Tijuana neighborhood called Ind[e]pendecia. It is known as a place where undocumented people cross north, the pollos. *Bord[er] Swings/Vaivenes Fronterizos* opens with someone describing the discovery of this breast.

**You talked about the border as an imaginary line. What did it mean to you, during th[e] time you lived in Tijuana, to cross north?**

To cross the border north is not only to trespass by crossing the artificial national boundary. Crossin[g] through Tijuana means to cross north for at least three hours, the time it takes to arrive in Los Angele[s]. The border region, then, is a large territory that encompasses various cities between San Ysidro and L[A]. This territory is the arena for social and political mobilizations. Chicanos, who historically have bee[n] marked as immigrants, despite their presence in the U.S. for many generations, have incorporated t[he] human rights of the undocumented into their struggle for full citizenship. This important alliance is rel[e]vant, as it expands the rights and practices of citizenship.

There are Chicano organizations that have been working with Mexican workers since the twenties, a[nd] the participation of women in this movement has been fundamental. Their roles range from bein[g] union leaders, such as Dolores Huerta, to serving the double function as workers and mothers in hel[p]ing to maintain the strikes as long as necessary. Just recently, in New York City, undocumented Latin[o] workers unionized against their Korean boss who hired them for $2 per hour, 12 hours a day, seven day[s] a week. This case is really important in that it conflates human and civil rights and labor rights regar[d]less of the workers' legal status. Prejudiced practices, like the ones denying citizenship to U.S.-bo[rn] kids of undocumented people, are being contested through the everyday social and political mobiliz[a]tions of documented and undocumented migrants and natives. For me, to cross north meant learnin[g] that every time you crossed implicated the practice of a double consciousness. You cross from wher[e] to become what? I learned that identity is not given nor stable, rather it's a series of identifications a[nd] the undoing of these identifications that have real political consequences according to what side of t[he] border you are on. Once you cross, you become – whether you want to or not – responsible for what[s] in front and what's behind you. You cross the border, but the border, recalling Gloria Anzaldua, crosse[s] you too.

**I mainly know the situation in Ciudad Juarez, are there any major differences be[-]tween the border towns?**

From Matamoros to Tijuana, the historical realities vary a great deal. Tijuana is a century old and th[e] consequence of San Diego's navy formation, Nogales, dates back to before the U.S. border was draw[n]. However, the imposition of the maquiladora industry in the various Mexican border cities happene[d] fairly simultaneously as a structural consequence of U.S.-Mexico power relationships. It's not that th[e] maquiladoras are the result of a border condition. The border is constituted by the power relationship between the two nations and this relationship gets materialized in maquiladoras and in the bars for U.S. tourists and for the migrant workers on their way north. This has to be clear; otherwise the border gets naturalized as this place of excess, a place of prostitution and corruption.

**That needs to be controlled?**

Yes. Simultaneously with the good-neighbor gestures extended by the FTA you have the militarization of the border. While on the level of representation the message is that the North and the South get along, the reality is that we have to build a stronger wall, we have to put up brighter lights, and we have to double the number of INS officers in addition to drug enforcement officers and the military personnel. You have this discursive representational space and you have this material space, which again is constituted through the crossing of people and the halting of these people. It's a very contradictory space.

Essentially, the U.S. is always at war against somebody, so when there is no international war going on, they use the border because that's their "natural" place to rehearse or have a little war. When the Gulf War was over, former President Bush announced nationally that his next war was against drugs. Guess where! I'm quite interested in the idea of recycling and the border is a good storage place for recycling. How do you recycle a war mentality and the materials of war? When the contra affair ended in Central America, the military personnel got transported to the border. It's not a coincidence that after the Gulf War the U.S. built a wall along the border's 2,500 miles with what they had used as landing tracks for their airplanes in Desert Storm! For the U.S. the border is a recycling territory where it can practice and rehearse its war mentality. The macho U.S. State culture is articulated through masculinized, high-tech war games performed at the border. It is a highly gendered place.

So there is a war against drugs and a war of the skinheads using paint bullet guns against undocumented workers and you have the floodlight on the border, people using this light for and against the crossings of migrant workers. It embodies the idea of a combat zone. This representation is so violent, not in essence but in the way it has been constructed. I don't even want to reinforce or repeat these images. In a way the border is always represented as a wound that has to be healed, that has to be closed, that has to be protected, from contamination and from disease. Where is AIDS coming from? From the border. Where is all this disease, poverty, and contamination coming from? From the border. So we have to heal this wound through various systems of militarization, purification, cleansing, it's a surgical place, like an operating room. Guillermo Gomez Peña made an interesting statement about artists using the border as a laboratory. What kind of laboratory? The State too has always used it as a laboratory because it perceives the border as a wound, as a penetrable site.

So it's a very complicated space of representation and one performance and that re-enforces and re-informs the border constantly, whereby there is always the unidirectional idea that everything goes from South to North. The crossing from the North to the South is discursively non-existent, unless it's from a tourist perspective and stems from the good-neighbor mentality: "let's go to Tijuana, eat burritos, take our picture with the painted donkey, and just trash the city," because Tijuana has always been seen a[s] the dump of the U.S. Fortunately, things move in both directions, and culture along the border has bee[n] very creative in assimilating and acculturating these movements. Recycling has become part of every[-]day life and landscape. It is a way of doing, using, and thinking about what is given to us, but with th[e] critical difference being in the moment of montage. You should see how all the car and truck tires com[-]ing from the U.S. get recycled by stacking them into the hills to prevent the houses from sliding an[d] collapsing. I just tell myself, if I can't beat them, I might as well use them, learn their language and us[e] it to my advantage.

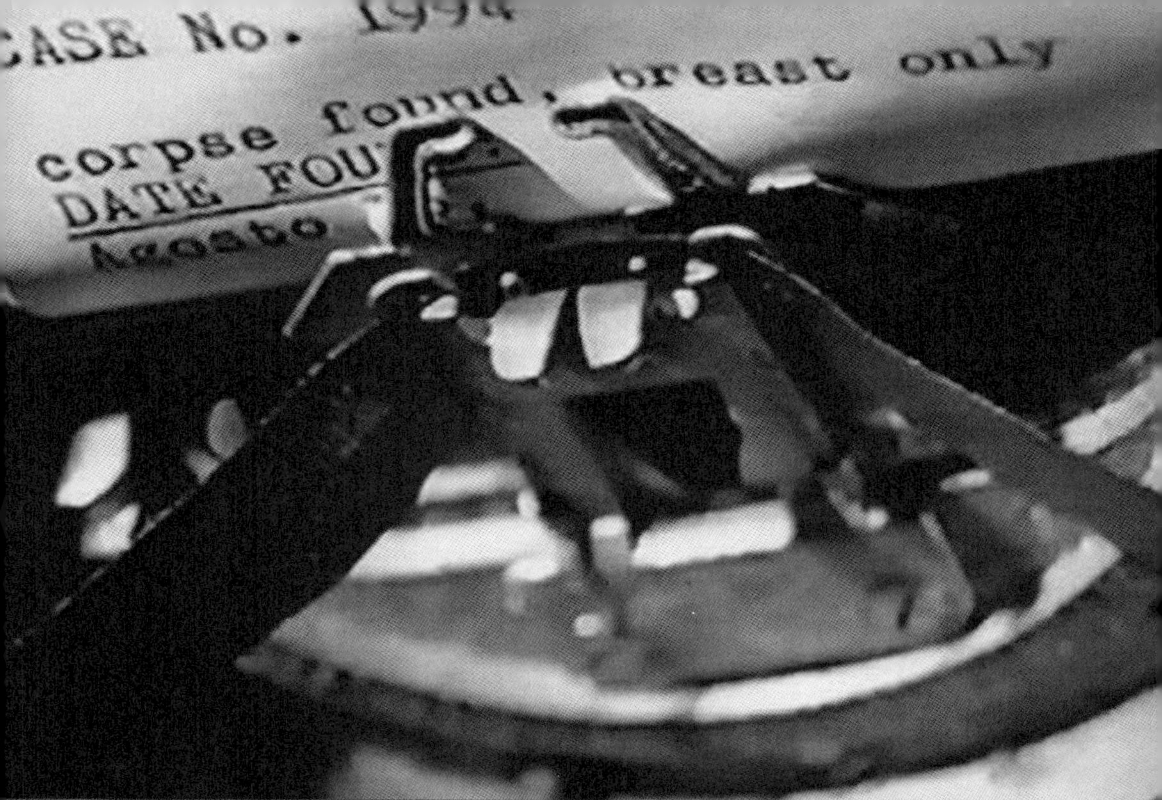

CASE No. 1994
corpse found, breast only
DATE FOU[ND]
Agosto

# Lexicon Hispanica

# _LEXICON HISPANICA
# AN ETHNOGRAPHIC COLLECTION
# 1989

The object of this series of works is the Hispanic alimentary brand, Goya, produced by a New Yorker Jewish family who picked the Spanish painter's name to market its products to Hispanic consumers. At the same time, Goya is also the Hebrew word for a non-Jewish woman. So that the name of the trademark simultaneously features female, negative, artistic, and commercial attributes. Like any minority group in New York, the Hispanic culture most noticeably distinguishes itself by eating habits and the foods sold at its local grocery store, the Spanish bodega, which is stocked with Goya products from black beans to virgin olive oil. The bodega also characterizes the appearance and atmosphere of the barrio street culture. As a hangout to observe the comings and goings and a meeting point to chat with your neighbors, the bodega contributes significantly to the urban public space in these neighborhoods. For *Lexicon Hispanica* I took stock of the existing bodegas in an extended radius from my residence on Grand Street in Williamsburg.

With this series of works I started to get more seriously involved in a critique of ethnography and the art-culture system according to which objects from non-Western origins are being classified by Western science. *Lexicon Hispanica* has become a kind of ethnographic collection which escapes most scientific criteria and value judgments by bringing cultural signifiers with no collectible value into the art space. The idea was not to gather "traditional" values in distinction from modernity, but to produce a contemporary expression of an emergent culture which establishes itself by a wealth of quotidian features. I was particularly interested in relating the two reference systems of anthropology and contemporary art with their respective criteria of interpretation.

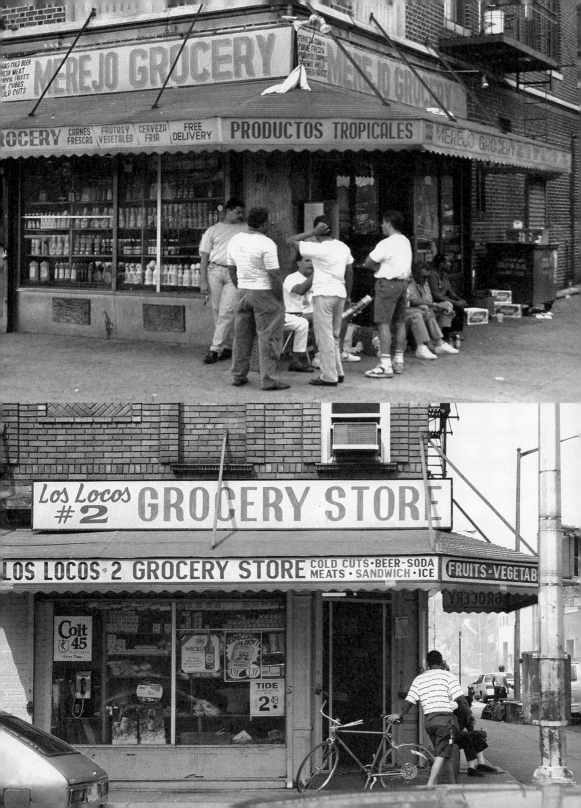

# _LEXICON HISPANICA
# EINE ETHNOGRAFISCHE SAMMLUNG
# 1989

Gegenstand dieser Recherche ist die hispanische Lebensmittelmarke Goya, die von einer jüdischen New Yorker Familie produziert wird. Den Namen des spanischen Malers haben sie gewählt, um ihre Produkte an hispanische KonsumentInnen zu vermarkten. Goya ist aber gleichzeitig auch das hebräische Wort für eine nicht-jüdische Frau. Mit dieser Benennung erhält das Andere gleichzeitig weibliche, negative, künstlerische und kommerzielle Attribute. Wie jede Minorität in New York hat auch die hispanische Kultur ihre eigenen Essgewohnheiten und Lebensmittel in den Läden und in den spanischen Bodegas, die – von den schwarzen Bohnen bis zum kaltgepresstem Olivenöl – mit Goya-Produkten bestückt sind. Die Bodega prägt das Erscheinungsbild und die Stimmung der Barrio-Strassenkultur. Als Ort, wo die Menschen herumhängen, das Kommen und Gehen beobachten und wo sie sich für ein Gespräch mit den Nachbarn treffen, ist die spanische Bodega ein wichtiger Raum des städtisch-öffentlichen Lebens in diesen Vierteln. Für *Lexicon Hispanica* machte ich eine Bestandsaufnahme der Bodegas, ausgehend von meinem Wohnort an der Grand Street in Williamsburg.

Mit dieser Serie von Arbeiten beginnt eine ernstere Auseinandersetzung mit der Kritik an Ethnografie und dem Kunst-Kultur-System, die Objekte nicht-westlicher Herkunft in der westlichen Wissenschaft klassifizieren. *Lexicon Hispanica* wurde eine Art ethnografische Sammlung, welche den wissenschaftlichen Kriterien und Werturteilen entgleitet, indem sie Kulturträger ohne Sammelwert in den Kunstraum bringt. Es ging nicht darum, Traditionelles zusammenzutragen, das der Modernität prinzipiell entgegensteht, sondern vielmehr darum, einen aktuellen Ausdruck einer sich neu formenden und sich anhand vieler alltäglicher Zeichen etablierenden Kultur festzuhalten. Dabei interessierte es mich besonders, eine unmittelbare Verbindung zwischen den Referenzsystemen der Ethnologie und der zeitgenössischen Kunst mit ihren respektiven Interpretationskriterien herzustellen.

# Global Food

# _GLOBAL FOOD
# 1991

*Global Food* is an ethnographic study that examines the degree of cultural assimilation of a globally distributed product to local tastes and customs and analyses the corporate strategies of the local integration of these products. Many brands would be well suited for such an examination. I have opted for Knorr soups because they bring together a wide range of cultural assimilations to match local customs and tastes. Also, they are sold in the most unexpected and obscure corners of the world, from small Indian towns high in the Venezuelan Andes to the most remote rural areas in Thailand. Their globalizing strategies are not limited to the metropolitan centers but have been implemented on a large scale.

This study – the object of which is to compile a complete collection of Knorr instant soup packages produced worldwide – is the result of a request to all the regional producers and distributors. Every week new packages arrived in the mail. The comparison between these regional soup programs reveals how far the corporate image has to yield to the local taste both in terms of content and graphic presentation of the packaging. *Global Food* reproduces the global trend of transcending national limits while maintaining a minimum of cultural distinctions. In the process of globalization, language remains the most pertinent and reliable carrier of ethnic characteristics. For the purpose of the installation a selection had to be made among the packages produced in 47 countries: Arabic, Chinese, Thai, Malayan, Spanish (Venezuela), Portuguese (Brazilian), English/Afrikaans (South Africa), Greek, Slavic, and Turkish. The use of the local language is always the first ethnic distinction made, but this only happens under the condition that a market is considered important enough to be "individualized." Kenya will have to make do with English packages, since their market is not considered significant enough to print a Swahili version. In terms of content, there are certain "universal" runners that appear in every program worldwide: the tomato soup and the mushroom soup are translated into just about every language.

In a more advanced stage of assimilation, the program is expanded by local specialties such as the tiger lily and mushroom soup in Malaysia or the Hungarian dumpling soup. Generally speaking, these dishes are exclusively produced for a particular market: the "semoule tomatée" is made for the Arabic space; it won't be sold in Hong Kong. However, there are peculiar exceptions, like in the case of Greece which produces a Mexican black bean soup served in a terra cotta bowl and packaged using Mayan pyramid imagery. The Hungarians feature a totally different version of "Mexicana"; the Mexicans don't carry anything like it. In some countries "foreign" specialties have become so much a part of daily eating culture that they have entered the individualized national program, and in others, the "exotic" quality is simply a good argument to sell. While European-style soups are served in white soup bowl, the Asian recipes are likely to be presented in small generic bowls or in the Chinese rice bowl with assorted porcelain spoons. The type of dish, the language, but also the quality of the image and the typography play an important part in courting a specific ethnicity.

Despite all the individual assimilations to match local taste, the corporate image demands to be recognizable at all times. In the case of Knorr, the corporate image relies graphically on a top third in yellow, lower two thirds in green (sometimes reversed), and a red logo. It's striking that the farther away the producing country is from the Swiss parent company, the more extravagant the packaging gets. China it seems to have abandoned almost all corporate prescriptions. Whereas in Malaysia the word Knorr is still written in Roman characters, the Chinese use two Chinese characters in the flag-shaped logo space. Only in Hebrew, Thai, and Chinese is the logo replaced by their script.

Knorr's strategy is to maintain a balance between corporate recognition and cultural integration. The tolerance appears to differ from country to country. Intergration means nothing else but recognizing one's own culture in the new product and associating this recognition henceforth with the corporate logo. Culturally speaking, however, this strategy is still more complex than the traditional type of imperialism Coca Cola conducts by moving in like a bulldozer and dominating any importing culture with its unmistakable taste, logo, and message of "the free world." The message it comes with is another one. Just as instant food brought the promises of modern life to the Western housewife in the fifties, these dehydrated soups may continue to present modern lifestyle to women in the developing world today.

These products also shape consumption practices in places where the local production and consumption of food are still organically connected and thus don't require hard currency which has to be earned one way or another. That's how rural and remote parts of the population get tied into the economy without lucrative jobs being created there that would help them afford this modern lifestyle. The purchase of a Knorr instant soup is never merely an expression of existing eating customs; it introduces structural changes in a local consumer culture.

## Ezo Gelin Çorbası

Ezo Gelin Soup     Ezo Gelin Suppe

4 Kişiliktir
Servings
Teller

โจ๊กรสไก่

CHICKEN FLAVORED RICE PORRIDGE

NET WT. 65 GMS.

كنور

كشك مصرى
Egyptian Kishk

Bag
Servings

١ كيس
٤ أطباق

康寶

雲耳干貝濃湯

港式手藝    料多味美

# 康寶

## 髮菜豆腐濃湯

港式手藝　料多味美

打一個蛋花
濃湯香噴噴

煮5分鐘
即可食用

4人份

Knorr

# _GLOBAL FOOD
# 1991

*Global Food* ist eine ethnografische Studie, die einerseits das Ausmass der kulturellen Anpassung eines global vertriebenen Produktes an die lokalen Gebräuche und Gewohnheiten erforscht und sich andererseits die Integrations-Strategien von globalen Konzernen etwas genauer anzuschauen will. Viele Markenprodukte würden sich gut für diese Untersuchung eignen. Ich habe mich schliesslich für Knorr-Suppen entschieden, weil Nahrungsmittel stärker als jedes andere Produkt in die Kultur des Bestimmungslandes eingreifen und Knorr eine relativ grosse Bandbreite kultureller Assimilationsformen entwickelt hat. Ausserdem sind Knorr-Produkte in bald jedem verstaubten kleinen Supermarkt der Welt erhältlich, vom Dorf in den venezolanischen Anden bis zum abgelegenen Hinterland in Thailand. Ihre Globalisierungsstrategie hat sich nicht nur auf die Metropolen beschränkt, sie hat sich auch flächendeckend durchgesetzt. Der Gegenstand dieser Recherche, d. h. die vollständige Sammlung der weltweit hergestellten Knorr-Suppenpackungen, ist in wochenlanger Arbeit zusammengetragen worden. Jede Woche kamen neue Pakete mit der Post. Erst der Vergleich aller regionaler Packungen zeigte, wie weit das Firmenbild dem einheimischen Geschmack (von Suppen *und* Verpackungsdesign) nachgeben muss. In gewissem Sinne reinszeniert *Global Food* den globalen Trend, sich über nationale Grenzen hinwegzusetzen und dennoch ein Minimum an kulturellem Unterschied zu wahren.

Auch im Globalisierungsprozess bleiben die Landessprachen bedeutende und verlässliche Träger ethnischer Eigenheiten. Für den Zweck der Installation musste unter den Knorrpackungen, die in 47 Ländern hergestellt werden, eine Auswahl getroffen werden. Ich wählte die folgenden Sprachen: arabisch, chinesisch, thai, malaysisch, spanisch (Venezuela), portugiesisch (Brasilien), englisch/afrikaans (Südafrika), griechisch, slowenisch und türkisch. Die Verwendung der einheimischen Sprache ist immer die erste ethnische Unterscheidung, die gemacht wird, sobald ein Markt wichtig genug ist, um "individualisiert" zu werden. Kenya wird sich mit englischen Packungen begnügen müssen, weil der Markt für eine Swahili-Version nicht als bedeutend genug befunden wird. Was den Packungsinhalt angeht, gibt es gewisse "universelle" Renner, die in jedem nationalen Programm erscheinen: Die Tomatensuppe und die Pilzsuppe werden in alle erdenklichen Sprachen übersetzt.

Eine fortgeschrittenere Stufe im Assimilationsprozess drückt sich zusätzlich in der Wahl der lokalen Spezialitäten aus: So gibt es in Malaysia Tiger-Lily–Pilz-Suppe oder in Ungarn Dumpling-Suppe. Generell werden solche Gerichte exklusiv für einen bestimmten Markt produziert; die "semoule tomatée" wird speziell für den arabischen Raum hergestellt und nicht in Hongkong oder Mexiko vermarktet. Es gibt aber auch sonderbare Ausnahmen: In Griechenland wird eine mexikanische schwarze Bohnensuppe angeboten, die in einer Terrakotta-Schale serviert wird und deren Verpackung mit Bildern von Maya-Pyramiden dekoriert ist. Die Ungarn haben eine ganz andere Vision von "Mexicana" entwickelt, und die Mexikaner haben nichts von alledem in ihrem Sortiment. In einigen Ländern sind ausländische Spezialitäten so sehr Teil der einheimischen Küche geworden, dass sie sich in das individualisierte nationale Programm eingefügt haben, und in anderen ist die exotische Qualität einfach ein gutes Verkaufsargument. Während die europäischen Suppentypen in klassischen weissen Suppentellern abgebildet sind, werden die asiatischen Rezepte eher in einer kleinen, gewöhnlichen Schale oder in chinesischen Reisschüsseln mit dazu passenden Porzellanlöffeln serviert. Die Art des Geschirrs, die Sprache, aber auch die Qualität der Typografie spielen eine wichtige Rolle bei der Umwerbung einer bestimmten Ethnizität.

Trotz all der individuellen Assimilationen an den Lokalgeschmack muss das Firmen-Image stets erkennbar bleiben. Knorr basiert grafisch auf einem oberen in gelb gehaltenen Drittel, zwei unteren Dritteln grün (manchmal auch umgekehrt) und einem roten Logo. Die Packungen werden extravaganter je weiter weg sich das Produzentenland vom Mutterhaus befindet. Während in Malaysia das Wort Knorr noch in römischen Buchstaben geschrieben ist, setzen die Chinesen nur noch zwei chinesische Zeichen in den fahnenförmigen Logoraum. Einzig in hebräisch, thai und chinesisch wird das Firmenlogo durch die entsprechende Schrift ersetzt.

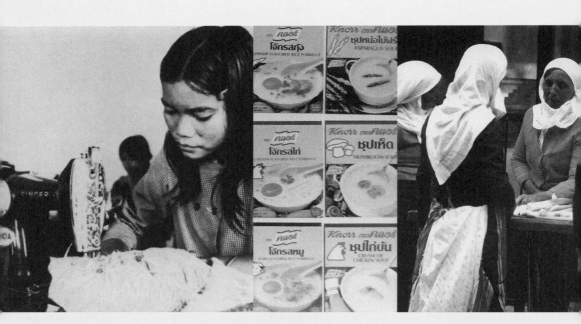

Knorrs Strategie ist es, das Gleichgewicht zwischen Firmen-Wiedererkennung und kultureller Integration zu erhalten. Die Toleranz ist offenbar von Land zu Land verschieden. Integration heisst hier eigentlich nichts anderes als im neuen Produkt die eigene kulturelle Identität zu erkennen und diese Wiedererkennung fortan mit dem Firmenlogo in Verbindung zu bringen. Kulturell gesprochen ist dieses Vorgehen dennoch komplexer, sensibler als der herkömmliche Kulturimperialismus, wie ihn z. B. Coca Cola betreibt, die jede Importkultur mit dem unverkennbaren Geschmack, dem Logo und der Botschaft "der freien Welt" dominiert. Die mitgetragene Botschaft ist bei Knorr eine andere. So wie die Sofort-Suppe für die Hausfrau der 50er-Jahre das Ende der Kochmühsal und den Anfang des modernen Komforts verhiessen, so versprechen heute dieselben Trockensuppen den Frauen in den Entwicklungsländern die Vorzüge des modernen Lebens. Diese Produkte formen die Konsumpraktiken auch in Orten mit, in denen die lokale Nahrungsproduktion und der Konsum noch organisch verbunden sind und somit keine harte Währung erfordern, die auf die eine oder andere Art erwirtschaftet werden muss. So werden ländliche und abgelegene Bevölkerungsteile in die Markwirtschaft eingebunden, ohne dass gleichzeitig lukrative Arbeitsstellen geschaffen würden, dank derer sie sich den modernen Lebensstil leisten könnten. Der Kauf von Knorr-Sofort-Suppen ist nie nur der Ausdruck von bestehenden Essgewohnheiten, er führt immer auch strukturelle Veränderungen in die lokale Konsumkultur ein.

# Zwischenräume
# Interstices

# _INTERSTICES - INTERESPACIOS 1992/1993

Images and texts by women in foreign place
A community project with Latinas in Zuric

Upon my return to Europe I looked for an institution that defined cultural work more broadly than a st dio-based art practice and engaged in activities linking social, cultural, and political concerns. Followir my previous project with Mexican women, I was interested in a collaboration with Latin Americans Zurich. Femia, a local center for culture and education for migrant women, became the partner wi whom this project was conceived and realized. Interstices was my first collaborative community pr ject, motivated by the fact that I didn't want to work on "Third-World" women but with them. It was co cerned with psychological and social aspects of identity as the result of cultural displacement. In E rope, like elsewhere, the situation of physical and cultural dislocation characterizes the daily lives many. Exile, and the split sense of self it entails, is how millions experience their sense of identit Where does one start addressing the marginalization of experience in a culture which denies the r presentation of anything that goes beyond identification with the national entity?

The title of the project suggests a plurality of spaces that can be inhabited and occupied, rather than gap to get stuck in. It implies a cultural interstice, i.e. the space that opens up between two cultures the occasion of cultural displacement or migration. The project started off as a visual communication seminar for Latin American women and it proposed to reflect on their position as women and migrant and to articulate it in the visual-verbal language of photography and text. I saw my role as a visual arti intervening in symbolic processes rather than a social worker setting out to help people find solution for their social problems. This art-driven idea turned into a turbulent one-year project that challenge many a personality, brought about identity crises, and triggered tough negotiations in a cultural stru gle that was larger than our project. What turned out to be larger than ourselves can be described general terms as the power relation between the two continents. Even though the project consiste mainly of what happened during those twelve months, a perhaps more tangible manifestation also r sulted from it in the form of a photo/text book.

Lyana Amaya, poet and language teacher from Colombia; Santusa Herbas, psychologist from Bolivi: Jacqueline Isler dos Santos, tourist guide from Brazil; Monica Senn Zegarra, Peruvian painter from A gentina; and Pierrette Malatesta, publicist from Peru participated in the seminar and Carmen Real, A gentine writer and performer, wrote an introduction for the book. The participants came up with a topi they were free to treat in a socially critical, poetic, or psychoanalytical manner. Culturally or socially sig nificant as the topics were, it soon became apparent that they also had deep personal roots. With some participants it was an obvious and conscious decision from the beginning that on a deeper level they were really reporting about themselves, while with others, it took several weeks or months to become immersed. The work could only begin once the personal connection had been made and accepted.

Three examples:

## Santusa Herbas

from Bolivia had been a psychologist with a rich professional and social curriculum before she left her country to look for new horizons. Now she works as a cleaning lady at a hospital in Zurich. Without hesitating, Santusa decided to write about the discrepancy between the education and skills she had acquired in her home country and the lack of professional opportunities available to her in Europe, an experience, as she describes, that brought about an identity crisis, feelings of inferiority, and depression. Through the effort of formulating her ideas, Santusa found tremendous strength in her roots and expressed this visually in her portrait for Mama Juana, a Bolivian friend and role model of hers. Furthermore, her involvement in this visual communications seminar gave her the self-confidence to approach and exchange ideas with a fellow psychologist at the University of Zurich.

## Angela Ceballos

a very young women from Colombia who literally threw herself into her research on Latin American women who are lured to Europe by agencies with promises of a glamorous life as models only to be channeled directly into the networks of topless bars. I greatly admired her fervor in writing about these women's predicament and accompanied her often to take undercover photographs of go-go girls and streetwalkers. One day I confronted her because I was curious to learn why this subject was so fascinating to her. A week later she suddenly remembered the traumatizing story of her cousin from Cartagena who had gone through this nightmare herself, risking her life to escape from a Dutch brothel, being rejected by her family, and never returning to her native country again. "Oh, I had completely forgotten about her," Angela told me. We decided to fit this personal story into her critical documentation and to mark the segments visually.

## Monica Zegarra

tried really hard, but five months into the project she still had not come up with a text, photograph, or even a single useful idea to pursue. She knew that if she didn't produce anything decent soon, she wouldn't be able to be in the book. I was anxious about deadlines and she was desperate. On the day before I was to present the project to the publishers, she came to the group radiating. She had written a number of stories she called *Just Another Flop*. They go like this: A Latina falls in love with a Swiss man, preferably blond, who is vacationing on tropical beaches. Invariably this man convinces her to come to the new world of opportunities with the promise to marry her. Once she is here, however, her dependency gets on his nerves, he loses interest and abandons her. Monica wrote subtle variations of this quotidian drama in a monotonous narrative style and complemented them with the isolating bareness of her photographs. Of all the pieces, I think of hers as one of the more successful ones. She must have carried the stories inside her the whole time and was only willing to release them under considerable pressure.

Taking the courageous step of moving to another continent often requires a radical break with the pa[st]. By the same token this also means disconnecting oneself from one's social and psychological roots. [In] a way these women were floating in a cultural limbo. By opening up a space of critical reflection b[e]tween their cultural heritage and the new and strange Swiss context, the project offered them their fi[rst] opportunity to reconnect the past with the present, and in doing so, to lay a sounder foundation for th[e] future trajectory. Very soon, our workshop came to represent this interespacio, and we set out to fil[l] with names and cultural signs, making it a space where their path and motivation, their history and ide[n]tity-building past were welcome. For several women in the group, engaging in this work initiated a d[is]turbing process of reorientation that they simply hadn't been exposed to as long as they had remain[ed] comfortably embedded in their self-confirming culture of origin. In this process, a highly idealiz[ed] image of motherhood had to give way to a more realistic assessment of their own reality. Besides in[di]vidual struggles over redefining one's identity, every individual project contributed to the articulation [of] a perfectly legitimate cultural position: that of vacillating between fixed identities associated with a si[n]gular national concept. In the realm of symbolic representation, our art production located itself in t[he] new spaces opening up in the cracks of nations. A third place challenges the monolithic concept of n[a]tions. The homogenous nation state has become a highly contested terrain, on the one hand for bei[ng] populated by an ever-increasing diversity of people, and on the other for being forced to yield power a[nd] influence to global formations. Where could a woman reorient herself in relation to these major cult[u]ral shifts? Merely celebrating deracialization and free-floating identities was clearly not the strategy [of] our project. Rather, the articulations attempted to recreate and legitimatize the cultural interstice in i[ts] own right.

A critique of representation cannot only state that Latinas are invariably represented by engrained st[e]reotypes. Indeed, the present images of Latin American women in Switzerland are either dominated [by] Christian funding agencies that are active in Latin America or by the tourist industry, which promot[es] sensual or adventurous vacations. Given this predicament it is crucial to intervene in the symbolic pr[o]duction from a perspective of a self-defined position. But it is equally important to understand ho[w] these misrepresentations work within the field of forces that constitute the domain of cultural struggl[e]. Starting from personal situations, the texts in Intersticies draw the connections to the wider contex[t] framing the experience of the subaltern. The texts tell stories of how illegality and isolation facilitate e[x]ploitation, how patriarchal attitudes and economic interests abuse romantic and professional expect[a]tions, and how legal regulations can be equated with pimping on a state level.

In the course of a few months, the deep involvement with issues of colonial oppression and relations [of] dependency both as colonized beings and as women triggered outrage and revolutionary feelings in th[e] group. The participants went through a thrilling process of liberating themselves ideologically and em[o]tionally and the closest subject at hand was the group's figure of authority. I was called to account f[or] my controlling the process of production and appropriating the project for my own art career. And the[n] work contained in this volume confirms that they were right. On the other hand, everyone in the grou[p] used this project for her own benefit, whether it was to forge new professional contacts, verbalize the[ir] messages, get social recognition, publish their poetry, or exhibit their photographs for the first time. A[f]ter this debate, the product and its distribution seemed to rest more firmly in their hands and my ro[le] became that of a participant.

If the prime purpose of this project had been to emancipate the participants, we can surely say the project was a success. But I have to recognize that, as a group, we fell short of transcending all the conflicts raised by power relations that we addressed in the book. However, the collaborative project d provide a space for negotiating a relationship with a long and painful history. It did so on a level of re lity that affects our lives, and it set into motion for all of us a more prosaic process of political and ps chological awareness that – as trying and challenging an experience as it at times may be – still in pro ress today.

Edited version of a paper presented at *Citizenship, Identity, Community: Feminists (re)Present the Political*, cc ference hosted by the Women's Caucus of York University's Graduate Program in Political Science, Mar 19/20, 1994, York University, Toronto.

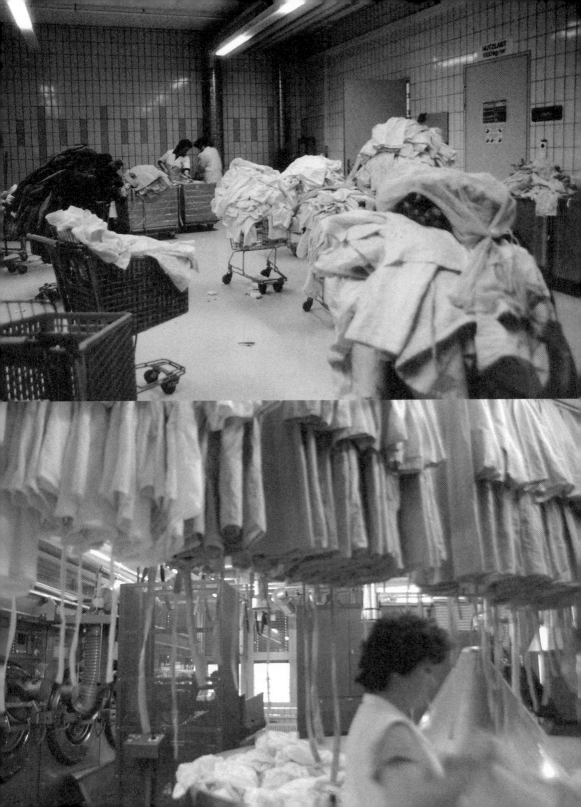

# _ZWISCHENRÄUME - INTERESPACIOS 1992/1993

Bilder und Texte von Frauen in der Fremd
Ein Community-Projekt mit Latinas in Züric

Nach Europa zurückgekehrt suchte ich eine Institution, die Kulturarbeit breiter formulierte als eine a
Atelier-Galerie begrenzte Kunstpraxis; eine Institution also, die durch ihre Aktivitäten soziale, kulture
und politische Anliegen verband. Im Anschluss an mein Projekt mit mexikanischen Frauen war ich a
einer Zusammenarbeit mit Lateinamerikanerinnen in Zürich interessiert. Femia ist das Zentrum für B
dung und Kultur für Migrantinnen, mit dem dieses Projekt schliesslich konzipiert und durchgeführt wu
de. Zwischenräume-Interespacios war mein erstes kollaboratives Community-Projekt. Es ging darin u
psychologische und soziale Aspekte von Identität als Resultat von kultureller Verschiebung. In Europ
wie auch sonstwo charakterisiert die Situation physischer und kultureller Verschiebung das Alltagsl
ben vieler Menschen. Exil und die Spaltung des Selbsts sind Identitätserfahrungen von Millionen v
Menschen. Wie können wir die Marginalisierung dieser Erfahrung in einer Kultur angehen, welche jed
Repräsentation, die sich nicht mit einer nationalen Einheit identifiziert, verneint?

Der Titel *Zwischenräume* bezieht sich auf die vielfältigen Räume zwischen zwei Kulturen, die durch ku
turelle Verschiebung oder Migration geöffnet werden und die bewohnt und besetzt werden können. Da
Projekt begann mit einem 3-monatigen visuellen Kommunikations-Workshop für Lateinamerikaneri
nen, die über die Position als Frau und Migrantin reflektieren und dies in einer visuell-verbalen Sprach
von Fotografie und Text artikulieren wollten. Ich verstand meine Rolle als Künstlerin, die in symbolisch
Prozesse eingreift und nicht als Sozialarbeiterin, die Lösungen für soziale Probleme sucht. Aus dies
"künstlerischen" Idee entstand ein turbulentes einjähriges Projekt, das manche Persönlichkeit auf d
Probe stellte, Identitätskrisen auslöste und Anlass zu harten Verhandlungen gab auf einem kulturelle
Kampffeld, das weit grösser war als unser Projekt. Daraus entstand die Publikation *Zwischenräum
Interespacios - Bilder und Texte von Frauen in der Fremde*, in der alle Beiträge zusammengefasst sin
An verschiedenen Foren konnten wir das Ergebnis unserer Arbeit öffentlich präsentierten.

Lyana Amaya, Poetin aus Kolumbien, Santusa Herbas, Psychologin aus Bolivien, Jaqueline Isler dos Sa
tos, Reiseleiterin aus Brasilien, Monica Senn Zegarra, Malerin aus Argentinien, und Pierrette Malatest
Publizistin aus Peru, nahmen am Seminar teil und Carmel Real, Schriftstellerin aus Argentinien, schrie
die Einleitung des Buches. Jede Teilnehmerin wählte ein Thema, das sie aus sozialkritischer, poetisch
oder psychoanalytischer Perspektive bearbeitete. So kulturell und sozial bedeutsam diese Themen wa
ren, es stellte sich früher oder später heraus, dass sie tiefe persönliche Wurzeln hatten. Bei den eine

war es von Anfang an offensichtlich und bewusst, bei anderen tauchte dieses Bewusstsein nach mehreren Wochen oder Monaten auf. Die Arbeit konnte erst dann richtig losgehen, als die persönliche Verbindung zum Thema bewusst hergestellt und akzeptiert wurde.

Drei Beispiele:

### Santusa Herbas

war Psychologin in Bolivien und hatte ein ausgefülltes professionelles und soziales Leben, als sie ihr Land verliess, um neue Horizonte zu suchen. Jetzt reinigt sie Spitalböden in Zürich. Ohne zu zögern entschloss sich Santusa, über die Diskrepanz zwischen ihrer Bildung und ihren Fähigkeiten, die sie sich in ihrem Herkunftsland angeeignet hatte, und den Mangel an beruflichen Gelegenheiten in Europa zu schreiben; eine Erfahrung, die eine Identitätskrise, Gefühle von Minderwertigkeit und Depression auslöste. Durch die Anstrengung, ihre Ideen in Worte zu fassen, und durch den Zugang zu ihren Wurzeln fand Santusa eine Kraft, die sie im Portrait von Mama Juana, bolivianischer Freundin und Rollenmodell zugleich, visualisierte. Ihre Teilnahme am Seminar gaben ihr auch das Selbstvertrauen, eine Kollegin aus der Psychologieabteilung der Universität Zürich zu kontaktieren und ihre Ideen auszutauschen.

### Angela Ceballos

eine sehr junge Frau aus Kolumbien, warf sich regelrecht in die Recherche über Lateinamerikanerinnen, die von Agenturen nach Europa gelockt werden, denen ein bezauberndes Leben als Fotomodell versprochen wird, nur um sie direkt in die europäischen Netzwerke von Gogo-Bars zu schleusen. Die Leidenschaft, mit der sich Angela in diese Recherche gab, war bewundernswert, und ich begleitete sie oft in die Gogo-Bars und auf den Strich, um undercover zu fotografieren. Eines Tages, sagte ich, würde ich bestimmt erfahren, warum dies so faszinierend für sie ist. Eine Woche später erinnerte sie sich plötzlich der traumatischen Geschichte ihrer Cousine aus Cartagena, die diesen Horror selbst erlebt hatte und ihr Leben riskierte, als sie nach einem Jahr Gefangenschaft aus einem holländischen Bordell ausbrach, von ihrer Familie verworfen wurde und nie in ihr Heimatland zurückkehren konnte. "Hatte ich ganz vergessen", meinte Angela zu diesem traumatisierenden Erlebnis. Sie nahm die persönliche Geschichte in ihre kritische Dokumentation auf.

### Monica Zegarra

strengte sich wirklich an. Aber fünf Monate nach Beginn des Projektes hatte sie weder einen Text noch ein Bild oder auch nur eine brauchbare Idee gefunden. Sie wusste, dass sie nicht im Buch mit dabei sein könnte wenn sie nicht bald etwas "Anständiges" produzieren würde. Mich machten die Deadlines nervös und sie war verzweifelt. Am Tag, bevor ich das Projekt dem Verlag vorstellen musste, kam sie in die Gruppe, strahlend. Sie hatte eine Reihe Geschichten geschrieben, die sie "Un fracaso mas", "ein Misserfolg mehr" nannte. Die gehen so: Eine Latina verliebt sich in einen Schweizer, vorzugsweise blond, der sich an tropischen Stränden erholt. Stets überzeugt er sie in die Neue Welt der unbegrenzten Möglichkeiten zu kommen und sie zu heiraten. Wenn sie einmal hier ist, geht ihm ihre Abhängigkeit auf die Nerven, verliert das Interesse an ihr und verlässt sie. Monica schrieb subtile Variationen dieses sich täglich ereignenden Dramas in einer monotonen Erzählung und verband sie mit der isolierten Kargheit ihrer Fotografie. Von allen Beiträgen schien mir dieser immer einer der erfolgreichsten. Monica Zegarra musste diese Geschichten all die Zeit mit sich herumgetragen habe[n] und war erst gewillt, sie unter beträchtlichem Druck freizugeben.

Der mutige Schritt in einen anderen Kontinent fordert oft den Bruch mit der Vergangenheit, was ebe[n]falls heisst, sich von den eigenen gesellschaftlichen und psychologischen Wurzeln zu trennen. Irgen[d]wie befanden sich diese Frauen in einem kulturellen Schwebezustand. Mit der Öffnung eines Raum[es] zwischen ihrer Herkunftskultur und dem neuen, fremden schweizer Kontext bot ihnen dieses Proje[kt] eine Gelegenheit, die Vergangenheit mit der Gegenwart zu verknüpfen und so eine solide Grundla[ge] für den weiteren Verlauf ihres Daseins zu legen. Sehr bald kam unser Workshop für diesen Zwische[n]raum zu stehen, den wir mit Namen und kulturellen Zeichen besetzten und so zu einem Ort werden lie[s]sen, in dem ihr Weg, ihre Motivationen, ihre Geschichte und eine identitätsbildende Vergangenheit wi[ll]kommen waren. Für mehrere Frauen in der Gruppe hiess die Teilnahme an diesem Projekt der Begi[nn] eines beunruhigenden Prozesses der Reorientierung, dem sie nicht ausgesetzt waren, so lange sie ko[m]fortable in ihrer selbstbestätigenden Herkunftskultur eingebettet waren. In diesem Prozess musste z.[B.] ein höchst idealisiertes Bild von Mutterschaft einer realistischeren Einschätzung der eigenen Wirklic[h]keit Platz machen.

Gleichzeitig trugen die individuellen künstlerischen Projekte zur Artikulation einer legitimen kulturelle[n] Position bei, die zwischen fixen, mit einem singulären nationalen Konzept verknüpften Identitäten a[n]gesiedelt ist. Die Realität eines homogenen Nationalstaates ist zu einem umstrittenen Terrain gewo[r]den. Als symbolische Repräsentation ist unsere Kunstproduktion in diesen neuen Räumen, den Risse[n] in dem Begriff Nation situiert, der immer mehr Terrain der Macht und des Einflusses an globale Form[a]tionen überlassen muss. Wie kann sich eine Frau in Beziehung zu diesen schwerwiegenden kulturelle[n] Verschiebungen orientieren? Einzig die Entwurzelung und die frei schwebenden Identitäten zu feiern, i[st] nicht die Strategie dieses Projektes. Die Artikulationen versuchten vielmehr den kulturellen Zwische[n]raum neu zu kreieren und als etwas eigenes zu legitimieren.

Repräsentationskritik kann nicht nur konstatieren, dass Latinas ständig durch eingefahrene Stere[o]typen repräsentiert werden. Tatsächlich sind die Bilder von Lateinamerikanerinnen in der Schweiz e[nt]weder von der Tourismusindustrie, die sinnliche oder abenteuerliche Reisen anpreist, oder von de[n] christlichen Hilfswerken dominiert, die in Lateinamerika aktiv sind. Die einen erzeugen ein Bedürfni[s,] die anderen versprechen Hilfe: zwei Ideologien, die sich immer schon gegenseitig bedingt haben. In di[e]ser misslichen Lage ist es ganz wichtig, aus der Perspektive einer selbstdefinierten Position in die sy[m]bolische Produktion einzugreifen. Doch ist es ebenso entscheidend zu verstehen, wie diese Missrepr[ä]sentationen im Kräftefeld funktionieren, das den Bereich des kulturellen Kampfes konstituiert. Von pe[r]sönlichen Situationen ausgehend ziehen die verschiedenen Beiträge in *Zwischenräume* die Verbindu[n]gen zum weiteren Kontext, der die subalterne Erfahrung kennzeichnet. Sie erzählen Geschichten vo[n] Illegalisierung und Isolation für eine erhöhte Ausnutzung, von patriarchaler Haltung im Missbrauch vo[n] romantischen und professionellen Erwartungen und von gesetzlichen Regulierungen, die der Zuhälter[ei] auf Staatsebene gleichkommen.

Im Laufe weniger Monate löste die intensive Beschäftigung mit Themen der kolonialen Unterdrücku[ng,] mit den Abhängigkeitsbeziehungen als Kolonisierte und als Frau, Empörung und "revolutionäre" Gefüh[le]

in der Gruppe aus. Die Teilnehmerinnen liessen sich auf einen spannenden Prozess der ideologischen und emotionellen Befreiung ein, wobei das nächstbeste Subjekt, von dem sie sich befreien konnten, die Autoritätsfigur der Gruppe war. Ich wurde zu Rechenschaft gezogen, den Produktionsprozess zu kontrollieren und das Projekt für künstlerische Zwecke anzueignen. Die Präsenz des Projektes in diesem Buch bezeugt, dass sie recht hatten: Ich habe das Projekt immer auch als ein Kunstprojekt gesehen, das ich initiiert hatte. Auf der anderen Seite hat jedes Gruppenmitglied dieses Projekt unterschiedlich funktionalisiert und zu ihrem Vorteil genutzt, sei es um berufliche Kontakte zu knüpfen, sei es um eine Botschaft zu verbalisieren, um gesellschaftlich anerkannt zu werden oder um Gedichte oder Fotografien erstmals zu publizieren. Nach dieser Debatte nahm die Gruppe das Produkt und dessen Vertrieb stärker in die eigenen Hände und meine Rolle wurde eher die einer Teilnehmerin.

Wenn das Hauptziel dieses Projektes die Emanzipation der Teilnehmerinnen gewesen wäre, könnten wir sicherlich sagen, dass es ein Erfolg war. Aber wir mussten auch erkennen, dass wir als Gruppe nicht alle Konflikte überwinden konnten, die wir im Buch ansprechen. Das kollaborative Projekt bot uns allerdings einen Handlungsraum, in dem wir die Beziehung, der eine lange und schmerzliche Geschichte vorausgeht, auf eine Art verhandeln konnten, die eine Wirkung auf unsere Leben hat und einen prosaischeren Prozess politischer und psychologischer Bewusstwerdung auslöste – so schwierig und herausfordernd das Experiment auch manchmal war –, der heute noch in Gang ist.

Redigierte Version des Vortrages gehalten anlässlich der Konferenz *Citizenship, Identity, Community: Feminis (re)Present the Political*, Women's Caucus of York University's Graduate Program in Political Science, York Universität, Toronto, im März 1994.

# Mediale Identitäten

This project has been conceived as part of *Art Strategies in the Nineties*, an exhibition that took place at the Glarus Art Museum in the summer of 1996. The project comprises the installation of a collection of media images of women from the South and a one-week workshop with migrant women held in a mountain house in Klöntal, a nearby alpine valley. The workshop focused on media representations of gender and ethnicity and brought forth two collaborative productions: a fotonovela and a video, which, upon completion, were included in the installation at the museum.

Dieses Projekt wurde für die Ausstellung *Strategien der Kunst in den 90er-Jahren* konzipiert, die im Sommer 1996 im Kunsthaus Glarus stattfand und sich auf das Klöntal, ein Bergtal in den Glarner Alpen, bezog. Das Projekt bestand zum einen aus einer Sammlung von Medienbildern über Frauen aus dem Süden, die im Kunsthaus installiert wurde, und zum anderen aus einem Workshop zur Darstellung von Gender und Ethnizität in den westlichen Medien. Im einwöchigen Seminar in einem Berghaus im Klöntal entstanden eine Fotonovela und ein Video zur Repräsentationspolitik in den Medien.

# _MEDIATED IDENTITIES
# 1995

It is to a large extent media images from television, magazines, or travel brochures, and not personal experience that define Western mainstream attitudes towards women from other cultural contexts. These representations fail to articulate the complexity of a person, communicate her ideas, her socialization, sexuality, or her relationship with the cultural context. Indeed, media images reflect an imaginary action that is being performed on the person being represented. The images reinforce the woman as a part of nature by decorating her with flowers, fruit, or butterflies as well as by juxtaposing her with cultivating, active, intervening, male characteristics; they chastize her by representing her as the pregnant, breastfeeding, overly fertile body responsible for global overpopulation; they divide, classify, and stratify women to maintain hierarchical orders; they order to control; they infantilize and incapacitate to create the need for care, food, shelter, and education; they modernize to tie her to mechanical, electronic, and digital work; they technologize to insure progress, globalization, and international competition; they sexualize to create notions of possession and power and, of course, to trigger desires for a number of other kinds of consumption; they eroticize and orientalize to give themselves narcissistic satisfaction.

In both the advertisement and the editorial section of a variety of media, representations of women from the South are used as a metaphor for a condition in which she supposedly finds herself, such as proximity to nature, poverty, fanaticism, or backwardness. The veiled woman may stand for the inaccessibility of the models of Islamic life that reject Western values, whereas depicted in Western fashion and hairstyle she advertises technological progress, democratic values, and safe investments. In such reductionist representations, the image of one person can come to stand for the alleged state or ambition of an entire nation. Because women are always already symbols, they are considered particularly effective substitutes. In this function, images cater to specific political and economic interests.

## Reformulations

The question was how to intervene in the power relations established and enacted through representations. As important as the deconstruction of paternalizing media images was for understanding the underlying messages and effects, it appeared most unattractive as a proper artistic strategy. There was a strong desire to create other images. As soon as a channel opens for minority representations in the press or the electronic media, the first impulse is always to contradict the criminalizing, stigmatizing images by posing positive ones. Producing positive images is an obvious motivation. But such counter-representations are relatively ineffective because they don't really counteract the other reductive media images, since these are already positive in the articulation of very specific, albeit diverging, interests. Critical media producers therefore feel it is extremely necessary to portray their own community in its entire complexity – including inner conflicts, even at the risk of once again being perceived as a trouble spot. The Indian media professional Gita Saghal, for example, makes television productions for Channel 4 in which she attacks fundamentalist actions within the Indian community in London. The same actions are criticized by British television, too, but with the effect that the entire Indian population in Britain is stigmatized. Gita Saghal's anti-fundamentalist critique conveys the multi-voiced nature of her community, which is both multi-ethnic and multi-religious. Simultaneously she makes reference to the fact that Britain is not a religiously neutral state, as it would have it, but a Christian state which marginalizes Muslim behavior as un-British. Her media work is both constructive – in that it provides an opening towards a new ethnic multiplicity – and deconstructive of British mainstream culture.

Yet an identity-building community is not always at hand nor is it even always desirable. Our seminar group was made up of women from a variety of backgrounds, political perspectives, and ages who joined out of interest in visual representation and who had, apart from their migration experience, no common denominator. The objective of our intervention, therefore, could not consist of differentiating between inner-communal debates, but it was clear that we would have to introduce divergent, multiply coded subjects in the image.

To avoid naive identity reconstructions we first had to discuss and define our interests in producing an image, particularly a self-representation. We used the notion of cultural identity formulated by Stuart Hall and Bell Hooks. Accordingly, it is no longer a matter of emphasizing or rediscovering an original essence which has been lost in the process of acculturation but increasingly one of positioning: a historical, geographic, cultural location has an empowering potential. It allows for a self-positioning – a willing production of identity – and opens new spaces for action, particularly in the field of representation. Here it becomes necessary to produce a more elaborate and divergent representation of women who have been consistently deprived of subjectivity.

The video *It's Only a Beginning* and the fotonovela *With Love from the Hike* are visual reformulations of identity as positioning which emerged from this seminar. It became evident in the work process, which ranged from the resistance to the production and publication of images to the recognition of the emancipating possibilities of representation as a distinct, effective field of politics, that identity is nothing essential but, on the contrary, that it is a field of contestation. Indeed, it is a new field of action in which migrant women, who in principle are denied a political voice, can become involved.

# _MEDIALE IDENTITÄTEN
# 1995

Es sind nach wie vor Medienbilder aus Fernsehen, Zeitschriften oder Reisebroschüren, und nicht persönliche Erfahrungen, welche die westliche Mainstream-Haltung gegenüber Frauen aus anderen kulturellen Zusammenhängen bestimmen. Dabei geht es nicht nur darum, dass die Repräsentationen die Komplexität von Personen durch ihre Denkweise, Sozialisierung, Sexualität und durch ihre Beziehung zum kulturellen Kontext unterschlagen würden. Die Abbildungen reflektieren vielmehr eine imaginäre Handlung, die an der Person vollzogen wird. Die Abbildungen naturalisieren die Frau, indem sie mit Früchten, Blumen und Schmetterlingen geschmückt wird, und neutralisieren sie in der Gegenüberstellung mit einer kultivierenden, aktiven, eingreifenden, männlichen Haltung; sie disziplinieren sie in den Darstellungen von schwangeren, stillenden, überfruchtbaren Körpern, welche als Ursache für die globale Übervölkerung stehen; sie teilen, klassifizieren und schichten sie, um eine hierarchische Ordnung beizubehalten; sie ordnen sie, um zu kontrollieren; sie infantilisieren und entmündigen sie zur Schaffung von Bedürfnissen nach Pflege, Nahrung, Schutz, Erziehung und Bildung; sie modernisieren sie für die Einbindung in mechanische, elektronische und digitale Arbeit; sie technologisieren sie als Zeichen für Fortschritt, Globalisierung und internationale Konkurrenz; sie exotisieren und orientalisieren sie zur narzistischen Befriedigung; sie sexualisieren sie als Besitzergreifung und Machtbeweis und natürlich als Auslöser von Begehren für jeden erdenklichen anderen Konsum.

Nicht nur in der Werbung, auch im redaktionellen Teil unterschiedlicher Medien werden Abbildungen von Frauen aus dem Süden als Metapher für einen Umstand verwendet, in dem sie sich angeblich befinden: Naturverbundenheit, Armut, Fanatismus oder Rückständigkeit. Während z. B. eine verschleierte Frau für die Unzugänglichkeit islamischer, sich dem Westen widersetzender Lebensentwürfe steht, wird eine in westliche Mode und Coiffure gestylte Frau gerne als Symbol für technologischen Fortschritt, demokratische Werte und zukunftssichere Investitionen ausgehängt. In solch reduzierten Darstellungen kann das Bild einer einzelnen Person für den vermeintlichen Zustand oder die Ambitionen einer ganzen Nation stehen. Weil die Frau immer schon ein Zeichen ist, gilt sie als effektvolles Substitut. In dieser Funktion dienen Bilder politischen und ökonomischen Interessen.

### Neuformulierungen

Die Frage war, wie wir in die Machtbeziehungen intervenieren können, die durch die Repräsentation etabliert und ausgespielt werden. Die paternalisierenden Medienbilder zu dekonstruieren war zwar für das Verständnis ihrer unterschwelligen Message und Wirkung wichti[g], schien aber allen als eigene künstlerische Strategie unattraktiv. Der Wunsch nach eigenen Bildern wa[r] gross. Sobald sich ein Kanal für Minoritätendarstellungen öffnet, sei es in der Presse oder in den ele[k]tronischen Medien, ist der erste Impuls immer der, endlich den kriminalisierenden, stigmatisierende[n] Bildern etwas Positives entgegenzustellen. Positive Bilder erzeugen zu wollen ist verständlich, solch[e] Gegendarstellungen sind aber schon deshalb relativ unwirksam, weil sie den anderen, reduktiven M[e]dienbildern nicht wirklich etwas entgegensetzen, denn jene sind bereits positiv d.h. affirmativ, wen[n] auch im Artikulieren anderer Interessen. Kritische MedienproduzentInnen sehen deshalb die Notwe[n]digkeit, die eigene minoritäre Gemeinschaft in ihrer Komplexität mitsamt ihren inneren Konflikten z[u] zeigen, auch wenn sie damit riskieren, einmal mehr als kultureller Unruheherd zu gelten. Die indisch[e] Medienfrau Gita Saghal z. B. produziert Fernsehsendungen für Chanel 4, in der sie fundamentalistisch[e] Aktionen innerhalb der indischen Gemeinschaft in London kritisiert. Dieselben Aktionen werden vo[m] Britischen Fernsehen ebenfalls kritisiert, das damit aber die ganze indische Bevölkerung in Englan[d] stigmatisiert. Gita Saghals anti-fundamentalistische Kritik vermittelt hingegen die Vielstimmigkeit ihre[r] Gemeinschaft, die ihrerseits multi-ethnisch und multi-religiös ist. Gleichzeitig statuiert sie die Tatsach[e,] dass England nicht, wie es gerne dargestellt wird, ein religiös neutraler, sondern ein christlicher Staa[t] ist, der muslimische Gepflogenheiten als unbritisch ausgrenzt. Gita Saghals Medienarbeit ist konstru[k]tiv in der Öffnung einer neuen ethnischen Multiplizität und gleichzeitig dekonstruktiv gegenüber d[er] Mainstream-Kultur.

Eine identitätsbildende Gemeinschaft ist aber nicht immer vorhanden oder auch nur erstrebenswe[rt.] Unsere Seminargruppe bestand aus Frauen ganz unterschiedlicher Herkunft, politischer Ausrichtun[g] und unterschiedlichen Alters, die aus einem Interesse an visueller Repräsentation zusammenkame[n] und ausser der Migrationserfahrung keine gemeinsamen kulturellen Nenner aufzuweisen hatten. Da[s] Ziel unserer Intervention konnte also nicht darin bestehen, innerkommunitäre Debatten auszudiffere[n]zieren, sondern vielmehr differenzielle, mehrfach codierte Subjekte im Bild zu konstituieren.

Um naive identitäre Rekonstruktionsversuche zu vermeiden, musste also erst unser Interesse hinter e[i]ner Bildproduktion, besonders einer Selbstdarstellung, diskutiert und definiert werden. Wir gingen vo[n] Identitäts-Begriffen aus, wie sie von Stuart Hall oder bell hooks formuliert werden, in denen es nicht da[r]um geht, etwas ursprünglich Wesenseigenes hervorzuheben oder wiederzuentdecken, was im Prozes[s] einer Akkulturierung verschüttgegangen wäre. Mit kultureller Identität ist vielmehr eine Positionierun[g] gemeint, eine geschichtliche, geografische, kulturelle Verortung. Dass mit dieser neuen Formulierun[g] von Identität auch eine Selbstpositionierung möglich wird, macht sie so geeignet. Sie öffnet neue Hand[-]lungsräume, insbesondere im Feld der Repräsentation, in dem es nach wie vor wichtig ist, differenzie[r]tere Darstellungen von Frauen zu schaffen, denen bisher jegliche Subjektivität abgesprochen wurde.

Das Video *Es fängt erst an* und die Fotonovela *Wandergrüsse* sind visuelle Neuformulierungen von Ide[n]tität, also Positionierungen, die aus diesem Seminar hervorgegangen sind. Dass Identität nicht[s] Wesenseigenes ist, sondern ein Feld der Auseinandersetzung, zeigte sich im Arbeitsprozess, der vo[m] Widerstand reichte, Bilder machen und öffentlich zeigen zu wollen bis zur emanzipierenden Möglichkei[t,] die Repräsentation als ein effektives Feld der Politik zu verstehen – ein Handlungsfeld, in dem auch M[i]grantinnen aktiv werden können, denen im nationalen Kontext die politische Mitsprache versagt ist.

chnologisieren > entkörpern
chnologize > disembody

teilen > schichten
devide > classify

modernisieren > industrialisieren
modernize > industrialise

erotisieren > aneignen > mystifizieren
erotisize > appropriate > mystify

# Salon

odernisieren > naturalisieren
odernize > naturalize

aturalisieren > mystifizieren
aturalize > mystify

werben > verkaufen
advertise > sell

sexualisieren > konsumieren
sexualize > consume

DIE POST bringt Ferienkataloge.

Tages Anzeiger
Abo-Telefon: 01-404 64 64

# Stellen Sie sich vor ...

Sie befinden sich auf einer Insel im Herzen der Karibik, rund neun Flugstunden von Europa entfernt. Sie sind an einem Strand, kilometerlang, weiss... und ruhig. Sie sind überrascht und begeistert. Die Sonne scheint ..., ein kühler Passatwind weht. Die Insel schickt Ihnen warme Grüsse. "Bonbini" (Willkommen). Die Freundlichkeit, der Strand ... die Ruhe, das herrliche Wetter:

# Das ist Aruba!

**Koyo** ...Da ich leider dieses System nicht verändern kann, habe ich mich entschieden, alle Ausweispapiere zu nehmen, die ich kriegen kann. Ich werde mich also immer darum bemühen, mir die Papiere zu besorgen, die ich gerade brauche, um mich in einem Gebiet aufzuhalten. Als freier Mensch sollte man auf der Erde zirkulieren können, ohne sich ständig rechtfertigen zu müssen, warum man sich gerade in dem Gebiet aufhalten möchte.

Ausweispapiere, die vom Staat herausgegeben werden, können die verschiedenen Identitäten, die ich mit mir herumtrage, gar nicht wiedergeben. Ich wurde von verschiedenen Leuten und Kulturen beeinflusst, von verschiedenen Lebensschemen und Lebensarten, die meine Person natürlich auch prägen und dadurch habe ich viele Identitäten entwickelt. Die wechsle ich bewusst aus oder setzte sie ganz bestimmt ein, je nach Situation. Ein Ausweis allein zeigt eigentlich nur, wie mich das System sieht aber nicht wie ich wirklich bin.

Ja, mit den Pässen. Jetzt bin ich schon bei drei und es fängt erst an.

**Cevahir**   Ich bin eine kurdische Frau ohne anerkanntes Heimatsland. Seit meiner Kindheit lebe ich immer im Exil...

Ich habe keine Identiätskarte, in der Schweiz können nur Schweizer Bürger und Bürgerinnen eine Identitätskarte haben. Nach Schweizer Politik heisst das, dass ich ohne Identität bin. Ich habe eine Karte und vorne steht Ausländerausweis und der Buchstabe B. Damit hat man mich markiert und eingestuft. Das Wort Ausländerausweis passt mir auch nicht. Als Geschlecht bin ich weiblich und man versucht, mich mit männlichen Formen zu bezeichnen. Man hat mich also als Ausländerin markiert, und mir mit B-Einstufung gesagt, welche Pflichten und Rechte ich in der Schweiz, ohne Identität, habe.

Ich bin als politische Frau in die Schweiz gekommen. Meine Erwartung war, dass man mich als politische Frau anerkennt und akzeptiert. Mit dem Ausweis B verstehe ich, dass sich meine Rechte und Pflichten auf ökonomische Interessen beziehen. Ich kann konsumieren, ich kann produzieren, dafür kann ich mich qualifizieren, aber das starke politische Interesse, das ich mitgebracht habe, hat man mir weggenommen.

**Iren**  Ich wurde im Iran geboren und lebe seit langem im Ausland, in verschiedenen Orten und Ländern. Gerade deshalb kann ich mich nicht mit einer Nationalität oder mit einer Kultur zufriedengeben, weil die nicht mehr meiner ganzen Identität entsprechen.

Seitdem ich ausserhalb von meinem Herkunftsland lebe, merke ich, wie wichtig diese Identitätskarte geworden ist. Es ist nicht so, dass ich diesen Ausweis als wichtig empfinde, sondern er ist mir wichtig gemacht worden. Jedesmal wenn ich ihn vorzeigen muss, werde ich wieder darauf aufmerksam gemacht, dass ich nicht zu dieser Gesellschaft gehöre Aus eigener Erfahrung kenne ich, dass ich eine Nationalität aufgeben muss, um die andere übernehmen zu können. Meine letzte Identität muss i aufgeben, damit ich die neue beantragen kann...

**Corinne**  Ich bin als Kind von Schweizern hier in der Schweiz aufgewachsen und lebe auch jetzt noch hier. Ich hatte eigentlich nie Probleme mit dem Schweizer Pass, weil die Behörden mich in Ruhe gelassen haben. Ich hatte auch keine grossen Probleme als ich ins Ausland reiste, weil die Schweiz zur Ersten Welt gehört.

Obwohl ich hier in der Schweiz lebe, möchte ich nicht immer hier bleiben und auch im Ausland arbeiten können, weil ich mich sonst in der Schweiz wie in einem Gefängnis fühlen würde. Und ich weiss genau, dass wenn ich mir diesen Wunsch erfüllen möchte, dass ich dann Probleme haben werde, weil es nicht so einfach ist, im Ausland länger zu leben und zu arbeiten, besonders weil die Schweiz nicht in der EU ist.

Ich möchte keine Einheimische sein.

**Aysel**  Ich bin Sozialpädagogin und arbeite im Sozialbereich. Dort nehme ich die Machtverhälnisse zwischen einheimischen Frauen und nicht-einheimischen Frauen sehr stark wahr. Wenn Du die Sprache nicht kannst, wenn Du in der Umgebung neu bist, heisst es gleich, dass Du nicht kompetent bist. Dann sieht man nur noch, dass Du Migrantin bist.

Ich möchte erst mal bei mir anfangen, mich analysieren, meine Bilder überprüfen. Überprüfen, ob die Bilder, die ich von meiner Familie, der Schule, Religion und der Gesellschaft erhalten habe, ob die für mich stimmen. Das ist ein ständiger Prozess, den ich mitbestimmen will.

Ich weiss, dass ich die Gesellschaft nicht verändern kann wie ich will, es liegt nicht in meiner Macht. Aber ich weiss, dass es Sachen gibt, au die ich Einfluss nehmen kann. Was ich rede, was ich diskutiere, das beeinflusst auch andere. Ich gebe auch Bilder weiter, wie ich es jetzt gerade mache.

Ich möchte meine Identität selber definieren.

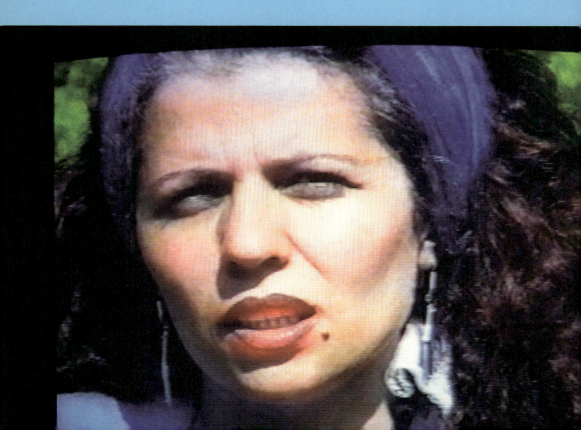

**Workshop vom 15. bis 20 Juli 1996 im Klöntal**
**Teilnehmerinnen:**

**Video**
Iren Delpasand, Iranerin
Cevahir Örnek, Kurdin
Corinne Haffner, Schweizerin
Koyo Koutt, Kamerun
Aysel Duman, Türkin

**Fotonovella**
Maritza Le Breton, Chilenin
Ursula Marx, Schweizerin
Delia Krieg, Bolivianerin
mit
Erna Platzmann, Roma
Nihal Karaboya, Türkin
Sudabeh Kasraian, Iranerin

# _VIDEOS BY
# SIMIN FARKHONDEH AND SIKAY TANG

In the video works by the Chinese-New York artist Sikay Tang *In Search of an Aliso* and *I Dream of Jeanie Complex* by the German-Iranian video artist Simin Farkhonde identity is presented as a complex, socially constructed fabric within which the vide makers have positioned themselves.

In a meticulous, well-rehearsed process of putting on makeup in front of the mirro Sikay Tang transforms her features into more Western-looking ones, a process sh learned as a child by watching her mother, who had undergone eye and nose sur gery in order to appear more European. Her mother's values as well as events expe rienced as a child, like the time one of her teachers demanded that she take on a English name, are influences that forged her present identity. In much the same way circumstances at a New York film school would later give Sikay the means to decon struct these influences.

*I dream of Jeanie Complex* brings to light the interests and mechanisms of dissemi nating specific images. The short and fast paced video montage features sequence of the beloved TV series of the genie in a bottle whose master is a NASA officer an who strangely resembles the imaginary fifties American housewife. The series wa first aired through the worldwide military network of the American army and provide a good example of how exoticized gendered representations of the Western image of the "orient" started getting disseminated in ideological and commercial medi productions on a global scale in the sixties. The artist grew up both in Germany an Iran. She noticed, therefore, that reception of the series differed greatly from on country to the other. In Iran, the audience was amazed by this Western a-thousand and-one-nights female embodiment of the "orient" who succeeded in subverting he rather awkward NASA space conqueror.

# _VIDEOS VON
# SIMIN FARKHONDEH UND SIKAY TANG

In den im Workshop diskutierten künstlerischen Videoarbeiten der New Yorker Chinesin Sikay Tang *In Search of an Alison* und *I Dream of Jeannie Komplex* der deutsch-iranischen Medienkünstlerin Simin Farkhondeh wird Identität als ein komplexes, gesellschaftlich konstruiertes Gefüge vorgestellt, in dem sich die Filmemacherinnen situieren.

In einem peinlich genauen, gut einstudierten Schminkvorgang verwandelt sich Sikay vor dem Spiegel in eine westliche Erscheinung. Dass ihre Mutter durch Augen- und Nasenoperationen europäischer erscheinen wollte oder ihre Lehrerin einen englisch aussprechbaren Namen von ihr verlangte, waren Erlebnisse, die ihre heutige Identität ebenso prägten wie der Umstand, dass sie sich später in der New Yorker Filmschule Mittel aneignete, um diese zu dekonstruieren.

In ihrem Video bringt Simin Farkhondeh die Interessen an der Verbreitung von ganz bestimmten Bildern ans Licht. Dieser kurze, rasante Videozusammenschnitt zeigt Sequenzen aus der Fernsehserie von Jeannie, einem weiblichen Flaschengeist, der mit einem NASA-Offizier verheiratet ist und etwa der Vorstellung der US-amerikanischen Hausfrau der fünfziger Jahre entspricht. Die Serie wurde erstmals vom militärischen Mediennetzwerk der US-amerikanischen Armee ausgestrahlt und ist ein gutes Beispiel dafür, wie exotisierte Gendervorstellungen des westlichen Fantasmas "Orient" in ideologischen und kommerziellen Medienproduktionen weltweit vertrieben werden. Simin wuchs teils in Deutschland, teils im Iran auf und rezipierte dieses Programm jeweils ganz unterschiedlich. Im Iran staunte man nicht schlecht über die westliche Tausendundeine-Nacht-Vorstellung des "Orients" in Gestalt einer Frau, die ihren etwas ungeschickten NASA Weltraum-Eroberer mit subversiven Tricks zu unterwandern versteht.

# _IN SEARCH OF AN ALISON
## SIKAY TANG

When I was younger I used to sit next to my mom and watch her put on her makeup. If we had to go at twelve, she would start her makeup at eleven. It was a very regimented step-by-step process.

My mother had a nose job, she had an operation on her eyes too. She never liked to talk about it too much. I think it was supposed to be a secret. One time I was told that my mother had a nose job, she got real mad. We asked her if that was true and she said that we kids should not be so nosy.

Everyone used to give my mom compliments about her looks. All my friends thought she was very pretty. But they always asked if she was entirely Chinese, they thought she was of mixed parentage. I guess that meant you were pretty in Hong Kong.

And as far as Miss Hong Kong was concerned, they would always have the least Chinese looking girls as winners. And Mommy used to say, "Well if you don't have the features, then you have to be nice so that you can at least be crowned Miss Friendship."

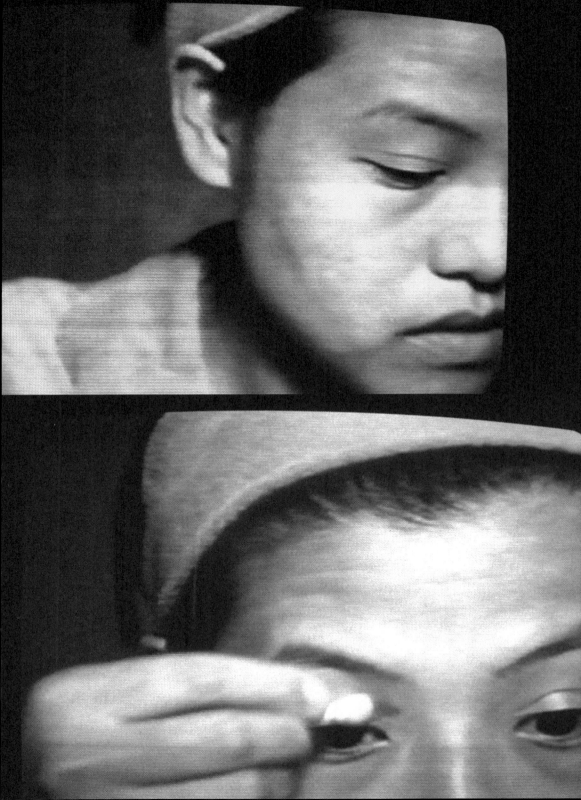

When I entered the first grade, my teacher asked me if I had an English name and I said, "Yes, Sikay Tang." She laughed and said, "No, an English name that's not translated." I felt bad and went home and told my Mom I needed an English name. Then she bought a book with all the English names of boys and girls and decided we should all have a name starting with the letter A.

She determined that I should be an Alison. I couldn't pronounce it very well at first, it took me a while to say it and to spell it. But then I went to my school and told all my teachers and friends that my name was Alison. Though you know at home I would always remain a Sikay to my parents, I felt more confident to step into the outside world with a European name so people wouldn't think of my name as being awkward.

For my sixth birthday, my mother wanted to give me a present. She wanted me to have a doll so we went to a store. I wanted a doll that talked but my mother said dolls that talk were not gentle enough and she gave me this pink baby doll and named it baby Mimi for me, but I think it was really more for her than it was for me. So I learned to love baby Mimi and she was very cute, but I was always sad that baby Mimi could not talk. And also I was never as cute as baby Mimi because she had this beautiful silky blond hair.

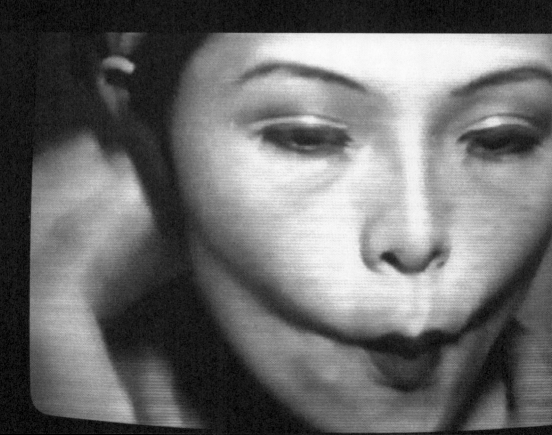

# _I DREAM OF JEANIE KOMPLEX
# SIMIN FARKHONDEH

In den sechziger Jahren kam das Fernsehen in den Iran. Die meisten Programme waren damals nordamerikanisch und zeigten eine westliche Lebensweise, die den meisten IranerInnen unbekannt war. Sie machten vor, wie man sich verhalten, wie man sich anziehen sollte.

Diese komischen Sendungen wie *Flipper*, *I love Lucy*, *I dream of Jeanie*, *The wild wild West*, *Bewitched*, *Payton Place*, *My Favorit Marcian*, wurden durch die U.S. Militär-Netzwerke zu uns ins Haus gebracht. Eine ganze Generation wuchs mit diesen Sendungen auf und wurde zum Konsum erzogen.

Als Kind sah ich mir diese Filme an. *I dream of Jeanie* machte einen besonderen Eindruck auf mich. Sie war die einzige nahöstliche Figur, die es in den Fernsehserien gab. Doch sie war blond, blauäugig und konnte zaubern. Sie hatte das Potential, mächtig zu sein, doch sie war an den Willen ihres Herrn, einem U.S. Militärpiloten und NASA Offizier gebunden. Sie ist und bleibt Sklavin ihres Herrn. Er machte sie zu dem, was sie ist. Er ist es, der sie im Weltall in ihrer Jeanie-Flasche gefunden hat.

Der U.S. Offizier zeigt der unwissenden Jeanie ständig, wie sie als authentische Jeanie zu handeln hat und lehrt ihr damit gleichzeitig, eine gute Hausfrau zu sein.

Es ist eine seltsame Mischung von Patriarchat und Orientalismus am Werk in dieser Sendung. Doch wie stellt Jeanie das "Andere" dar? Wie versteht man durch sie den Nahen Osten? Diese und andere Sendungen wurden auf Farsi synchronisiert. Natürlich kennt man diese Art Sendungen überall auf der Welt, wo es Fernsehen gibt. Welche Einflüsse haben diese Sendungen auf europäische Zuschauer? Im Iran förderten sie eine Art kapitalistische Konsumkultur und eine "Westoxikation".

Die Frage ist, wann kann sich Jeanie, der weibliche Flaschengeist, endgültig von der Flasche befreien?

# Afghan Collection

# _AFGHAN COLLECTION
# 1991

It's war in Afghanistan between the Mujahedin and the State forces that are backed by the Sovjet Union. For a passage across the border, the nomads in the highlands trade in their century-old family treasures: their clothes, chests, jewelry and carpets. Behind the border, the dealers with connections to the West are already waiting. In deserted villages they remove the doors, the carved columns and entire porches. One container after another is filled with Afghani artifacts and shiped to the U.S. They enter the fairs and galleries and finally reach private homes in California and Texas.

Es ist Krieg in Afghanistan zwischen den Mujahedin und den von der Sowjetunion gestüzten Regierungskräften. Für eine Flucht über die Grenze geben die NomadInnen im Hochland ihren jahrhundertealten Familienschatz her: ihre Kleider, ihre Truhen, ihren Schmuck und ihre Teppiche. Hinter der Grenze warten schon die Händler, die Verbindungen zum Westen haben. In den verlassenen Dörfern werden Holztüren, geschnitzte Pfeiler und ganze Balkone abgebaut. Ein Container nach dem anderen wird mit dem afghanischen Kulturgut gefüllt und in die USA geschifft. Dort kommt es auf Messen und in Galerien und endet schliesslich in kalifornischen und texanischen Privathäusern.

Chals

Chand-dar

Chhat

Chhali

Chhang

Cchos-khor

Charkha

Chasnak

Chashm

Chancha

Tribal

# Art

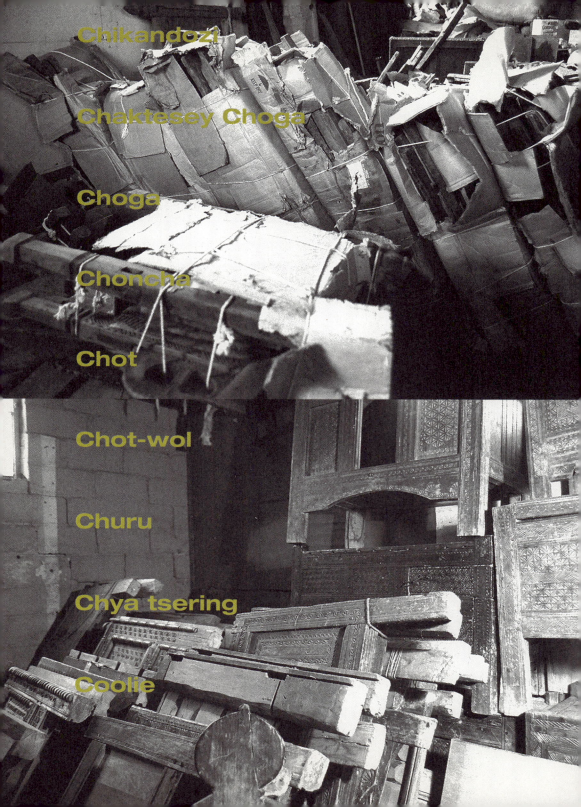

Chikandozi

Chaktesey Choga

Choga

Choncha

Chot

Chot-wol

Churu

Chya tsering

Coolie

# Platzwechsel

# _PLATZWECHSEL
# 1995

Platzwechsel/Changing Places is the title of an exhibition designed for the Kunsthall[e] Zurich as a site-specific joint project with Tom Burr, Mark Dion and Christian Philip[p] Müller. Platzspitz is the name of a small peninsula formed by the confluence of th[e] Limmat and Sihl rivers at the center of Zurich. The park has made international head[-] lines for more reasons than for just being the largest open drug scene in Europe. Th[e] four of us have chosen analogous methods, each from a different point of view, t[o] convert the park and the adjoining National Museum into a model of public space[.] The investigations focused on strategies of possession, exclusion, changing places[.] An extension of the exhibition is found at the Swiss National Museum, where the firs[t] National Expo took place.

Platzwechsel ist der Titel der Ausstellung, die als ortsspezifisches Gemeinschafts[-] projekt mit Christian Philip Müller, Tom Burr und Mark Dion für die Kunsthalle Züric[h] erarbeitet wurde. Platzspitz heisst der Park am Zusammenfluss von Limmat und Sih[l] im Zentrum Zürichs, der als ehemals grösster offener Drogenumschlagplatz Europa[s] weltweit in die Schlagzeilen geriet. Zu viert untersuchten wir methodisch analog[,] aber je unter anderen Gesichtspunkten das Platzspitz-Arial samt Landesmuseum al[s] Modell eines öffentlichen Raumes. Im Fokus der Untersuchungen standen insbeson[-] dere die Strategien der Inbesitznahme, des Ausgrenzens, des Platzwechsels. Ein Ne[-] benschauplatz der Ausstellung bildet auch das Landesmuseum auf dem Platzspit[z] wo die erste Landesausstellung stattfand.

# _ETHNO-X-CENTRIC REFLECTIONS ON THE NATIONAL EXPO AND THE NATIONAL MUSEUM

Inspired by the spectacular World Fairs in London, Philadelphia, and Paris in the mid-19th century, Switzerland was determined to organize its own major exhibition. In May 1883 the first Swiss National Expo was held at Platzspitz where the National Museum was to be opened a few years later. Industrialization was in full swing, bringing countless new products and technologies onto the market. This National Expo was intended as the first sweeping survey of the country's latest achievements in the field of industry, commerce, arts and crafts, and as a means of elucidating the increasingly complex social fabric. The products and machinery representing the ceaseless march of progress provided a suitable vehicle by which the organizers of the 1883 exhibition could project the desired image, for, after all, national and international exhibitions not only served to promote the interests of trade and technology, but were also self-aggrandizing showcases for the new nation states with their claims to international power. The position of other peoples in this Eurocentric weltbild can be seen clearly in the example of the Samoyed exhibition held to coincide with the National Expo in Zurich's Plattengarten.[1]

Presenting people of other ethnic origins was an attraction that formed part and parcel of the world fair and colonial exhibitions of the 19th century. These ethnic shows could also be seen in the pleasure parks and zoological gardens of Switzerland from 1879 onwards. The proprietor of the restaurant Zur Platte offered a wide range of entertainment in his garden pavilion, in the menagerie and in the Platter theater, and had already caused a sensation in previous years with troupes of Nubians and Patagonians, particularly as most of the Patagonians died during the exhibition. For the opening of the National Expo he now presented a Samoyedic caravan, a group of Lapps and four reindeer. On a meadow near the Platte, they demonstrated the daily life of nomads, breaking camp and moving with their tents from one end of the meadow to the other.[2] The Samoyeds then went on to the Basel Zoo, where they were presented to visitors along with "Bonny the Austral-Negro."[3] Although these ethnic shows were organized predominantly by German livestock traders, most of whose supplies came from German colonies, Switzerland, with no colonies of its own, nevertheless shared in this spectacle of imported cultures.

The second National Expo, held in Geneva in 1896, forged an unequivocal link between nascent national consciousness and the otherness of the "exotic." In addition to an industrial and technological show, the Genevese organizers constructed a "Swiss Village" and a "Negro Village" with 227 Sudanese from 15 different tribes. The "Swiss Village" reassuringly affirmed the image of rural idyll and primitive purty that had formed in the mind's eye of an industrialized urban society. It was a patriotic ode treated with reverence by the visitors. The "Negro Village," on the other hand, set in an amusement park, was a source of curiosity and laughter.[4] The difference between the two forms of presentation reveals the blatant segregation of these Africans who had been wrenched from their familiar surroundings and were being displayed in an alien cultural context to show how funny and backward they were. These live shows underlined the assumption that Europeans, in contrast to these "primitives," were at the very apex of mankind's cultural and technological evolution. Organized encounters with non-European cultures in ethnic shows made the intended relationship clear right from the start. Balthasar Staehlin, writing on the relationship between the spectacle and the spectators, has noted that by presenting these people in the setting of a zoo, the organizers were relying on the public being attuned to a certain "way of seeing" based on the observation of animals and the registration of physical features.[5] The gulf created in this way between those "looking" and those "being looked at" was so great in the minds of the spectators that any form of personal contact was inconceivable.

Scholars are known to have used the participants in these ethnic shows during their brief sojourn as research objects for anatomical "race studies." Professor Kollmann,[6] for example, sought to deduce intellectual capacities on the basis of anatomical features and cultural behavior. Kollmann claimed that the Samoyeds and the Australian, Bonny, were savages whose level of intellectual development was equivalent to that of Europeans thousands of years earlier.[7] Such reports clearly indicate the dubious ideological background of these exhibitions. They reveal the kind of "scholarship" applied to lend plausibility to the concept of European superiority and leave no doubt as to who bore the brunt of building up a sense of national self-esteem in this way. It is no coincidence that the desire to consolidate national consciousness should have gone hand in hand with the scientific categorization and evaluation of foreign peoples, for growing mobility in Europe and overseas resulted in cultural contacts regarded as "amusing" and at the same time as threatening. This, on the other hand, strengthened the need to retain the "specific characteristics" and strengthen national consciousness through mutual observation and confirmation of the same. It was on this basis that ethnic studies became an acknowledged new discipline at the University of Basel in 1989, the very year in which the Swiss National Museum was opened at Platzspitz in Zurich.[8]

Even if the projection of national identity at the cost of others was not always quite as heavy-handed as it was in these ethnic shows, the concept of "being Swiss" continued to be pitted against all that was "foreign." This called for an institutional distinction between the Historical Museum and the Ethnographic Museum, for, as one may imagine, the two did not operate according to the same principles, even though both addressed questions of culture and civilization. Whether an object is shown in one or the other of these institutions has a considerable impact on the way it is interpreted. Today, non-European cultural theorists are critical of the fact that art and artifacts from non-Western cultures are displayed in museums of ethnology where they continue to be placed in a natural science context. Such criticism is well founded, considering that "Indian Art, Oceanic Art and Tropical Aquarium"[9] are still mentioned in a single breath and shown in an anthropo-zoological context. The ground prepared in the late 19th century continues to form the basis on which we evaluate and interpret the artifacts of non-European culture.

My work is situated at the crossroads of conventional museum practice, which allocates objects to ar[t] history, or ethnology. It presents the three systems of reference as not only linked but even mutuall[y] dependent, and places them within an obvious context. Which system of reference applies to compo[-] nents of Anatolian costume if they are exhibited in an art gallery? And which applies to traditional S[t.] Gall hats if they are photographed by a woman from St. Gall who is of Turkish-Kazakh origin?[10] Wha[t] relevance can the construct of nationality and national history have today if it fails to take into accoun[t] the increasing dissolution of ethnically defined identity? The days when a "people" formed a homo[-] genous society within national borders is, at best, a thing of the past. Must a National Museum restric[t] itself to ever-narrower stereotypes far removed from reality, which exclude far more than they actuall[y] pretend? Or are there ways of dismantling these defunct categories?

Translation: Ishbel Flett
This essay first appeared in the catalog *Platzwechsel/Trading Places*, Kunsthalle Zurich, 1995

Footnotes at the end of German text.

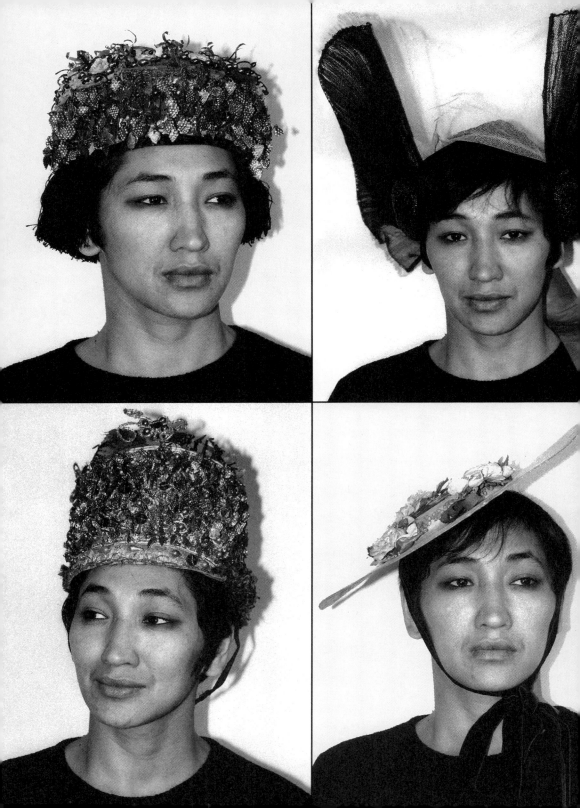

# _ETHNO-X-ZENTRISCHE ÜBERLEGUNGEN ZU LANDESAUSSTELLUNG UND LANDESMUSEUM

Inspiriert von den spektakulären Weltausstellungen in London, Philadelphia und Paris Mitte des letzten Jahrhunderts, entschloss man sich auch in der Schweiz zu einer grossangelegten Ausstellung. Im Mai 1883 wurde auf dem Platzspitz-Areal, wo wenige Jahre später das Landesmuseum zu stehen kommen sollte, die erste Schweizer Landesausstellung feierlich eröffnet.

Die eben angelaufene Industrialisierung hatte unzählige neue Produkte und Technologien auf den Markt gebracht. Diese Landesschau sollte nun erstmals umfassend die neuesten nationalen Errungenschaften aus Industrie, Gewerbe und Kunst zeigen und ihren Anteil zur Vermittlung einer zunehmend komplexen Gesellschaft leisten. Die Veranstalter der Ausstellung 1883 fanden in Produkten und Maschinen, die einen unaufhaltsamen Fortschritt suggerierten, eine für die moderne Industriegesellschaft passende Form der Selbstdarstellung. Denn Landes- und Weltausstellungen dienten schliesslich nicht nur der Förderung von Handel und Technologie, sondern sie waren gleichzeitig gigantische Selbstdarstellungen der neugebildeten Nationalstaaten und ihres Weltanspruchs. Welche Stellung andere Völker in diesem eurozentrischen Weltbild einzunehmen hatten, zeigte sich am Beispiel der Ausstellung von Samojeden im Zürcher Plattengarten, die parallel zur Landesausstellung lief.[1]

Die Zurschaustellung von Menschen anderer Ethnien war eine Attraktion, die von Welt- und Kolonialausstellungen im letzten Jahrhundert kaum wegzudenken war. In Vergnügungsparks und Zoologischen Gärten, waren diese Völkerschauen von 1879 an auch in der Schweiz zu sehen. Der Inhaber des Restaurants Zur Platte, der in seinem Gartenpavillon, in der Menagerie und im Plattentheater ein dichtes Unterhaltungsprogramm anbot, hatte mit den Truppen von Nubiern und Feuerländern bereits in den Vorjahren Aufsehen erregt, als die meisten Feuerländer während der Ausstellung starben. Zur Eröffnung der Landesausstellung wartete er nun mit der "Samojeden-Caravane" auf, einer Gruppe Menschen vom nördlichen Eismeer und vier Rentieren. Sie liessen sich auf der Wiese neben der Platte nieder und führten dem Publikum ihren Nomadenalltag vor, indem sie täglich ihre Zelte abbrachen und am anderen Ende der Wiese wieder aufschlugen.[2] Anschliessend reisten die Samojeden in den Basler Zoo weiter, wo sie zusammen mit "Bonny, dem Austral-Neger" den Zoobesuchern vorgestellt wurden.[3] Obschon die wichtigsten Organisatoren der Völkerschauen ursprünglich deutsche Tierhändler waren, die hauptsächlich aus deutschen Kolonialgebieten beliefert wurden, nahm die Schweiz – selbst ohne Kolonialbesitz an diesem spektakulär aufbereiteten Kulturimport teil.

Die zweite Landesausstellung in Genf 1896 brachte dann das aufkommende nationale Bewusstsein und die Abgrenzung vom "Exotischen" in einen direkten Zusammenhang. Abgesehen von der industriellen Expo konstruierten die Genfer Organisatoren ein "Village Suisse" und ein "Village nègre" (Negerdorf) mit 227 Sudanesen aus 15 verschiedenen Stämmen. Mit dem Schweizer Dorf rekreierten sie das versichernde Bild bäuerlicher Idylle und primitiver Reinheit, das direkt der Vorstellungskraft einer urbanen, industrialisierten Gesellschaft entsprang. Es war eine Hymne ans Vaterland, dem die Besucher mit Andacht begegneten. Das "Negerdorf" war bezeichnenderweise im Vergnügungspark angelegt und löste bei den Besuchern Neugierde und Gelächter aus.[4] Die Kontrastierung der beiden Darstellungen diente einer krassen Abgrenzung, wobei sie die dislozierten, aus ihrem Kontext gerissenen und zur Schau gestellten Afrikaner als besonders kurios und rückständig erscheinen liess. Solche Live-Inszenierungen unterstützten die Annahme, dass Europäer, im Gegensatz zu den "Primitiven", an der Spitze kultureller und technologischer Evolution der Menschheit stünden. Die organisierte Begegnung mit aussereuropäischen Kulturen in Völkerschauen machte das Verhältnis, in dem sich der persönliche Austausch abspielen würde, von anfang an deutlich. Zur Beziehung zwischen Ausgestellten und BesucherInnen bemerkt Balthasar Staehlin, dass das Publikum durch den Kontext Zoo auf ein bestimmtes "Sehen" eingestellt war, das sich an die Tierbeobachtungen anlehnt und vorab physische Besonderheiten registriert.[5] Die Distanz zu den Ausgestellten war im Denken der Zuschauer so gross, dass eine persönliche Annäherung ausser Betracht fiel.

Es ist bekannt, dass Wissenschaftler die TeilnehmerInnen von Völkerschauen während ihren kurzen Aufenthalten auch als Forschungsobjekt für rassenanatomische Untersuchungen benutzten. So Professor Kollmann[6], der von seinen anatomischen Vergleichen auch sofort auf geistige Fähigkeiten schloss, welche er dem kulturellen Verhalten dieser Menschen entnahm. Zu den Samojeden und zum Australier Bonny meinte Kollmann, dass diese wilden zeitgenössischen Völker in Bezug auf die geistigen Fähigkeiten alle nur auf derselben Stufe stünden, auf der wir vor Jahrtausenden uns befunden hätten.[7] Solche Berichte machen deutlich, vor welch fragwürdigem ideologischen Hintergrund diese Ausstellungen stattfanden, mit welchen naturwissenschaftlichen Mitteln die Vorstellung der eigenen Superiorität glaubwürdig gemacht wurde, und auf wessen Kosten die nationale Aufwertung stattfand. Es ist kein Zufall, dass der Wunsch nach einer Festigung des nationalen Bewusstseins mit dem wissenschaftlichen Bearbeiten (Einstufen und (Ab)werten) von fremden Völkern einherging, denn die wachsende Mobilität in Europa und Übersee bewirkte Kulturkontakte, die man zunächst als amüsant, dann wieder als bedrohlich empfand. Dies wiederum schürte das Bedürfnis, das "Eigentümliche" zu wahren und das nationale Bewusstsein durch ein gemeinsames Betrachten und Bestätigen desselben zu stärken. Unter diesem Vorzeichen wurde 1898 die Volkskunde an der Universität als neue Wissenschaft anerkannt und im gleichen Jahr das Schweizer Landesmuseum auf dem Platzspitz in Zürich eröffnet.[8]

Obschon die Selbstdarstellung nationaler Identitäten auf Kosten Anderer später kaum mehr so schwerfällig wie in den Völkerschauen betrieben wurde, es blieb doch die Tatsache bestehen, dass sich der Begriff des "Schweizerischen" nur in der Abgrenzung zum "Fremdländischen" definieren kann. Dies erfordert von Anfang an eine institutionelle Trennung in Geschichtsmuseum und Völkerkundemuseum, die, wie man vermuten kann, nicht nach denselben Kriterien operieren, obwohl es sich in beiden Disziplinen um die Aufzeichnung und Darstellung von Kultur handelt. Ob nun ein Gegenstand in der einen oder anderen Institution zu betrachten ist, hat auf dessen Interpretation einen wesentlichen Einfluss. Heute äussern sich KulturtheoretikerInnen aussereuropäischer Herkunft kritisch gegenüber der Tatsache, dass Kunstgegenstände aus nichtwestlichen Kulturen in Völkerkundemuseen abgeschoben werden, wie

sie weiterhin in den naturgeschichtlichen Kontext gestellt sind. Zurecht, denn nocht heute wird "Art 
dien, Art Oceanique und Aquarium Tropical"⁹ im gleichen Atemzug genannt und in einem anthropol
gisch-zoologischen Zusammenhang gezeigt. Die Weichen, welche Ende des 19. Jahrhunderts geste
wurden, leiten auch jetzt noch unsere Einschätzung und Auslegung von aussereuropäischen Kulturg
tern. Meine Arbeit positioniert sich an der Schnittstelle der gängigen musealen Praxis, welche Objek
entweder der Kunst, der Geschichte oder der Ethnologie zuordnet. Sie stellt die drei Referenzsystem
die nicht nur miteinander verknüpft sind, sonder sich geradezu gegenseitig bedingen, in einen offe
sichtlichen Zusammenhang. Welchem Referenzsystem gehören nun anatolische Kostümteile an, wer
sie in der Kunsthalle ausgestellt sind? Oder St. Galler Trachtenhauben, wenn sie an einer St Gallerin F
tografiert sind, die türkisch-kasakischer Herkunft ist?[10] Wie lassen sich solche alltäglichen Verschi
bungen wissenschaftlich erfassen? Welche Relevanz kann das Konstrukt des Nationalen und dam
auch des Nationalgeschichtlichen heute noch haben, wenn es der Realität einer zunehmenden Aufl
sung der ethnisch definierten Identität nicht Rechnung tragen kann? Die Zeit, in der ein "Volk" innerha
von Landesgrenzen eine homogene Gesellschaft bildet, gehört bestenfalls der Geschichte an. Muss sic
ein Landesmuseum auf immer engere, realitätsfremde Stereotypen beschränken, die mehr ausschlie
sen als sie vorgeben, oder zeichnen sich Möglichkeiten ab, diese überholten Kategorien aufzubrecher

Der Text erschien erstmals im Katalog *Platzwechsel*, Kunsthalle Zürich, 1995

[1] Rea Brändle, *Wildfremd, Hautnah.* Völkerschauen und Schauplätze Zürich 1880-1960, Rotpunktverlag, 199
[2] i.b.i.d., chapter 1 / a.a.O., 1. Kapitel
[3] Balthasar Staehlin, *Völkerschauen im Zoologischen Garten Basel 189-1935*, Basler Afrika Bibliographie 1993
[4] Gerald Alettaz et.al., *Les Suisses dans le miroir (Les expos nationales suisses)*, Verlag Payot, Lausanne 199
[5] Stahelin, p 102
[6] Julius Kollmann, professor of anatomy at the University Basel 1978 - 1913. Stahelin, p. 116
[7] Schweizer Volksfreund 10.07.1883, in: Staehelin, op.cit., p. 121
[8] Lotti Schürch, Louise Witzig, *Trachten der Schweiz*, Edition Kolibri, Bern 1978
[9] A few weeks ago, I received a postcard from Jean-Hubert Martin, curator of the exhibition *Les Magiciens d* 
*la Terre* bearing the stamp of his museum with this wording.
Vor wenigen Wochen erhielt ich eine Karte von Jean-Hubert Martin, Kurator der Ausstellung *Les Magiciens d 
la Terre*, die mit dieser Aufschrift seines Museum gestempelt war
[10] Saadet Türköz, experimental singer, Zürich

# Kültür

# _KÜLTÜR
# 1996/1997

Kültür is a research and exhibition project involving eight women from Istanbul wh[o] are artists and/or social scientists of the media and urban studies fields engaged i[n] cultural analysis and art production on the subject of urban space, the correlatio[n] between centre and periphery and the position of women within these social an[d] economic structures, particularly women in the garment industry. We developed thi[s] project together, first for an exhibition at the Shedhalle, Zurich, later for a publica[-] tion, and finally for another project at the Istanbul Biennial in the Fall of 1997. Th[e] Biennial project focused on issues of migrancy, urban politics and Istanbul's plan t[o] become a global city.

Kültür ist ein Forschungs- und Ausstellungsprojekt von acht Künstlerinnen, Sozio[o-] loginnen und Medienarbeiterinnen aus Istanbul, die sich mit kultureller Analyse un[d] Kunstproduktion in Bezug auf den öffentlichen Raum, mit den Wechselbeziehunge[n] zwischen Zentrum und Peripherie sowie mit der Stellung der Frau innerhalb diese[r] sozioökonomischen Strukturen – insbesondere in der Textilindustrie – beschäftigte[n.] Wir haben dieses Projekt gemeinsam entwickelt, zunächst für eine Ausstellung in de[r] Zürcher Shedhalle, danach für eine Publikation und anschliessend, im Herbst 1997[,] für ein Projekt auf der Istanbuler Biennale. Das Projekt für die Biennale zentriert[e] sich um die Themen Migration, Kommunalpolitik und Istanbuls Ambitionen, sich al[s] globale Stadt zu entwickeln.

# _OUTSOURCING AND SUBCONTRACTING

Even though the categories West and non-West have become pervious in many ways and don't seem so useful anymore when describing the situation in metropolitan centres, the conflict between these two world narratives continues nonetheless on similar terms. With the opening in 1991, this discourse has taken new directions, and I will discuss, using the example of a two-year project, what curating might entail in this field. The notions of outsourcing and subcontracting are borrowed from the new economic order which we are facing since the breakdown of the socialist structures.

From a curatorial perspective, I intended with this project to intervene in these transnational relations on various levels. First of all, I mediated between a European art institution and artists from other contexts in an attempt to eliminate the biased contract between Western curators in possession of the concept of funding and decision-making power on the one hand, and the artists hungry to participate in the international art scene they had been excluded from for many years on the other.

I went to Istanbul with the idea of presenting a different kind of art practice that operated on a concept of art that claims a social commitment and is strongly context-oriented, gender specific and collaborative in its mode of production. If Western art was being presented to Istanbul in a big way, someone needed to be on the spot to introduce a different strategy, a critical practice with a different understanding of the role of the artist. The intention was to acquaint some artists with an option that would also provide the tools to deconstruct what seemed so attractive at the moment, namely the white master discourse. Then, I wanted to intervene in the stereotyped image of the Turkish woman in Switzerland. The Turkish woman wearing a scarf often stands for women's submissive role in Muslim societies. Her image is that of a backward, uneducated, rural woman. Generally speaking, representation of migrant women in Switzerland is still dominated today by Christian funding agencies. There is very little self-representation except for some programmes on free radio stations. Also, I wanted to find out what gender discourse, if any, was taking place among women artists in Istanbul. It turned out that the term feminist art practice had very negative connotations at the Academy: It was associated with screaming street activists with whom the institution simply couldn't identify. Also, Atatürk had let women believe that he had resolved the problem of gender specific inequality in his modern nation by giving them the right to vote in 1923. The feminist approach in art thus far had consisted in unearthing women artists from an unwritten history. By contrast, the cultural studies department was, of course, familiar with gender theories. Thus a project aim became the attempt to combine these perspectives and come up with gendered strategies for an art practice.

And finally, there was the delicate question of cultural repression with regard to the Kurdish issue which needed to be addressed in one way or another. During the preparations, I had the chance to accompany a delegation of journalists and feminist activists to Diarbakir to investigate women's conditions in the war in the Kurdish regions. I felt that I needed firsthand information to understand the situation in depth. On that occasion I was able to make contact with the Kurdish cultural centre in Istanbul which became an important link in this project.

## Western curators in foreign services

Postcolonial theories represent an important frame of reference for this project. The problem with this discourse is that the majority authors relate to British conditions or to North American minority cultures. In practice, however, it is essential to analyse every situation precisely, in order to avoid talking in unreflective, established terms that describe power relations of a different historical moment.

For us the question was how far postcolonial discourse was applicable to the specific situation of Kültür. It was important to take a close look at these historical images. The art space is indeed a place where the relations resulting from the colonial experience can and should be represented and di

cussed, since this is the place where cultural codes are being negotiated. But the art institution is also one of the sites where the postcolonial process materialises. As a curator, I have the choice of either critiquing and transforming the existing power relations or reproducing them. Not asking this question usually leads to reproducing them.

To develop new strategies it is necessary to understand how established Western curators proceed in extra-European contexts. As in many countries, the opening in 1991 had a strong impact on Turkey. Changes were noticeable immediately. Twenty new private TV channels joined the single state channel. Also, the art scene in Istanbul attracted the interest of European curators who came to pick and choose within the local art scene those artists whose work corresponded best to Western criteria and concepts. A new and rather competitive climate started to spread in the small Istanbul art circle.

On the other hand, Western curators also stage large scale, on-site exhibitions where the concepts hardly distinguish themselves from the exhibitions they curate in the West. These shows come across as gigantic advertising campaigns for Western art, and it's not surprising that they create the desire to take part in them. It cannot be overlooked that this kind of globalisation of Western high art also has a colonising impact in other geopolitical contexts or on minority cultures. Similar to other media, art too devalues existing cultural signs through the validation of Western aesthetics and symbolic values in a sheer and financially overwhelming onslaught.

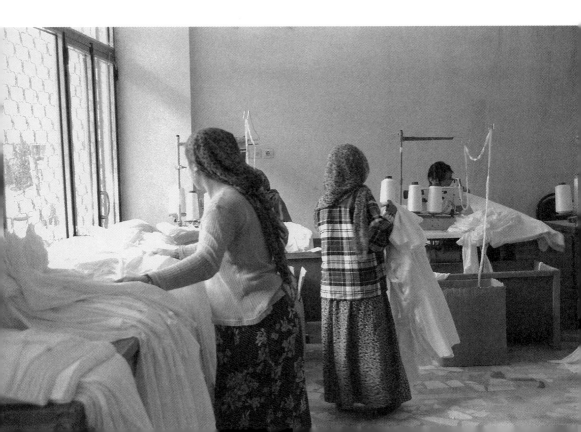

## Negotiating the terms

For a curator, to tackle a different cultural context and to work with those cultural producers automatically means to engage in a power relationship which is described in the theory books as postcolonial. I realised that, I couldn't simply extract myself from the dynamic nor theorise somewhere in the safety of an unchallenged centre... that on the contrary, such a collaboration would personally involve me as the curator in this relationship which demanded to be negotiated and reformulated "live", as it were, with all its participants. Until then I had formulated a critique of representation, now I was suddenly a party in the postcolonial relationship, I was in the middle of this problematic programme. It became clear that if Kültür wasn't going to remain a descriptive exhibition practice, if it was to aim at transposing theoretical critical strategies into its work method, then it needed to allow space for this negotiation. The critique of Kültür needed to set aside the normative Western art quality standard in favour of an analysis and elaboration of the specific situation in Istanbul and an unravelling of the artists' ties with their geopolitical contexts. Also, due to the relative ineffectiveness of the deconstructive approach in the art discussion – an approach that didn't politicise the gender relations but merely shifted them to the level of cultural signification – we intended to once again tie feminism to political interests lying outside the academic ones. From the initial discussions in Istanbul through the research and production phases and the week of presentation in Zurich, the project took place in a workshop structure. We decided to focus on the relations between cultural centre and periphery, dynamics which are particularly relevant in the context of the Turkish metropolis, where the tension between what we call the modern, democratic, Western centre and the post-modern, migrated

illegal realities on its borders is constantly increasing. Kültür situated itself on the periphery, as it were, and drew from there a cityscape, which derived from the social spaces, the migrant histories and trajectories of the people who occupied that space..

Outsourcing and subcontracting

At the core of the project was the research itself. Field trips to textile sweatshops, interviews, home visits, chats, video recordings. The suburbs are often as far away as a two-hour bus ride in one or the other direction from the commercial centre. The garment industry is an informal, grey-market, semi-legal industrial sector employing mainly women who have migrated to the big city. It is very labour-intensive and frequently operates by subcontracting to smaller shops that hire workers on a short-term basis. A migrated, informal, precarious and completely deregulated life is the norm in these neighbourhoods. They have no communal structures, no history other than the migration stories we recorded on video and photographed. We focused on invisible cultural expressions and on the cultural process of marginalisation per se. If a contemporary discourse expects to be successful, it cannot be formulated exclusively from a perspective of the Western observer. A critique needs to emerge from the sites of production, from "the country of origin". Outsourcing curatorial activities becomes a necessity in this particular discourse.

Istanbul as a geopolitical site at the crossing between the Balkans, Asia Minor, the Eastern Mediterranean and the Black Sea area is virtually predestined to bring to light the alliances of contradictions and

existential struggles. It is in a particularly strategic location; a chaotic giant, a city forcefully striving for modernism and suppressing its Ottoman history that keeps cropping up everywhere. It is a city that denies the multiplicity of its cultural composition, which spans from Sephardic to Uzbek influences, an enchanting city with a skyline of utmost beauty, a site of violence, where power uses medieval measures to coerce people into the nation's narrow scheme.

I have asked myself if it's tenable to engage with a place that conducts untenable politics including massive human rights violations or if we should impose a cultural embargo. I came to the conclusion that it is more effective to engage with the democratic forces on the spot, strengthening the critical dialogue and opening up new possibilities of action within the field of representation. After all, it's through interpersonal relations, educational institutions, symbolic representations and cultural work that power relations are produced as well as challenged.

## Politics of representation

With the massive entry of the media, it was very obvious that the field of representation was a new battle ground to be taken seriously. We recognised that in particular the conflict of ethnicity and the right to express oneself culturally has shifted increasingly into the area of art, media and education. For a cultural practice, particularly in postcolonial projects, it's important to keep in mind that these forces are embodied in totally ordinary work relations and contents on which we can have a direct impact. The local integration of art projects has become an important strategy in the resistance against a globalisation of Western aesthetics and values. It is a resistance against a relentless evacuation of art works and against their random interchangeability at international art exhibitions.

Based on the arguments of institutional criticism, as mentioned earlier, and of the interchangeability and marketability of art, I refrained from offering a neutral exhibition space, from selecting promising talents and from presenting finished positions. In fact I didn't judge and select at all but tried to navigate the project, at times just floating along I tried to yield control as much as I could, e.g. the budget for the entire project was openly posted, a big lump was handed over to the participants to be self-managed. It became a subcontract.

The Kültür participants decided to research the condition of migrant women at the urban and social periphery of Istanbul and by doing so they placed themselves firmly at the centre. This choice led them to question not only their own privileged positions, but also the means by which the migrant's existence is devalued. They questioned the role the Academy plays in excluding their narrative and in pushing these subjects to the margin. It turned out, for example, that certain methods like field work and recording oral histories were being repressed at the sociology department, where these methods were reserved for use by higher ranking faculty members only. Up until then, research for these younger sociologists had consisted of library work. This project brought them into the field and into personal contact with people whose work and existence are not represented elsewhere. With the work on Kültür, the participants broke the taboos and brought minority representation into the academic context in a lively way.

Dealing with the diplomatic aspects of this cultural and political situation influenced a number of my decisions. As an outsider I could afford more risky positions than a local initiative would have dared. Knowing that we had to face Kurdish refugees in Zurich motivated me during preparations to carefully integrate a member of MKM, a Kurdish cultural centre in Istanbul, into the project. At that moment three participants left the group, seven stayed. It is not a harmless thing to be associated with MKM, considering the police force makes regular raids on the centre, arrests and tortures its members and destroys its archives. Including a Kurdish element in Kültür was the most delicate and diplomatically difficult move I was to make. It could have shattered the whole project, yet it was a necessary decision since excluding this element, once again, would have meant reproducing Turkish State policies.

## A city project

A year later, we were invited to participate in the International Istanbul Biennial. Adapting Kültür for this setting triggered a whole range of new reflections and discussions on both sides. This required the application of major diplomatic skills. It was a move worth making, since this is yet another site where postcolonial processes are wont to manifest themselves. As the only project of its sort at the Biennial we dealt directly with the urban situation in Istanbul. Migrancy may be the key issue in Istanbul, which registered an increase of population from 7 million to over 15 million over the last few years. Istanbul's major changes in the last few years raised questions of intertextualities and displacement in the contemporary metropolis at the Biennial's symposium, How do we understand the meaning of and the dynamics behind migrancy, the changes in the cultural topography, the erasure of

the distinction between cultures and places? For us the question was also, How can we, as cultural producers, make sense of the drastic transformations or even intervene in the process? From the outset it was clear that we wouldn't think of intertextuality and displacement as merely a philosophical or discursive subject but we would also think of them as a result of financial, political and military decisions which become apparent in the way cities are transforming. The speedy reorganisation and segmentation of social groups in terms of function and status is only one of the visible marks which have been made on the urban fabric in recent years. Particularly striking is that the majority of people now living in Istanbul leads a village-type life and doesn't even attempt to integrate in the cosmopolitan idea anymore. In turn, new conglomerations of lifestyles emerge; communities consolidate both among the migrant settlers in gecekondus as well as among the affluent cosmopolitans who leave the inner city to move into newly built American, country-style, high-security suburban areas. The model of interweaving cultures and dissolving cultural differences may be appealing, but in view of these developments they tend to be overly optimistic and don't advance us much in understanding the larger scenario. And the larger scenario is, of course, to turn Istanbul into a global city.

So we decided to organise an open-air night forum on city politics in one of the gecekondus, a slum neighbourhood called Karanfilköy which is always under threat of demolition and evacuation. The forum was organised together with civil organisations and an association of progressive architects and urban scholars. At the Biennial exhibition space we had an information wall with videos and texts.

# Writing oneself into international relations

Art and culture especially when detached from local conditions, lend themselves outstandingly well to upgrading the image of a city and promoting the objective of becoming internationally attractive to trade and finance. That's the practice we are involved in when exhibiting aesthetic productions in art-defined spaces, when engaging in the art discourse at panels and symposiums and particularly when disseminating them internationally through the daily press, art magazines and Biennial catalogues. It may be no coincidence that the Istanbul Biennial was founded simultaneously with the globalisation trend, as were many large scale art exhibitions and festivals in other ambitious cities at that time.

Migrant settlements, as they clearly don't correspond to an ideal vision of the global city, come under pressure. There is a real conflict of interest over urban territory, which is carried out on two fronts: the symbolic and the urban space. A critical art practice could consist therefore in making visible the links between these two discourses, i.e. the public space of (symbolic) representation of international art and media and the public space of communities like Karanfilköy where the urban struggle takes place. These two sites are tightly connected – feeding each other – and Kültür situates itself in both them, which has not been without conflict, since the two sites operate according to their own politics and priorities. In Karanfilköy, the site of our forum, where the police force had bulldozed over fifty self built houses to clear the way for a financial district, the globalisation scenario has an incisive effect on real peoples' lives. Thus opening a public space, a forum of self-representation, could be a valid cultural strategy against privatisation and dislocation. Yet the point of this project in the art exhibition may not be so much to draw the attention to the existential struggle of several million citizens, but rather to understand how international art is not just in line with certain global changes but that it actually constitutes those very relations within which it operates.

Today, postcolonial art and curatorial practices could bring the identity politics of the eighties – which sought to deal with cultural difference either by emphasizing multiple identities or by showing the constructed nature of national identity – into the context of wider transformations of the very public sphere that has been created by this new cosmopolitanism.

This city project made us move in many spaces, addressing many publics, taking multiple positions, speaking many languages and learning new ones. We travelled the distance between the public space of the Forum on Urban Politics in Karanfilköy and the public space of International Art at Darphane as many times as we engaged in conversations with the gecekondu community, in conversations among ourselves, when reading theoretical texts, when listening to the migrant settlers, when writing our proposals and articulations, when participating in organizations and in political meetings, when tracing the conviviality and simultaneity of all these activities.

To travel these different venues connects the ambiguous sites of globalisation and places us within it. Our participation in this exhibit means to include the voice of a marginalized "gecekondu" site but also to take a part in enhancing Istanbul's image and reputation. Both are the contradictory outcomes of the same global city dream.

# _AUSLAGERUNG UND ZULIEFERUNG

Zwar gelten Kategorien wie die westliche oder nicht-westliche Welt mittlerweile als allzu durchlässig und überholt, um die Verhältnisse in den urbanen Zentren adäquat zu beschreiben, doch der Konflikt zwischen diesen beiden Welterzählungen wird unter ähnlichen Bedingungen fortgesetzt. Seit der Öffnung Osteuropas 1991 nimmt dieser Diskurs eine neue Richtung ein. Anhand eines zweijährigen Projekts habe ich die spezifischen Möglichkeiten und Voraussetzungen eruiert, die das Ausstellungsmachen auf diesem Gebiet mit sich bringen kann. Die Begriffe Auslagerung und Zulieferung – outsourcing and subcontracting – sind der neuen ökonomischen Ordnung entnommen, mit der wir es seit der Auflösung der sozialistischen Strukturen zu tun haben.

Aus kuratorischer Perspektive wollte ich mit *Kültür* auf verschiedenen Ebenen in diese transnationalen Beziehungen intervenieren. Erstens wollte ich in die Beziehung zwischen einer europäischen Kunstinstitution und KünstlerInnen aus anderen Kontexten eingreifen, in das Missverhältnis zwischen westlichen KuratorInnen auf der einen Seite, ihrer Macht über Konzepte, Finanzierung und Entscheidungen, und den KünstlerInnen auf der anderen Seite, ihrem Hunger nach einer Teilnahme an der internationalen Kunstszene, von der sie jahrelang ausgeschlossen waren.

Ich bin mit der Idee nach Istanbul gegangen, eine etwas andere Kunstpraxis zu präsentieren, die auf einem Kunstkonzept basiert, das sich sozial engagiert und dessen Arbeit kontextorientiert, geschlechterspezifisch und kollaborativ ausgerichtet ist. Da westliche Kunst in Istanbul seit kurzem im grossen Rahmen präsentiert wurde, war es auch nötig, vor Ort eine andere Strategie mit einem anderen Verständnis der Rolle der KünstlerIn vorzustellen. KünstlerInnen sollten mit einer Option vertraut gemacht werden, das zu dekonstruieren, was im Moment so attraktiv erschien, nämlich den westlichen Meisterdiskurs. Zudem wollte ich das stereotype Bild der türkischen Frau in der Schweiz in Frage stellen. Die türkische Frau mit ihrem Kopftuch steht häufig für die unterdrückte Rolle der Frau in der muslimischen Gesellschaft, ihr Image ist das einer unselbständigen, ungebildeten Landfrau. Ganz allgemein gesagt, wird das Bild der eingewanderten Frauen in der Schweiz immer noch von den christlichen Organisationen bestimmt. Es gibt, ausgenommen von einigen Programmen freier Radiosender, kaum die Möglichkeit der Selbstrepräsentation. Weiter wollte ich herausfinden, wie Künstlerinnen in Istanbul untereinander über Gender-Fragen diskutierten. Es stellte sich heraus, dass in der Akademie der Begriff feministische Kunst äusserst negative Konnotationen beinhaltete, wie etwa schreiende Strassenaktivistinnen,

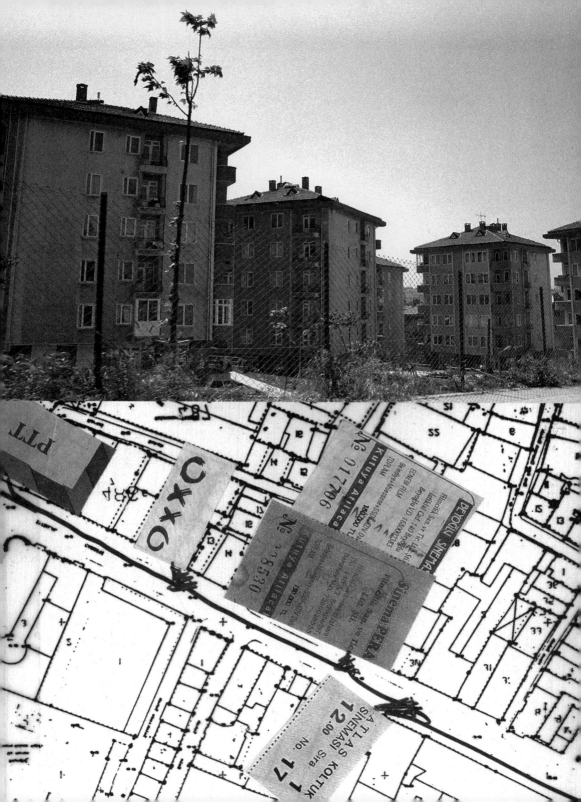

mit denen sie sich nicht identifizieren konnten. Zudem hatte Atatürk Frauen den Glauben gegeben, d[as] Problem der geschlechterspezifischen Unterdrückung in einem modernen Staat gelöst zu haben, als [er] ihnen 1923 das Wahlrecht gab. Ein feministischer Ansatz in der Kunst beschränkte sich daher allein da[r]auf, Künstlerinnen aus einer ungeschriebenen Geschichte überhaupt erst auszugraben. An der Cultu[ral] Studies Abteilung der Universitäten hingegen waren die Frauen mit Gender-Theorien vertraut. So kon[n]te der Sinn dieser Kollaboration darin bestehen, diese Perspektiven zu verbinden, um eine geschlechte[r]spezifische Strategie für eine Kunstpraxis zu entwickeln.

Und schliesslich galt es, die schwierige Frage der kulturellen Unterdrückung der KurdInnen auf die ei[ne] oder andere Weise anzusprechen. Während der Vorbereitungen hatte ich Gelegenheit, eine Gruppe v[on] Journalistinnen und Feministinnen, welche die Situation der Frauen in den kurdischen Kriegsgebiete[n] untersuchten, nach Diarbakir zu begleiten. Ich hatte den Eindruck, dass ich mir ein eigenes Bild vor O[rt] machen müsse, um die Situation zu verstehen. So konnte ich Kontakte zum kurdischen Zentrum in Is[t]anbul aufbauen, das zudem eine wichtige Verbindung in diesem Projekt darstellte.

### Westliche KuratorInnen im Aussendienst

Für dieses Projekt bilden pos[t]koloniale Theorien einen wichtigen Referenzrahmen. Das Problem dieses Diskurses liegt darin, dass d[ie] meisten AutorInnen sich auf britische Bedingungen oder nordamerikanische Minderheiten beziehen. [Es] ist allerdings in der Praxis wichtig, jede Situation genau zu analysieren, um nicht unreflektiert Begrif[fe] zu übernehmen, die Machtverhältnisse in einer ganz anderen historischen Situation beschreiben.

Für uns stellte sich die Frage, wieweit der postkoloniale Diskurs auf die spezifische Situation von *Kült*[ur] übertragbar sei. Es war wichtig, die Geschichtsbilder genau zu betrachten. Der Kunstraum ist tatsäc[h]lich der Ort, an dem die aus der Kolonialbewegung hervorgegangenen Beziehungen repräsentiert u[nd] diskutiert werden sollten, da er der Ort ist, an dem kulturelle Codes verhandelt werden. Aber Kunsti[n]stitute sind auch Orte, an denen sich die postkoloniale Bewegung materialisiert. Als KuratorIn kann ic[h] die bestehenden Machtbeziehungen kritisieren und transformieren, wenn ich sie nicht reproduziere[n] will. Sich diese Frage nicht zu stellen, läuft normalerweise auf ein Reproduzieren heraus.

Um neue Strategien zu entwickeln, ist es wichtig zu verstehen, wie westliche KuratorInnen sich bishe[r] im aussereuropäischen Kontext bewegt haben. Die Öffnung Osteuropas 1991 hatte, wie für viele and[e]re Länder auch, eine grosse Bedeutung für die Türkei. Die Veränderungen waren sofort sichtbar. In kü[r]zester Zeit kamen zu dem einen staatlichen Fernsehsender 20 Privatstationen hinzu. Zugleich zog di[e] Kunstszene Istanbuls westliche KuratorInnen an, die aus der lokalen Kunstszene jene KünstlerInne[n] auswählten, die am ehesten westlichen Konzepten und Kriterien genügten. In der kleinen Künstlerge[-] meinde Istanbuls entwickelte sich ein neues, äusserst konkurrenzträchtiges Klima.

Auf der anderen Seite haben westliche KuratorInnen zahlreiche Ausstellungen vor Ort ausgerichtet, de[-] ren Konzepte sich kaum von denjenigen unterschieden, die sie im Westen kuratiert hatten. Diese Aus[-] stellungen wirkten wie gigantische Werbekampagnen für Westkunst, und es ist nicht überraschen[d,] dass sie die Sehnsucht weckten, daran teilzuhaben. Dass diese Art Globalisierung von "Westhochkunst[”] auch eine kolonisierende Wirkung auf andere geopolitische Zusammenhänge oder auf Minoritätskultu[r] ren haben muss, ist leicht auszumachen. Ähnlich wie andere Medien entwertet Kunst existierende kulturelle Zeichen durch die massive und finanzkräftige Gültigkeit westlicher Kunst und Symbole.

## Die Bedingungen verhandeln

Für einen Kurator, eine Kuratorin, die in einem fremden, kulturellen Kontext mit dessen ProduzentInnen arbeitet, bedeutet dies automatisch, sich in ein Machtgefüge zu begeben, das in den Theoriebüchern als postkolonial beschrieben wird. Ich stellte fest, dass ich mich dieser Dynamik weder entziehen konnte, noch aus einer unanfechtbaren Mitte heraus darüber theoretisieren konnte, dass – ganz im Gegenteil – eine derartige Zusammenarbeit mich als Kuratorin persönlich in eine Beziehung einband, die neu durchdacht und mit allen Teilnehmenden neu formuliert werden musste. Bis dahin hatte ich allein Kritik an der Repräsentation geübt, jetzt war ich auf einmal Teil dieser postkolonialen Beziehung. Ich war mitten drin in diesem problematischen Programm. Es wurde deutlich, dass *Kültür* Raum für diese Überlegungen brauchte, wenn es nicht innerhalb der deskriptiven Ausstellungspraxis verharren wollte, sondern darauf ausgerichtet war, die theoretische Kritik in eine Arbeitsmethode zu transformieren. Die kritische Ausrichtung von *Kültür* musste sich von dem normativen Westkunstbegriff lösen und statt dessen die spezifische Situation in Istanbul analysieren und genau darstellen, indem es die Verknüpfung der KünstlerInnen mit ihrem geopolitischen Kontext freilegte. Aufgrund des relativ unbefriedigenden dekonstruktivistischen Ansatzes innerhalb der Kunsttheorie, der das Verhältnis der Geschlechter nicht politisierte und es statt dessen auf der Ebene kultureller Repräsentation ansiedelte, beabsichtigten wir zudem, Feminismus ausserhalb des akademischen Diskurses wieder zu politisieren. Mit Beginn der ersten Diskussionen in Istanbul wie auch während der Zeit der Forschung, Produktion und anschliessenden Präsentation in Zürich bestand das Projekt als Workshop. Wir beschlossen, uns auf die Beziehungen zwischen dem kulturellen Zentrum und der Peripherie zu konzentrieren, eine Dynamik, die besonders in der türkischen Metropole eine Rolle spielt, wo die Spannungen zwischen dem, was wir modern, westlich und demokratisches Zentrum nennen, und der postmodernen, illegalen Einwanderungsrealität am Stadtrand, ständig wachsen. Kültür selbst situierte sich an der Peripherie und entwarf von dort aus ein Stadtbild, das von den Lebensräumen und Migrationsgeschichten der Frauen ausgeht, die diese Räume bewohnen.

## Auslagerung und Zulieferung

Das Zentrum des Projekts bildete die Forschung: Feldreisen in die Nähateliers der Textilindustrie, Interviews, Hausbesuche, Videoaufnahmen, Gesprächsaufzeichnungen. Die Vororte liegen, sowohl in der einen wie auch in der anderen Richtung, eine zweistündige Busfahrt vom Handelszentrum entfernt. Die Textilindustrie ist ein informeller, grauer Markt, ein halblegaler Industriezweig, in dem zumeist Frauen beschäftigt werden, die in die grossen Städte gezogen sind. Sie ist sehr arbeitsintensiv und wird zumeist von kleinen Subunternehmern (subcontractors) betrieben, die ihre Arbeitskräfte nur kurzfristig beschäftigen und grösseren Abnehmern zuliefern. In diesen Vierteln führen die Zugezogenen normalerweise ein inoffizielles, unsicheres und völlig dereguliertes Leben. Es gibt keine kommunalen Strukturen, keine Geschichte ausser den Geschichten der Einwanderung, die wir auf Video und Foto dokumentierten. Wir konzentrierten uns auf die unsichtbaren kulturellen Zeichen und auf den kulturellen Prozess der Ausgrenzung als solchen. Wenn ein zeitgenössischer Diskurs Sinn machen soll, dann darf er nicht allein aus der Perspektive des westlichen Beobachters formuliert werden. Die Kritik muss aus dem Raum der Produktion hervorgehen, aus dem

"Herkunftsland". Es ist in diesem spezifischen Diskurs unerlässlich, die kuratorischen Aktivitäten aus zulagern, d. h. zu outsourcen.

Es versteht sich, dass der geopolitische Ort Istanbul am Übergang zwischen Balkan, Kleinasien, der östlichen Mittelmeer und dem Schwarzmeerraum geradezu prädestiniert ist, kulturelle und politisch Widersprüche und die damit verbundenen existentiellen Kämpfe ans Licht zu bringen. Es ist ein beson ders strategischer Ort, ein chaotischer Gigant, eine Stadt, die kraftvoll nach Modernität strebt und da bei ihre überall hervorspringende osmanische Geschichte unterdrückt und gleichzeitig die Vielfalt de kulturellen Zusammenspiels negiert, das von Sephardim bis zu den Usbeken reicht. Istanbul ist eine be zaubernde Stadt mit einer Skyline von unglaublicher Schönheit und gleichzeitig ein Ort der Gewalt, w die Mächtigen mittelalterliche Mittel verwenden, um die Menschen in das enge Schema der Nation z zwingen.

Ich habe mich gefragt, ob es verantwortbar ist, sich an einem Ort zu engagieren, wo die politischen Zu stände massive Menschenrechtsverletzungen einschliessen, oder ob wir nicht ein kulturelles Embarg verhängen sollten. Ich kam zur Schlussfolgerung, dass es sinnvoller ist, sich dort mit demokratische Kräften zu verbünden, um den kritischen Dialog zu stärken und neue Aktionsmöglichkeiten im Bereic der Repräsentation zu eröffnen. Schliesslich sind es auch die persönlichen Beziehungen, Ausbildungs stätten, symbolischen Repräsentationen und kulturellen Arbeiten, die das Machtgefüge produzierer aber auch verändern.

# Politik der Repräsentation

Nach dem massiven Einzug der Medien seit 1991 war es nur zu offensichtlich, dass das Feld der Repräsentation ein neues, ernst zu nehmendes Feld der Auseinandersetzung wurde. Wir bemerkten, dass besonders der Konflikt der Ethnien und das Recht auf die eigene kulturelle Identität sich enorm auf das Gebiet von Kunst, Medien und Bildung verlagert hatten. Für kulturelle Praxis, besonders in einem postkolonialen Kontext, ist es wichtig, gewahr zu werden, dass diese Kräfte in völlig normale Arbeitsverhältnisse eingebunden sind, auf die wir direkt einwirken können. Eine wichtige Strategie im Kampf gegen die Globalisierung westlicher Ästhetik und Werte ist die lokale Integration von Kunstprojekten. Das ist ein Widerstand gegen die unentwegte Entleerung der Bedeutung eines Kunstwerks und gegen seine wahllose Austauschbarkeit auf den internationalen Kunstausstellungen. ·

Wegen der schon erwähnten Institutionskritik und der Austauschbarkeit und Vermarktung von Kunst habe ich davon Abstand genommen, einen neutralen Ausstellungsraum anzubieten, vielversprechende Talente auszuwählen und fertige Positionen zu präsentieren. Tatsächlich habe ich weder bewertet noch ausgewählt; vielmehr habe ich versucht, das Projekt durch die Gezeiten zu lenken und die Kontrolle so weit wie möglich aufzugeben. Z. B. war das Budget für das ganze Projekt allen einsichtig. Die Teilnehmerinnen erhielten einen grossen Brocken zur Selbstverwaltung. Sie wurden zu Subunternehmerinnen, zu Zulieferinnen.

Die Teilnehmerinnen von *Kültür* entschieden, dass sie die Lebensbedingungen von MigrantInnen a‹ städtischen und sozialen Rand von Istanbul untersuchen wollten, wobei sie sich selbst stärker ins Ze‹ trum rückten. Diese Entscheidung führte dazu, dass sie im Vergleich mit den Migrantinnen ihre eigen‹ privilegierte Position stärker in Frage stellten, aber auch die Rolle der Akademie, die deren Erzählunge‹ ausschliesst und diese Subjekte an den Rand drängt. Schliesslich wurde deutlich, dass Arbeitsmeth‹ den wie Feldforschung und Oral History am Soziologischen Institut unterdrückt wurden oder, genaue‹ gesagt, nur langjährigen Professoren vorbehalten waren. Bis dahin hatte Forschung für die jüngere‹ SoziologInnen vor allem Bibliotheksarbeit bedeutet, wohingegen dieses aktive Projekt sie nach drau‹ sen und in Kontakt mit Menschen brachte, deren Arbeit und Existenz nirgendwo repräsentiert ist. M‹ der Arbeit für *Kültür* haben sie mit diesem Tabu gebrochen und die Repräsentation von Minderheite‹ auf höchst lebendige Art in den akademischen Kontext hineingetragen.

Um mit der Diplomatik dieser kulturellen und politischen Situation umzugehen, traf ich einige Vorke‹ rungen. Ich konnte als Aussenstehende riskantere Positionen beziehen als eine heimische Initiative. D‹ wir in Zürich auch kurdischen Flüchtlingen begegnen würden, sah ich mich veranlasst, vorsichtig M‹ glieder des MKM, des kurdischen Kulturzentrums in Istanbul, in das Projekt zu integrieren. Daraufh‹ verliessen drei Teilnehmerinnen die Gruppe, sieben blieben. Es ist nicht ungefährlich mit dem MKM i‹ Verbindung gebracht zu werden in Anbetracht der Tatsache, dass die Polizei regelmässig Razzien i‹ Zentrum durchführt, seine Mitglieder verhaftet und foltert und ihre Archive vernichtet. Ein kurdische‹ Element zu integrieren, war sicher nicht nur die schwierigste Aufgabe in *Kültür*, sondern auch die, d‹

am meisten diplomatisches Geschick erforderte. Sie hätte das ganze Projekt zu Fall bringen können. Aber es war eine notwendige Aufgabe, da die erneute Ausgrenzung nur die offizielle türkische Politik reproduziert hätte.

## Ein städtisches Projekt

Ein Jahr später wurden wir zur Internationalen Biennale in Istanbul eingeladen. Um *Kültür* für diesen Kontext wieder aufzuarbeiten, bedurfte es auf beiden Seiten neuer Überlegungen und Diskussionen und verlangte ein ausgesprochenes diplomatisches Geschick. Aber das war es wert, da die Biennale ein weiterer Ort ist, an dem sich postkoloniale Prozesse materialisieren. Wir waren das einzige Projekt auf der Biennale, das unmittelbar eine Verbindung zur städtischen Situation Istanbuls herstellte. Migration ist vielleicht die Schlüsselfrage in Istanbul, einer Stadt mit einem EinwohnerInnenwachstum von sieben auf fünfzehn Millionen innerhalb nur weniger Jahre. Die grossen Veränderungen der letzten Jahre in Istanbul wurden auf dem Symposium der Biennale zum Anlass genommen, Intertextualität und Ausgrenzung in zeitgenössischen Grossstädten zu diskutieren. Wie verstehen wir die Bedeutung und die Dynamik von Migration, von Ausgrenzung? Welche Rolle spielt sie für die Topografie der Städte, für den Verlust der Unterscheidung zwischen Kulturen und Orten? Für uns KulturproduzentInnen stellte sich die Frage: Wie können wir diese drastischen Veränderungen sinnvoll beschreiben oder sogar in diesem Prozess vermitteln? Von Anfang an war klar, dass wir Intertextualität und Ausgrenzung nicht nur als philosophisches oder diskursorientiertes Thema verstanden, sondern auch als das Ergebnis finanzieller, politischer und militärischer Entscheidungen, die in den sich verän-

dernden Städten sichtbar werden. Die schnelle Reorganisation und Segmentierung sozialer Gruppen i Anbetracht ihrer Funktion und ihres Status hinterliessen in den letzten Jahren deutliche Spuren im städ tischen Gewebe. Es ist besonders auffällig, dass die Mehrheit der BewohnerInnen Istanbuls ein dör liches Leben führt und eine Integration in das kosmopolite Modell nicht einmal mehr anstrebt. Auf de anderen Seite entwickeln sich neue Lifestyle-Zusammenballungen, Gemeinden, die sich sowohl zw schen den Migranten in den *Gecekondus*, den Slums, bilden, als auch zwischen den wohlhabenden Ko mopoliten, die das städtische Zentrum verlassen, um nach US-amerikanischem Vorbild in neu erbauter scharf gesicherten Country-Style-Vororten zu leben. Das Modell der multikulturellen Gesellschaft, in de sich die kulturellen Unterschiede auflösen, mag zwar sehr ansprechend sein, aber angesichts diese Entwicklungen scheint es zu optimistisch und hilft uns nicht dabei, das grössere Szenario zu versteher Und dieses grössere Szenario ist der Versuch, Istanbul in eine globale Stadt zu verwandeln.

Daher entschieden wir uns, ein Open-Air-Forum über städtische Politik in einer der *Gecekondus* zu o ganisieren, einem Slum mit Namen Karanfilköy, der evakuiert und abgerissen werden sollte. Das Forur wurde zusammen mit BürgerInneninitiativen und einer Vereinigung progressiver ArchitektInnen un StadtplanerInnen organisiert. Auf dem Gelände der Biennale zeigten wir eine Informationstafel mit V deos und Texten.

### Sich in internationale Beziehungen einschreiben

Losgelös von lokalen Gegebenheiten eignen sich Kunst und Kultur ausgesprochen gut dazu, das Image eine Stadt zu fördern, und sie unterstützen das Ziel, ein international attraktiver Handels- und Finanzplatz z werden. In diese Praxis sind wir involviert, wenn wir ästhetische Produkte in einem Kunstraum ausste len, wenn wir am Diskurs über Kunst während einer Podiumsdiskussion oder eines Symposions tei nehmen und besonders wenn wir sie in Tageszeitungen, Kunstmagazinen und Biennale-Katalogen ver breiten. Es war sicher kein Zufall, dass die Biennale in Istanbul zeitgleich mit dem einsetzenden Tren zur Globalisierung gegründet wurde, genauso wie eine Vielzahl von Kunstausstellungen und Festivals i anderen ambitionierten Städten.

Da Siedlungen von Einwanderern nicht der idealen Vision einer globalen Stadt entsprechen, geraten si unter Druck. Es entsteht ein tatsächlicher Interessenkonflikt im städtischen Bereich, der an zwei Fron ten ausgetragen wird: im symbolischen und im städtischen Raum. Eine kritische Kunstpraxis könnt daher darin bestehen, die Verbindungen zwischen den zwei Diskursen sichtbar zu machen, d.h. den öffentlichen Raum der (symbolischen) Repräsentation internationaler Kunst und Medien und den öffentlichen Raum von Gemeinden wie Karanfilköy, in dem der urbane Kampf ausgetragen wird. Beid Räume sind eng miteinander verbunden, ernähren einander. Und *Kültür* situiert sich selbst in beide Räumen, was nicht ohne Konflikte geschieht, da beide Räume ihrer eigenen Politik und ihren eigener Prioritäten gehorchen. In Karanfilköy, wo die Polizei über fünfzig selbst gebaute Häuser niedergewalz hatte, um dort einen Finanzdistrikt zu errichten, hat die Globalisierung einschneidende Auswirkunger auf das reale Leben der Menschen. Dort einen öffentlichen Raum, ein Forum der Selbstrepräsentatio einzurichten, kann eine brauchbare kulturelle Strategie gegen Privatisierung und Vertreibung sein. Doch mag die Hauptfunktion dieses Projektes in der Kunstausstellung nicht so sehr darin liegen, die Auf merksamkeit auf den existentiellen Kampf von Millionen von Einwohnern zu lenken, als vielmehr sichtbar zu machen, wie internationale Kunst sich den globalen Veränderungen nicht nur anpasst, sondern gerade jene Beziehungen mitherstellt, innerhalb derer sie operiert.

Postkoloniale Kunst und kuratorische Praxis können heute die Identitätspolitik der 80er Jahre – die kulturelle Differenzen entweder durch die Betonung von multiplen Identitäten herausarbeitete oder die Konstruiertheit der nationalen Identität aufzeigte – in den Kontext grösserer Transformationen im öffentlichen Raum stellen, die durch den neuen Kosmopolitismus hervorgerufen wurden.

# Writing Desire

# _WRITING DESIRE
# 2000

*Writing Desire* is about the rapport between words and body and the creation of desire. It looks at writing by means of electronic communications technologies where the boundaries between private fantasy and the public sphere must be redefined. In this compressed electronic space the notion of the self undergoes transformations that also affect questions of boundaries, gender, and sexual relations. *Writing Desire* represents and practices communication of desire at a time when fantasies can freely travel the wires in a coded, textualized, disembodied manner. The isolated private space of writing inspires fantasies with simulated emotions which remain forever unfulfilled. In my video, Rosi Braidotti relates this disembodiment of sexuality with a long history of letter-writing women and their fantasized interlocutors. On a physical level she parallels the trend of the disappearing body with the ephemeral image of the anorexic, prepubescent, and pedophilic types of bodies prescribed by the fashion industry.

*Writing Desire* links the creation of romantic desire through writing to the production of desire in consumer culture by looking at the capitalization of these relations on and by the Internet. The bride market in general and the virgin market in particular are evidence of the booming commercialization of sexual relations: sites to shop for another body that represents desire and pleasure. The media of communication that, in the beginning, facilitated foreign relations and allowed one to fantasize, has quickly become a media of commerce where girls offer themselves for sale to complete strangers. *russianbride.com, tigerlilies.com,* and *blossoms.com* (the virgin cherry blossoms) are among the most popular sites that advertise large numbers of women from the former Soviet Union and the Philippines to the global male community. The sites include comprehensive picture databanks with anatomical information about the future bride. Some sites even feature short presentation videos in which the applicant can voice her personal qualities as well as her desires, although the part with her wishes is always left to the end and often gets cut short. In the digital representation of the Russian and Filipino women, bodies get reduced to a flat minimum of visual and textual information, and the digitized video net.cast technologizes the bodies even further. The slave of the colonial era is transformed into a post-Fordist robot. The "e-mail order bride," a positively thriving market segment in the nineties, draws on a historical narration of the female racialized body as an object of desire waiting to be conquered.

It is no coincidence that the female reservoirs of Novosibirsk and the Philippine islands are being tapped for women with traditional qualities as they become more and more difficult to find in the industrialized world. *getmarriednow.com* – a very selective, "business class" type of site which offers Russian models with a university education – announced the upcoming videos of 2000 women from Novosibirks, Siberia, Russia, and Ukraine as of April 2000. They offer a package deal for $199 which includes a round-trip from a U.S. city to Novosibirsk and the privilege of being a judge in the beauty contest – a bride lineup – organized for prospective grooms. So the human market on the net is thriving, resources are almost inexhaustible, and a lot of these enterprises are syndicated operations. The unscrupulous commercialization of the female body – visually, discursively, and physically – has gone public in a big way.

However, through the new possibilities of net.casting video clips, the brides are also able to voice their desires, and by doing so, they resist their total sellout. As subjects with desires they can no longer be reduced to mere objects of desire. This video is an attempt to articulate different writing positions and their respective desires. In Mexico City the virtual artist Maris Bustamante, who was tired of the local machismo, recently found an American husband via the Internet. For her, this is a way to formulate a different way of relating and to realize her desires in real life.

We know the Internet creates different subjectivities in the industrial and the developing worlds. But it is not enough to keep on lamenting that access is not available in the latter. From what I experienced during my last trip to Southeast Asia, Internet is not all that inaccessible anymore. In the metropolitan centers in the Philippines, one of the poorest countries in the region, young people have widespread access to the Internet. Every neighborhood has Internet cafes and they are always crowded with young people. Slum girls have access to the net here. It's not entirely inaccessible, but it is used differently. *Writing Desire* is an attempt to introduce these differing desires in the representation of virtual culture.

>Published in Socialtext 48, fall 1996, Roland B. Tolentino's insightful analysis of mail-order bride catalogs has been a vital resource for the video.

# _WRITING DESIRE
# 2000

*Writing Desire* handelt von der Beziehung zwischen Worten und dem Körper und der Erzeugung von Be gehren. Das Video befasst sich mittels elektronischer Kommunikationstechnologien mit dem Mediu der Schrift, wo Grenzen zwischen privaten Fantasien und öffentlichen Bereichen neu definiert werde müssen. In diesem komprimierten Raum unterzieht sich der Begriff des Selbsts Veränderungen, d auch Fragen von Grenzen, Geschlechtern und sexuellen Beziehungen betreffen. *Writing Desire* repr sentiert und praktiziert gleichzeitig die Kommunikation von Begehren zu einer Zeit, in der Fantasien fr und codiert, textualisiert, entkörpert das Kabelnetz bereisen können. Der isolierte private Raum de Schreibens inspiriert Fantasien und simuliert Emotionen, die für immer unerfüllt bleiben. Im Video brin Rosi Braidotti die Entkörperung von Sexualität mit einer langen (Literatur-)Geschichte von briefeschre benden Frauen in Verbindung, die ein Gegenüber fantasieren. Auf einer repräsentationellen Ebene fin det sie den Trend der verschwindenden Körper auch in den Bildern der verflüchtigten, anorexische narkotischen, vorpubertären, pädophilen Körpern wieder, welche die Mode vorschreibt.

*Writing Desire* verbindet die Kreation romantischen Begehrens durch die Schrift mit der Produktion vo Begehren in der Komsumkultur und untersucht die Kapitalisierung dieser Beziehungen im Internet. De Brautmarkt im Allgemeinen und der Jungfrauenmarkt im Besonderen, ist ein Ort der boomenden Kom merzialisierung sexueller Beziehungen: das Anbieten von Körpern, die Begehren und Genuss repräser tieren. Das Internet, das Austausch mit dem Ausland förderte und zu träumen erlaubte, ist zu einem Me dium des Kommerzes geworden, wo sich Mädchen vollständig Fremden zum Verkauf anbieten.

*russian.bride.com, tigerlilies.com* und *blossoms.com* (die jungfräulichen Cherry Blossoms), gehören z den populärsten Seiten, die eine grosse Anzahl von Frauen aus den ehemaligen Sovjet-Republiken un den Philippinen der globalen männlichen Kundschaft anbieten. Die Webseiten führen umfassende Bild archive mit anatomischen Information über die zukünftigen Bräute. Einige Adressen bieten sogar kurz Präsentationsvideos, in denen die Bewerberinnen ihre persönlichen Qualitäten sowie ihre Wünsche zur Ausdruck bringen können, wobei der Wunschteil immer an den Schluss gedrängt ist und oft zu kur kommt. In der digitalen Repräsentation der Russinnen und Filipinas werden die Körper auf ein Minimun visueller und textueller Information reduziert und die digitalen Netz-Videos technologisieren die Körpe noch stärker. Die Sklaven der Kolonialära haben sich in einen post-fordistischen Roboter verwandelt Die "e-mail-order Braut", ein äusserst blühendes Marktsegment in den neunziger Jahren, gründet au einer historischen Erzählung des weiblichen, farbigen Körpers als Objekt des Begehrens, das nur darauf wartet, erobert zu werden. Es ist kein Zufall, dass das weibliche Reservoir von Novosibirsk und den philippinischen Inseln für Frauen mit traditionellen Qualitäten angezapft wird, wenn diese in der industrialisierten Welt immer schwieriger zu haben sind. *getmarriednow.com*, eine sehr selektive "business class" Webseite, die russische Modelle mit Universitätsabschluss anbietet, kündete erst neulich an, dass sie per April 2000 weitere 2000 Videos von Frauen aus Novosibirsk, Russland, Sibirien und der Ukraine auf ihrer Webseite zur Verfügung stellen werden. Ihr 199$ Paket beinhaltet ein Rundflug von einer U.S. amerikanischen Stadt nach Novosibirsk und das Privileg, Richter beim Schönheitswettbewerb zu sein – ein Brautdéfilé, das für potentielle Ehemänner organisiert wird. Der Menschenmarkt boomt also auf dem Internet, die Resourcen sind fast unerschöpflich und die meisten dieser Unternehmen sind organisierte illegale Ringe. Die unverblühmte Vermarktung des weiblichen Körpers – visuell, diskursiv und körperlich – ist im grossen Stil an die Öffentlichkeit getreten.

Dank der neuen Möglichkeiten der übers Internet gebeamten Videoclips können die Angebotenen ihre Wünsche zum Ausdruck bringen und widerstehen somit einem totalen Ausverkauf. Als Subjekte mit Begehren können sie nicht länger auf ein Objekt des Begehrens reduziert werden. *Writing Desire* ist ein Versuch, verschiedene Schreibpositionen und deren Begehren miteinander zu verbinden. Die virtuelle Künstlerin Maris Bustamante in Mexico City, die dem lokalen Machismo zu entrinnen suchte, fand vor kurzem einen amerikanischen Mann übers Internet. Ihr hat das Medium dazu verholfen, eine andere Art von Beziehung zu formulieren und ihre Wünsche im materiellen Alltag umzusetzen.

Wir wissen, dass das Internet unterschiedliche Subjektivitäten bildet in der Industrie- und der Entwicklungswelt. Doch ist es meines Erachtens nicht genügend, den fehlenden Zugang in der zweiteren zu lamentieren. Während meiner letzten Reise nach Südostasien wurde mir klar, dass das Internet dort mittlerweile gar nicht so unzugänglich ist. In den städtischen Zentren in den Philippinen, die eines der ärmsten Länder in der Region sind, haben junge Leute breiten Zugang zum Netz. In jeder Nachbarschaft gibt es Internet Cafés, in die sich junge Leute drängen. Auch Slum-Mädchen haben hier Zugang zum Internet. Internet ist nicht unzugänglich, aber es wird anders gebraucht. *Writing Desire* ist so ein Versuch, diese unterschiedlichen Formen von Begehren in die Repräsentation virtueller Kultur einzubeziehen.

> Roland B. Tolentinos ausführliche Analyse von mail-order-bride Katalogen, publiziert in Socialtext 48, Herbst 1996, war eine wichtige Informationsquelle für das Video.

# _WRITING DESIRE

video script 23 min. 2000

With interviews with Rosi Braidotti, Yvonne Volkart, and Socorro Ballesteros

GEOGRAPHY IS IMBUED WITH THE NOTION OF PASSIVITY
FEMINIZED NATIONAL SPACES THAT AWAIT RESCUE
WITH THE PENETRATION OF FOREIGN CAPITAL

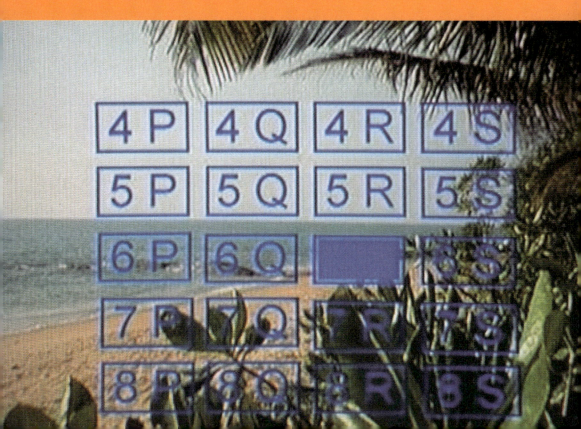

**Rosi**  The whole issue of writing and women's bodies of desire comes up in Western culture at a very particular moment in history. It comes up in late modernity, early postmodernity, if you wish, at a time when by all accounts the humanist culture is in a state of crisis. And then the issue of the emergence of female subjectivity or of all the subjectivities of other subjects, of different subjects is put on the agenda. So even the question "How do you write women's desire/How do you resignify the female body?" becomes itself a symptom of something in the phallogocentric system of representation not working anymore.

words prefigure the body

bodies are inscribed in words

pleasure is implicated through words

sex is consumed through words

that perform the body

that performs the words

the acts of providing words and bodies

and the act of consuming words and bodies

are entangled

the body is entangled

in words that recount

not a historical body

but a nostalgic body

in any case a narrated body

imbued with electronic desire

imbued with electronic pleasure

**Rosi** I do believe that bridging the distances and being able to create virtual or deferred connections and through that also doing collaborative writing and collective writing are definitely a possibility. Whether that in itself will resolve in a deepening or strengthening of women's exploration of body and desire, however, remains to be seen. What I'm worried about is the historical precedence, for instance, of epistolary literature, women writing the message in the bottle writing to far away non-existent loves, fantasizing interlocutors. With speed and simultaneity making their responses faster, there is some recognition coming in from them, at the same time, the fantasy level is pretty high. Nothing wrong with that, except that we have a long history of women fantasizing about love objects.

SAY, HAVE I TURNED INTO A PERMANENT LITTLE ICON ON YOUR SCREEN?

I THOUGHT OF RECORDING A VIDEO, SO I COULD SPEAK TO YOU. BUT THEN, IT WOULD SEEM SUCH A VIOLENT SHIFT FROM THE PURELY SEMANTIC LEVEL TO THE REPRESENTATIONAL IMAGE AND ELECTRONIC SOUNDS. IT'S ALL TOO WEIRD.

WE CAREFULLY TIMED THOSE INSTANCES WHEN WE ADDED A FURTHER LEVEL OF COMMUNICATION. DECRYPTING SLOWLY.

MUCH LATER WE EXCHANGED PICTURES THAT WEREN'T VERY REVEALING AND WE MADE FUN OF EACH OTHER'S DESIRE TO KNOW MORE ABOUT A PERSON THROUGH A PICTURE OF 72 DPI.

**Rosi** On the one hand, I think on a level of exploration it is interesting and experientially very rich but we have to look carefully at the fantasies involved in this. The fantasies of either bridging the distance or deferring it indefinitely, so you never need to confront the effect of your words upon the other, or the effects of the fantasy, or the effect of the collectively or jointly constructed fantasy. It may not be something that in itself is liberatory. I do think the Net is a very large scene of fantasy, a phantasmatic scene. Which is great, I'm all for it. Fantasies in the unconscious construct the social, so I'm not opposed to that, but to declare it sort of liberatory just because of that is really a little bit optimistic. I find that a lot of these long distance relationships do regenerate both the fantasy of the impossible object and a tremendous sort of melancholia. It engenders a culture of premature loss of the object and women are good at melancholia; we are very good at loss and mourning even before we get the object of desire. Although the aspiration of a long-distance, deferred fantasy can be productive, it does engender a culture of premature melancholia. I just do think the body needs the experience. I think that the physical embodied self needs the experience. Some of it can be produced and reproduced virtually, a lot of it not.

WHEN YOU GAVE ME A BODY IMAGE — YOU RELAXING IN THE BATHTUB — I WAS
DEBATING FOR A MOMENT WHETHER I SHOULD ACKNOWLEDGE IT OPENLY OR DOWN-
LOAD IT INTO THE SUBLIMINAL TEXT.
AND?
WELL, I DECIDED TO ADDRESS IT BECAUSE IT SEEMS A WAY OF FINDING A
LANGUAGE FOR QUESTIONS OF DESIRE AND SUBLIMATION. IT'S NOT THAT I
CAN'T STAND TO SUBLIMATE ANY LONGER, I THINK MY POTENTIAL IS A LOT
HIGHER THAN YOURS.
DON'T YOU EVER TRY TO OUT-SUBLIMATE ME.

IN THE ISOLATION OF THE PRIVATE SPACE OF WRITING, RELEASED FROM THE
EXPERIENCE OF PHYSICAL PROXIMITY, PERSONAL FANTASIES REACH A
HEIGHTENED INTENSITY. THE SENSATION OF PURE DESIRE. THE PERFECT ONE,
THE ONE EMANATING FROM NO IMAGE, NO AURA, NO VOICE, NO BODY, NO PHYSI-
CAL EXPERIENCE WHATSOEVER, ONE THAT EMERGES COMPLETELY FROM ONE'S
IMAGINATION. CULTURALLY CODED, OF COURSE. ALWAYS. SUSPENDED REALITIES
THAT SIMULATE A PERMANENT STATE OF BEING IN LOVE. A FANTASY FOREVER
UNFULFILLED IN ITS ENACTMENT. A SENSE OF ALWAYS APPROACHING BUT NEVER
REACHING.

emails conquer distance
emails maintain distance
emails mark exchanges
and promise fulfillment
the fulfillment of promise
the bride is the promise
the groom is the promise
no longer physically delivered
but electronically generated

in the sexual economy
the body is eroticized
is made generic
is made anonymous
emptied of its specific identities
to signify the collective exotic
to engender desire
the desire to be conquered

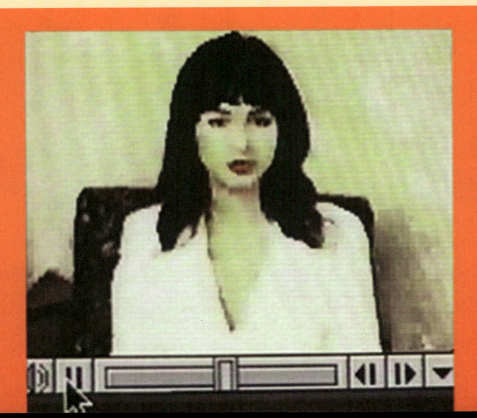

**Maris** Despues de tomar la decision de encontrarme un compañero y despues de hacer un minucioso estudio dentro de mi entorno mexicano al que he llamado "La Cuna del Machismo", me di cuenta de que una mujer como yo: 50 anios, artista no tradicional, feminista, viuda y madre, profesora universitaria y radical por voluntad propia, solo podia asustar como una Fem-Flasher, a los posibles varones de mi eleccion.

Estando el elenco a mi alcance muy "flaco" decidi que las hi-techs estar ahi para ayudarnos a encontrar a nuestros iguales, donde quiera que estos se encuentren. Prendi mi "interneta" y afloraron las famosas dating-online webs. Venciendo la culpa intelectual que me atosigaba y como se ofrece la proteccion del anonimato, otra vez como Fem-Flasher, coloque mi perfil para anunciarme como pareja ideal de un hombre muy especial.

John me encontro ahi, y despues de seis meses de escribirnos y vencer algunas dificultades como el miedo que me dio el saber que era militar, Teniente Coronel de los US Marine Corps y romper mis prejuicios de artista contemporanea mexicana, descubrimos que eramos iguales. Que buscabamos las mismas formas de seguir desarrollandonos como individuos de fin de siglo y asi llego el dia en que decidio venir para romper la virtualidad y entrar en la realidad. Realmente nos enamoramos much antes de vernos en persona. Y como la quimica fisica si funciono, nos comprometimos. Hoy tenemos una nueva familia.

**Maris** When I decided to find myself a companion I made a meticulous examination of my Mexican environment, which I would call the "Cradle of Machismo." I realized that a woman like me - fifty years old, untraditional artist, feminist, widow and mother, University professor and radical of my own will - would only scare any prospective man away for fear of a Fem-Flasher.

Since the listings within my reach were very meager, I decided that the hi-techs are here to help us find kindred spirits, wherever they may be. So I went on the Internet and the famous dating-online sites flashed up. I overcame the intellectual guilt that haunted me and thanks to the anonymity, I posted my profile, again as Fem-Flasher, and announced myself as an ideal partner for a very special man.

John met me there. First I was scared, when I found out that he was a lieutenant colonel at the U.S. Marine Corps. But after 6 months of corresponding and overcoming these difficulties, I broke my prejudice as a contemporary Mexican artist and we found out that we had a lot in common. At the end of the century, we were looking for the same kind of individual development. So the day came, when we decided to break the virtuality and enter reality. But we really fell in love much before meeting and since the physical chemistry worked well, we committed ourselves. Today we have a new family.

**Yvonne** Ich denke, dass die ganze e-mail Geschichte so ein narzistisches Element in einem beflügelt, dass man sich selber als aktiv Begehrende empfindet und sich gespiegelt bekommt und dass so ein wahnsinniger Begehrensstrom am Laufen gehalten wird, ohne dass er durch irgendwas getrübt würde, was in der Realität die Sache nochmals zum stoppen oder stocken oder umfliessen bringen könnte.

Das Besondere an der Sache ist eigentlich, dass man in diesen e-mails eine Liebesgeschichte kreiert, in der man selbst die Protagonisten ist. Das Interessante ist, dass man sich in diesen Liebesdiskurs einschreibt und gleichzeitig diesen Liebesdiskurs selbst weiterschreibt, mit einem schriftlichen Medium – also dieses Moment der Schrift in der Absenz der realen Körper – das Ganze ist eigentlich nur in der Schrift verkörpert. Gleichzeitig ist der sexuelle Diskurs so wichtig, weil er etwas Unmittelbares in einem auslöst und eine sexuelle Befriedigung suggeriert, wenn man ein sexuell aufgeladenes email liest. Es wäre aber falsch, daraus zu schliessen, dass es den Körper ersetzt. Der Körper verschwindet nicht, sondern ist total präsent in der Schrift.

**Yvonne** I think this whole story about e-mail inspires a narcissistic element in oneself. You experience yourself as an actively desiring person who gets mirrored and this maintains an incredible stream of desire, troubled by nothing, in reality, which would bring this stream to a halt or flag or redirect it.

What's special about it is that with the e-mails you create a love story in which you are the protagonists. That is what is so interesting about it. You inscribe yourselves into this love discourse at the same time as you continue writing it through e-mails: in a written medium. What is important is the act of writing while the bodies are absent, it's all embodied in the writing. At the same time, the sexual discourse becomes important because it inspires an immediacy in oneself, suggesting that one gets some sort of satisfaction from receiving a message that is sexually charged. It would be wrong to infer that it replaces the body. The body doesn't disappear but is strongly present in the writing.

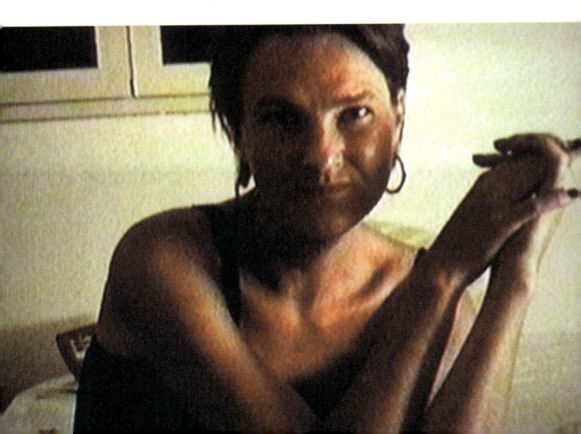

I DON'T THINK I WANT TO ENTER YOUR REALITY BECAUSE IT WILL COST WHAT W
HAVE NOW. AND SINCE THAT'S A LOT BETTER THAN WHAT I USUALLY GET, IT WOUL
BE FOOLISH.

**Rosi**   I think there are several factors involved in this disembodiment
of sexuality or this flight from the sexual body. The psychopathology of
the youth also tells a story. The most widespread disease is no longer
immediately sexually related. It is anorexia. It has to do with eating.
Eating disorders are the telling symptoms of the advanced population of
the world. And it tells a long story about the kind of bodies that are
being constructed in advanced societies like ours and the importance
of fitness and slimness and the skinny body. Consequently eating disorders are necessarily the ones that emerge.

It's a strange disembodiment that comes from a young culture that takes
sexuality for granted and that fits into an absolutely oppressive model
of the super-duper anorexic body, to a whole commodification industry
through the heroine chic of Calvin Klein, through anorexic Lolitas,
through a kind of narcotic culture which is camouflaged and latent and
never manifest, which flirts with these adolescent, ill-defined almost
androgynous bodies. We are flirting with bodies that aren't really
there, that are evaporating, that are as slim as possible, if possible

non-existent. There is almost a sociological rendition of it that you can see on a daily basis. The body is a contested zone. It is supposed to be constructed in a way that blurs sexual difference - androgeny - but in a sense it also blurs sexual desirability. It's almost a flirt with the ugly, the mutant, the illde-fined; it's deeply pedophilic in some way. It's quite disturbing in the advanced world. So, there is something in the social imaginary, but it is the flight from what we would call the body, a reduction of the body to something ethereal, sexually as non-adult as possible.

bodies move through various spheres
passing through transnational spaces
shopping for another body
that represents desire
that represents pleasure
bodies turn to images
bodies turn to words
bodies turn to codes
culturally coded
always
a simple electronic device
has allowed to order bodies
passing borders
passing officials
passing through transnational wires
to some proper place

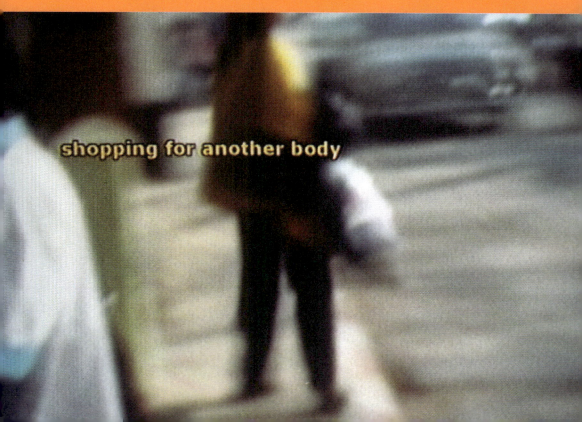

**Soki**  Isn't it that when you open a web page you have to pin in your card number and before you can have access to this information, you have to pay?

One day I chanced upon this homepage on the internet. I was really surprised to see high school students, I think they are friends, ten of them, advertising themselves, in their own handwriting and with their photos, to prospective husbands: We are looking for foreign husbands between the ages of 45 and 60. We are Catholics, we are industrious, we don't drink and we don't smoke, and we think that we can be better wives for foreigners.

In the context of the globalized economy, women are commodified due to this technology. It facilitates easy transport and information to the buyers and allows the agents to publicize women and children to their prospective buyers in the global community. There are agents that go from one community to another recruiting for mail-order brides. It started as just a pen pal club actually, a legitimate pen pal club, and even now many young girls and women are not aware that they are already being used and publicized and sold to the Internet. Most of them are syndicated operations.

she is beautiful and feminine
she is loving and traditional
she is humble and devoted
she likes to listen to mellow music
the smile is her rhetorical gesture
she believes in a lasting marriage
and a happy home
she is the copy of the First World's past

I would like to share my future
with a man who would
understand me completely
and help me in my life and in my work
good bye
so long

Rosi Braidotti, Philsopher, Utrecht University
Yvonne Volkart, Independent art critic and curator, Zurich
Maris Bustamante, Virtual artist, Mexico City
Socorro Ballesteros, International Organisation for Migration, Manila

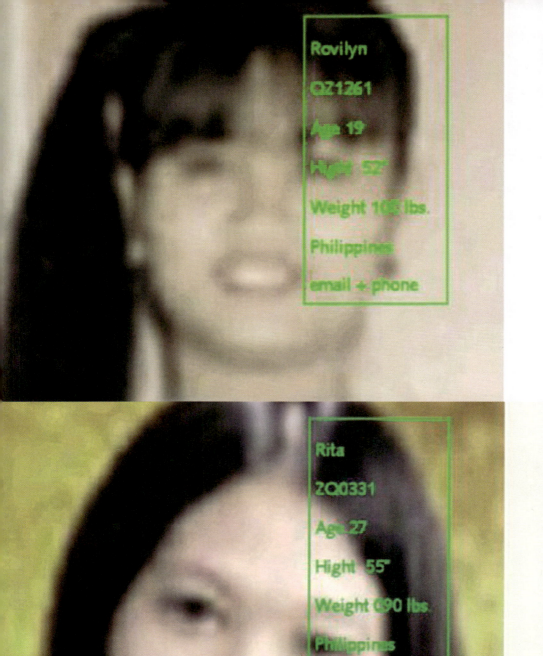

From an interview with Rosi Braidotti at the women's studies department of the University in Utrecht, summer 1999. Apart from the segments used in the script for *Writing Desire*, I was particularly interested in women's motivation to enter virtual relationships.

**The mail-order-bride market is a clear sign that Western men are frustrated with the equal roles women claim in postmodern relationships and that men are looking for traditional brides in the Third World to fill the domestic place that has been evacuated by the working woman. Do you think virtual relationships are also a sign of women's frustration with unchanged gender relations in everyday domestic life?**

R o s i    There is an escape-into-fantasy element: Emancipation has its limits so let's at least do that. I also think there is a general loneliness involved. I do think that particularly for heterosexual women of a certain generation, of say forty plus, who have done a certain itinerary or have gone through the left feminism in our part of the world and have changed tremendously - the generation that has changed themselves and the world – has a hard time finding male partners who have the same amount of challenge and imagination in them. You just have to open newspapers and look at dating services and read the stuff that's being written about the new single woman, watch the soap operas about single women of all kinds. They were divorcees, never married, career women, closet lesbians, out lesbians, others, teenagers, pregnant teenagers, all categories of single women who just don't find partners. And that has something to do with masculinity not wanting to change, not being able to change at the same rhythm as femininity. And this has created a new type of urban loneliness, not a dramatic, melancholic kind, but genuine. A lot of career women talk about this and if you look at how the career woman is represented in media and popular culture it's quite appalling. A few years ago there was a posthuman, postmodernist art exhibition, a critique of humanism, and at the entrance the representative of the status quo was the career woman in a blue suit carrying the attaché case. She has come to represent law and order. How that came to be is something I would really like to know. It's coming across in a lot of the cultural studies literature. The single career woman, aggressive, assertive who has difficulties finding a partner as the representative of law and order, and the men, of course, as the creative element.

It is the single woman that requires the escort services and the whole sex industry that would eventually cater to the needs of this new type of loneliness. It's a luxury problem of the advanced world but I think it's genuine. Particularly with the population growing older and these women living longer you are looking at a sexual desert, an erotic desert that wasn't there for non-emancipated generations because your sex life was over at 37 anyway and from there on you were old. But now, with the boundaries stretching, you are looking at much longer erotic lives and longer stretches of solitude for these women. So for this population, the electronic medium could be a very interesting one, an interesting way of constructing relationships. So it's not only about fantasy, it's also about getting out of this new hyper-individualized woman as a product of a whole system, the molecularization of the population which has happened as a result of post-industrialism. Somehow men can purchase love and partners a lot more easily and the different age couple is not symmetrical. A man with a younger woman is a banality; a woman with a younger man is blasphemy. Until this changes, the Internet is certainly a place for experiments.

# Trafficking and Trading

# _TRAFFICKING AND TRADING
# (WORKING TITLE)
# A DOUBLE FEATURE
# 2000

This collaborative video with Simin Farkhondeh is a work in progress to be released in fall 2000. The video is a double feature in the sense that each of us shot with her cameras and will edit an independent video from this footage; in the end we will simply stick them together. The project is the outcome of our common interest in tracing the migration of women for labor, particularly sex work. Girls and women are the precious new cargo of the nineties. We visited Manila and the U.S. army bases in the Philippines, Bangkok, and along the Thai border to Laos and Burma as well as the sex beach resorts in Phuket. Since the trafficking of women for commercial sex is internationally syndicated, it is only fitting that gender politics also be conducted with a transnational perspective.

The opening of borders to tourism and trade in the Mekong region has increased the flow of populations across borders for trade (licit and illicit) and labor, with major implications for the sex industry. It is an area characterized by ethnic diversity, cultural pluralism, and linguistic complexity. These minorities crosscut political boundaries. There are a vast number of distinct languages from different language families. Many of these are unwritten languages with no indigenous scripts. Highland women, who don't speak the major languages, are particularly vulnerable to trafficked or non-trafficked sex work and to the related threat of HIV/AIDS.

In any smuggling operation, the size of the product determines the methods of transport. Unlike drugs, which are easily concealed, human beings are a fragile cargo that calls attention to itself. Therefore, corruption is nearly always less costly than concealment. Most trafficked persons are moved across international boundaries in more or less plain view.

To understand the structural underpinnings and implications of the flow of women into the Thai sex industry it may be useful to distinguish conceptually between "trafficking" and "trade". Trafficking involves recruitment and transportation of women within and across national borders by means of violence or threat, debt bondage, deception, or other forms of coercion. "Trade," on the other hand, is merely descriptive of the exchange involved in the entry into sex work and makes no judgment about the cause or process of that entry. From speaking with trafficked women in a number of geographic and political contexts, it becomes evident that the line between these definitions is anything but clear-cut.

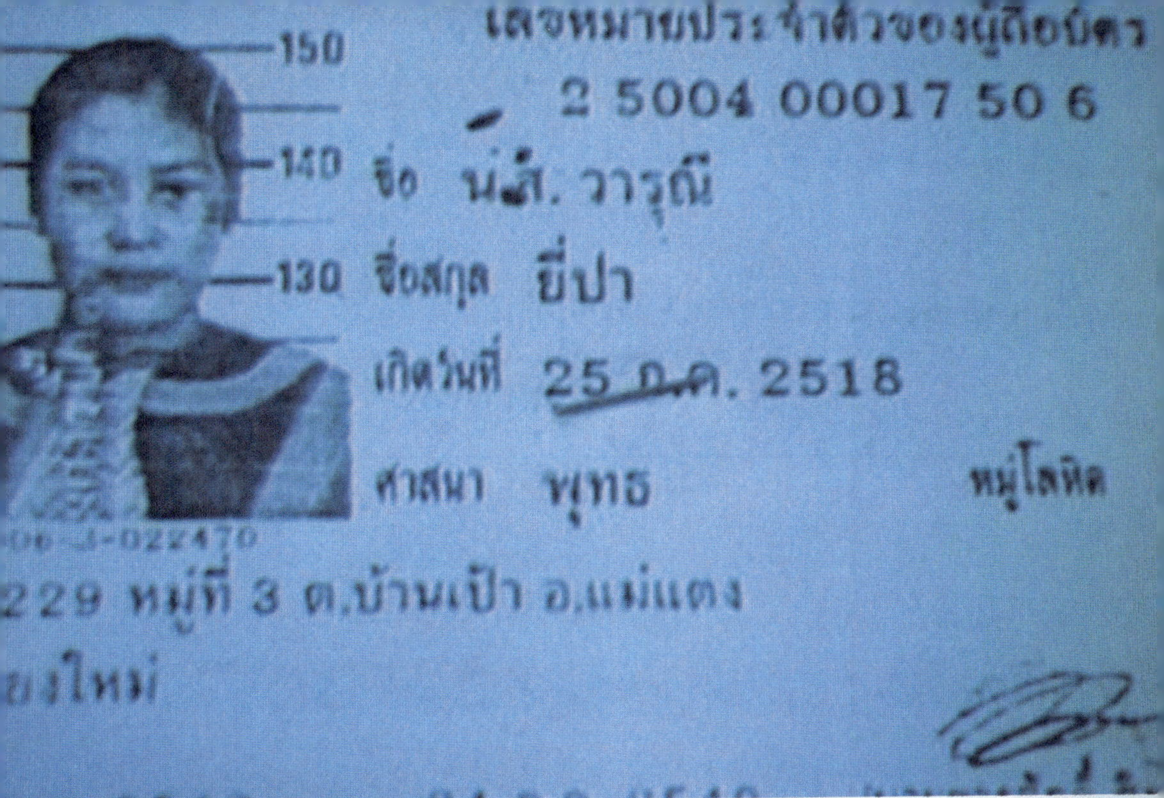

เลขหมายประจำตัวของผู้ถือบัตร
2 5004 00017 50 6

ชื่อ น.ส. วารุณี

ชื่อสกุล ยี่ปา

เกิดวันที่ 25 ก.ค. 2518

ศาสนา พุทธ    หมู่โลหิต

229 หมู่ที่ 3 ต.บ้านเป้า อ.แม่แตง
ชียงใหม่

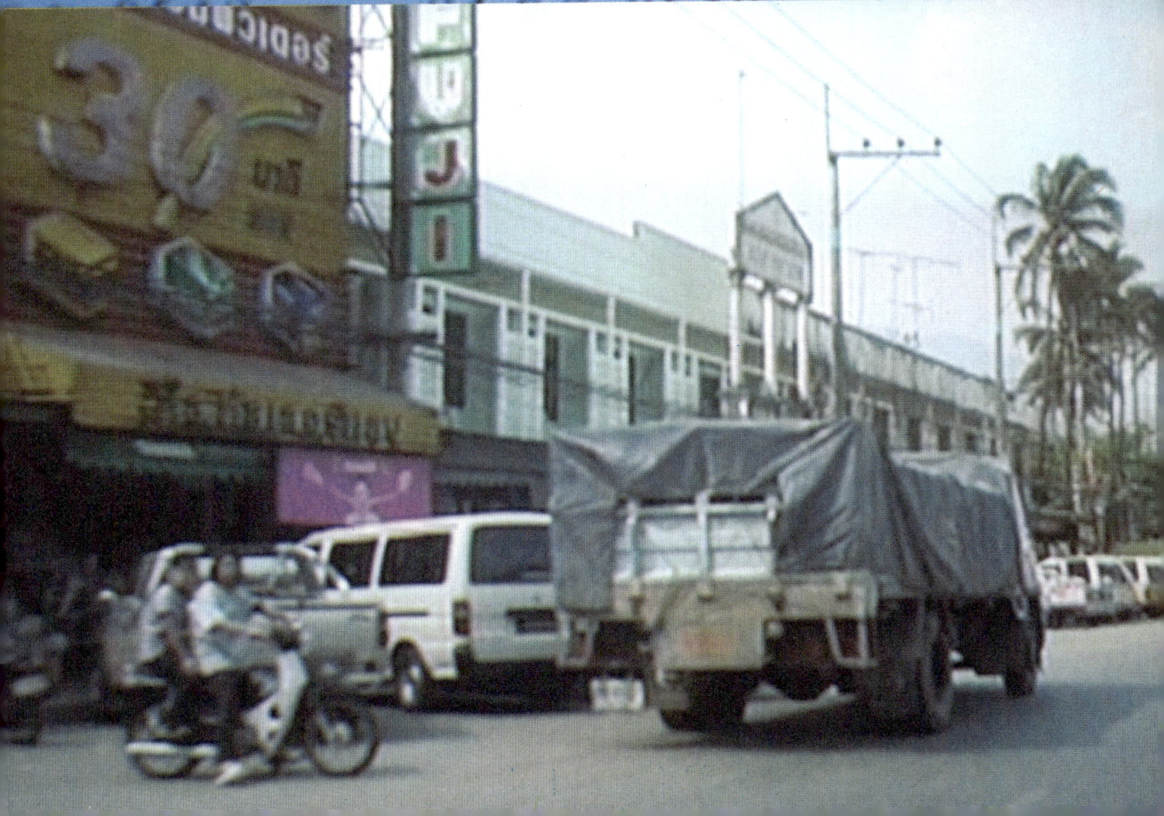

Thailand, which has been a sending country for a long time, has turned into a receiving country in recent years. Only a third of the prostitutes in Bangkok are Thai. Since 1991, a great number of women from the neighboring countries Laos, China, Vietnam, and Burma have entered Thailand, replacing the women who have gone abroad. Laos has become a transshipper of persons for Thailand. Hundreds if not thousands of Burmese girls and women have been trafficked over the border and into brothels. The entry of girls into sex work involves a complex of interlocking networks – both formal and informal, commercial and non-commercial – crisscrossing borders throughout the Upper Mekong region. There is a flow of females moving north in one area, south in another. Asia is in the midst of a crisis. For Burmese women the economic and political situation is so dismal that they make voluntary choices to start their journey and cross the border with the intention of entering the sex industry. Most of the Chinese girls and women who enter the region are not so much fleeing abject poverty and political oppression but pursuing a better, more exciting life.

In the Philippines, too, women have migrated in flocks to neighboring countries in recent years, despite and because of the Asian economic crisis. Since the Marco regime, both tourism and the export of labor have been pushed to gain foreign currencies. There are an estimated 400,000 Filipinos in Japan and 90% of them are women. Most of them work in the entertainment business. The bride market is a highly lucrative business in the Philippines. Filipinas are traded to husbands in Taiwan, Korea, China, Japan and Australia.

The video Writing Desire addresses the bride market on the Internet. Trading and Trafficking gets more into the structural conditions around this mega business. In Manila, high school girls and young women are recruited by neighbors, family members, and friends to become brides for foreigners or to go into the entertainment industry abroad. Around lunchtime, the most popular radio station in Metro Manila blasts trendy commercials recruiting girls to become online pen pals and put their photos on web sites. Many of these pen pal clubs are syndicated organizations for the trafficking of brides.

Subic Bay in Olongapo and Angeles City are two former U.S. military bases that played an important role during practically every war in Southeast Asia. When a ship docked in one of these harbors, 10,000 service men would go ashore. Around the camps Americans established a sex industry to cater to their soldiers. In 1991, the two governments signed a contract to close the bases, but recently talks on again being able to dock ships there and use the facilities have resumed. During the wars in Vietnam and Korea the American army used these areas for their rest and recreation programs. Some of the veterans have become expats, have settled in these areas, and continue to run brothels, bars, and restaurants.

Many of these long-term conditions have to be kept in mind if we are to understand the new forms of trafficking of women since the opening of markets and borders. For a great number of young women travel and seasonal movements between and across national boundaries will be an indispensable basis for survival.

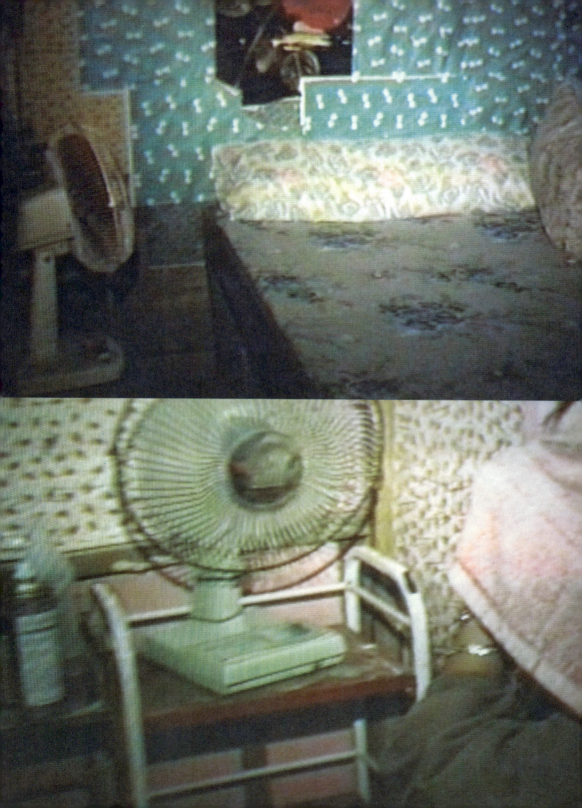

Angeles U.S. base, Philippines

# _TRAFFICKING AND TRADING
# (ARBEITSTITEL)
# EIN DOPPELVIDEO
# 2000

Dieses kollaborative Video mit Simin Farkhondeh ist zur Zeit der Publikation des Buches noch in Arbeit, es soll im Herbst 2000 fertig werden. Es ist insofern eine Doppelproduktion als dass wir zusammen gereist und jetzt im Begriff sind, zwei unabhängige Videos zu machen, die am Schluss zusammengefügt werden. Das Projekt ist das Resultat unseres gemeinsamen Interesses an Fragen der Arbeitsmigration von Frauen, besonders Sexarbeit. Mädchen und Frauen sind die wertvolle neue Fracht der neunziger Jahre. Wir haben Manila und die U.S.-amerikanischen Militärstützpunkte in den Philippinen besucht, Thailand und die Grenze zu Laos und Burma und die Sex-Strandorte Phuket im Süden bereist. Da der Schmuggel mit Frauen für kommerziellen Sex international organisiert ist, sollte Geschlechterpolitik ebenfalls mit einer internationalen Perspektive betrieben werden.

Die Öffnung der Grenzen für Handel und Tourismus in der Mekong-Region hat die Zunahme des grenzüberschreitenden Bevölkerungsflusses für den legalen und illegalen Handel und den Arbeitmarkt angetrieben, mit schwerwiegenden Folgen für die Sex Industrie. Diese Region ist von ethnischer Vielfältigkeit, kulturellem Pluralismus und sprachlicher Komplexität gekennzeichnet. Die Minoritäten überschreiten politische Grenzen. Es gibt hier eine grosse Anzahl unterschiedlicher Sprachen von verschiedenen Sprachbäumen. Die meisten sind ungeschriebene Sprachen, ohne eigene Schrift. Hochlandfrauen, die keine der Hauptsprachen sprechen, sind für den legalen und illegalen Frauenhandel für die Sexindustrie besonders anfällig und für die einhergehende Gefahr, sich mit HIV zu infizieren.

In jeder Schmuggel- und Schlepperoperation ist die Grösse des Objektes für die Methode des Transportes ausschlaggebend. Im Gegensatz zu Drogen, die einfach versteckt werden können, sind Menschen eine fragile Fracht, die Aufmerksamkeit auf sich lenkt. Deshalb ist Bestechung meist billiger als Verbergen. Also werden die meisten Leiten bei vollem Tageslicht über die Grenze geschleppt. Um die strukturellen Hintergründe und Folgen des Zustroms von Frauen in die Sexindustrie zu verstehen, ist es sinnvoll, zwischen "Trafficking" und "Trade" konzeptuell zu unterscheiden. Trafficking/Frauenhandel beinhaltet Rekrutierung und binnen- oder grenzüberschreitenden Transport von Frauen durch Bedrohung, Gewalt, Verschuldung, Täuschung oder andere Formen von Zwang. Trade/Handel hingegen beschreibt lediglich den Austausch von Sexarbeit und beurteilt weder Grund noch Vorgang des Eintretens in diesen Handel. In Gespächen mit gehandelten Frauen in verschiedenen geografischen und politischen Kontexten wird aber deutlich, dass die Linie zwischen diesen Definitionen nicht klar gezogen sind.

Thailand, das für lange Zeit ein Senderland war, hat sich in den letzten Jahren in ein Empfängerland verwandelt. Gerade noch ein Drittel der Prostituierten in Bangkok sind Thai. Seit 1991 sind eine grosse Anzahl von Frauen aus den benachbarten Ländern Laos, China, Vietnam und Burma nach Thailand gekommen, um die ins Ausland gezogenen Thaifrauen zu ersetzen. Laos ist mitunter zu einem Personentransport-Unterhändler für Thailand geworden. Hunderte, wenn nicht Tausende von burmesischen Mädchen und Frauen sind über die Grenze und direkt in Bordelle verkauft worden. Der Eintritt von Mädchen in die Sexarbeit bedarf ein komplexes, ineinandergreifendes Netzwerk – formell und informell, kommerziell und nicht-kommerziell – das sich kreuz und quer durch die Mekong-Region erstreckt. So kann sich ein Strom von Frauen in einem Gebiet gegen Norden bewegen, in einem anderen gegen Süden. Asien befindet sich inmitten einer Krise. Für Burmesinnen ist die politische und ökonomische Situation so trist, dass sie gar nicht mehr gezwungen werden müssen, sondern mittlerweile freiwillig nach Thailand in die Sexindustrie ziehen. Die meisten chinesischen Mädchen und Frauen, die im Norden einwandern, flüchten nicht vor Elend, Armut und politischer Unterdrückung, sondern um einem besseren, aufregenderen, städtischen Leben nachzugehen.

In den Philippinen sind viele Frauen in den letzten Jahren trotz Asienkrise ebenfalls in Nachbarländer gezogen. Das Marcos-Regime hat Tourismus und den Export von Arbeitskräften als Mittel zur Devisenbeschaffung angeheizt. Von den geschätzten 400'000 Filipinos in Japan sind 90% Frauen. Die meisten von ihnen arbeiten in der Unterhaltungsindustrie. Der Brautmarkt ist ebenfalls ein höchst lukratives Business in den Philippinen. Filippinas werden Männern in Taiwan, Korea, China, Japan und Australien vermittelt. Während das Video *Writing Desire* den Brautmarkt übers Internet behandelt, geht *Trafficking and Trading* stärker auf die strukturellen Bedingungen dieses Megadeals ein. In Manila werden Schulmädchen und junge Frauen von Nachbarinnen, Familienmitgliedern und Freunden rekrutiert, um Ausländer zu heiraten oder in die Unterhaltungsindustrie ins Ausland zu gehen. Der lokale Radiosender wirbt mit trendigen Musikanzeigen um Mädchen, die für on-line Briefclubs ihre Fotos einschicken. Viele dieser Clubs gehören organisierten Trafficking-Ringen.

Subic Bay in Olongapo und Angeles City sind zwei ehemalige U.S.-Militärstützpunkte, die praktisch in jedem Krieg in Südostasien eine wichtige Rolle gespielt haben. Wenn ein Schiff in einem dieser Hafen anlegt, gehen 10'000 Dienstmänner an Land. Um die Militärlager herum haben die Amerikaner eine Sexindustrie eingerichtet, die den Soldaten zudient. Während der Kriege in Vietnam und Korea haben die Amerikaner diese Zonen für ihre Erholungs- und Vergnügungsprogramme benutzt. Einige der Veteranen haben sich endgültig in dieser Gegend niedergelassen und leiten weiterhin Bordelle, Bars und Restaurants. 1991 haben die beiden Regierungen die Schliessung dieser Militärbasen vertraglich vereinbart, vor kurzem wurden aber wieder Gespräche über die Benützung der Anlagen aufgenommen. Die U.S.-Army verspricht der Philippinischen Armee Militärtraining und technologische Modernisierung, aber lokale Organisationen wehren sich gegen das come-back der Militärs.

Langjährige Bedingungen, sowie Handels- und politische Abkommen müssen jedenfalls berücksichtigt werden, wenn wir die neuen Formen von Frauenhandel, die sich seit der Öffnung der Märkte und Grenzen entwickeln, verstehen wollen. Für eine grosse Zahl von jungen Frauen ist Reisen und die saisonale Bewegung zwischen und über nationale Grenze eine unentbehrliche Überlebensgrundlage geworden.

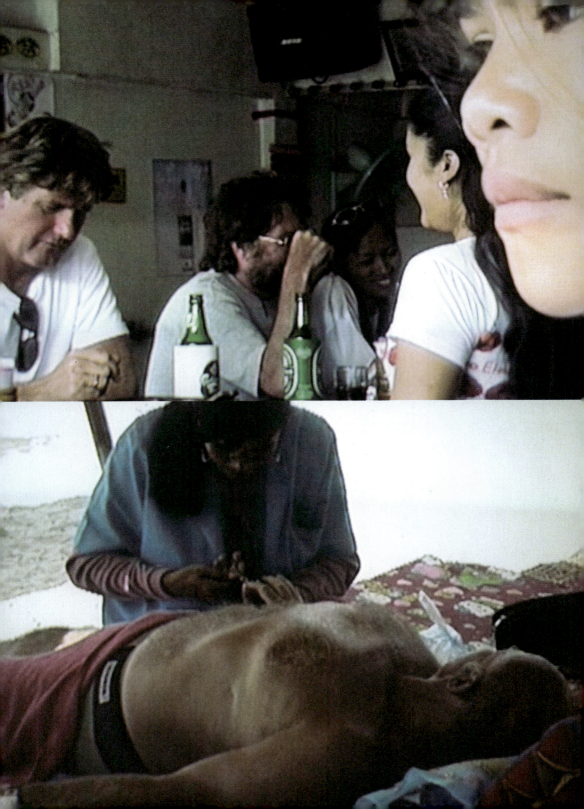

Patpong, Bangkok

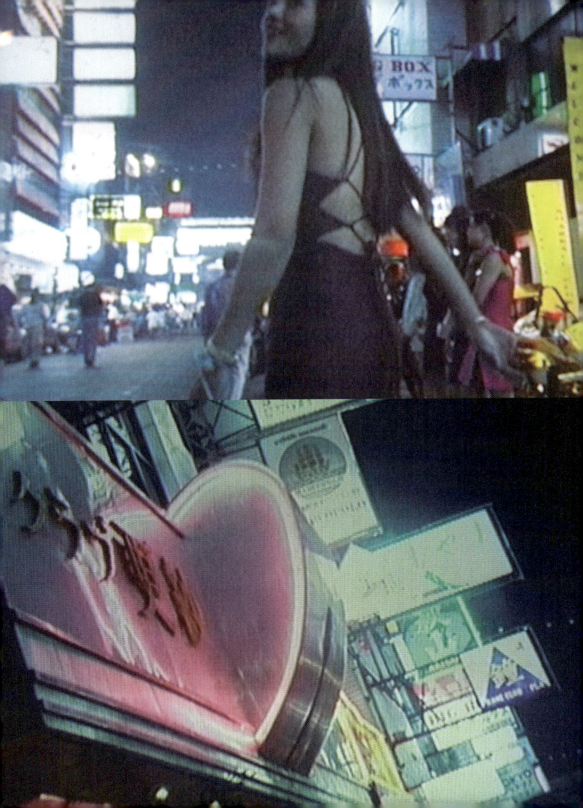

# _PROJECT INFORMATION

Exhibitions

**Border Project**
Whitney Independent Study Program, New York, 1987/88
Americas, Expo Sevilla 1992, Monasterio de Santa Clara, Moguer
When tekkno turns to sound of poetry, Kunstwerke, Berlin, 1995
Environ 27 ans (peutêtre un peu plus), Athenée, Geneva, 1997

**Lexicon Hispanica**
American Fine Arts Company, New York, 1989
The Elements: Sex Money Politics Religion, Real Art Ways, New Haven, 1989
Spent. Currency, Security and Art on Deposit, The New Museum, New York, 1990
White Columns, New York, 1991
The Third Rail, John Post Lee Gallery, New York, 1991

**Afghan Collection**
White Columns, New York, 1991

**Global Food**
Wann wird es kritisch in der Kunst? Helmhaus, Zürich, 1991
Museo Universitario del Chopo, Mexico City, 1992
Las Nuevas Majas, Contemporary Art Foundation, Mexico City, 1993

**Platzwechsel / Changing Places**
A collaborative exhibition project with Christian Philip Müller, Mark Dion and Tom Burr, curated by Mendes Bürgi at the Kunsthalle Zürich and the National History Museum, Mai-July 1995
Exhibition Catalog German/English

**Mediale Identitäten / Mediated Identities**
Strategies of Art in the Nineties
Exhibition at Kunsthaus Glarus curated by Annette Schindler, June-September
and media workshop in Klöntal, July 1996

**Kültür – A gender project from Istanbul**
Ayse Durakbasa, Ayla Yüce, Meral Özbek, Yasemin Baydar, Seyma Reisoglu, Meltem
Ahiska, Gülsün Karamustafa, Tül Akbal, and Nihan Turan, curated by Ursula Biemann
Shedhalle Zurich, April-May 1996

**Kültür – A city project**
A collaboration of Tül Akbal, Yasemin Baydar, Ursula Biemann, Meral Özbek,
and Seyma Reisoglu
5th International Istanbul Biennal, October 1997

**Performing the Border**
Video, 43 minutes 1999
Women Make Movies, New York, www.wmm.com
V-Tape for Canada, www.vtape.org
Lumpenvision netcast at www.lumpen.com
Biennial of the Moving Image, St-Gervais, Geneva, palmares award, 1999
Kasseler Film- und Video Festival, 1999
Women in the Director's Chair Festival, Chicago, 2000
Werkleitz Festival 2000

**Writing Desire**
Video, 23 minutes 2000
Swiss Institute New York, March 2000
Shedhalle Zürich, Juni 2000

# Video presentations/lectures

**1999**
Next Cyberfeminist Internat'l symposium, Rotterdam (trailer)
next 5 minutes conference, Amsterdam (trailer)
Studio One, Clocktower, New York
Video Cultures, Zentrum für Kunst und Medien, Karlsruhe
Depot, Vienna
Nations, Pollinations, Dislocations: Changing Imaginary Borders in the Americas,
The Americas on the Verge, Vancouver

Cerlac, York University, Toronto and Globalisation Institute, McMaster University, Toronto
Dialoge & Debatten, symposium on feminist positions in contemporary art, die Höge/Bremen
L'adieu au siècle, La Comédie de Genève
Burials on the Border, University of New Mexico
Encuentro Iberoamericano de Teatro, performance festival in Cadiz, Spain
Komunales Kino, Freiburg i.B., Germany
Shedhalle, Zurich

## 2000
Kunsthalle Basel
Clairmont College, Los Angeles; University of California, Los Angeles; University of California, San Diego
CalArts, Los Angeles, and Cinematik, Tijuana Mexico
International Frauenuniversität, Hannover/Hamburg
Fresa, Migration Seminar, Luzern
Crossroads in Cultural Studies, Birmingham
Manifesta 3, Ljubljana, Slovenija
American Studies Conference, Detroit
Dartmouth University
Pacific Film Archive, San Francisco
Brazilian tour of 12 cities

## Publications

### Zwischenräume / Interespacios
Bilder und Texte von Frauen in der Fremde
Imagenes y textos de mujeres en lo extraño

A German/Spanish photo-text book with contributions by Lyana Amaya, Santusa Herbas, Jacqueline Isler dos Santos, Monica Senn Zegarra, Angela Ceballso, Pierrette Malatesta with an introduction by Carmen Real in collaboration with Femia, Zurich
eFeF Verlag, Zürich and Düsseldorf, November 1993, ISBN 3-905493-52-7
website with the Institute of International Visual Arts, London
www.iniva.org/celluloid

### Kültür – ein Gender-Projekt aus Istanbul
Istanbul'dan bir "toplumsal cinsiyet" projesi
Kunst.Feminismus.Migration / Sanat.Feminizm.Göç

with texts by Ursula Biemann, Ayse Durakbasa, Ayla Yüce, Meral Özbek, Yasemin Baydar, Seyma Reisoglu, Meltem Ahiska, Gülsün Karamustafa, Tül Akbal and Nihan Turan and Sema Erder. Chronology of the Feminist Movement in Istanbul.
edited by Ursula Biemann, Shedhalle Verlag Zürich 1997, German/Turkish, ISBN 3-907829-06-9

distributed by b_books, Berlin  tel. +49306117844 / b_books@txt.de

Women's Library and Information Center, Fener Mahallesi, Fener P.T.T., Haliç, 34220 Istanbul. Tel +90 212 534 9550 / Fax +90 212 523 7408

**Hors Sol**
Reflexionen zur Ausstellungspraxis
Réflexions sur la pratique de l'exposition
with texts by Judith Barry, Ursula Biemann, Beatrice von Bismarck, Andrea Fraser, Sylvia Kafhesy, Stephan Geene and Renate Lorenz, Catherine Queloz, Philip Urspruch and others.
edited by Catherine Queloz and Ursula Biemann, Sous-sol Genève and Shedhalle Zürich 1996, shedhalle@access.ch
German/French, ISBN 3-907829-04-2

# Published Articles

Border Project photo piece in Below Texas/Below the Equator, The New Observations, no 89 (1991)
Positionen zur postkolonialen Diskussion MOMA (1995)
I do not intend to speak about, just speak nearby Die Filme von Trinh T. Minh-ha, Filmpodium (1995)
KunstproduzentInnen im Aussendienst Hors Sol (1996)
Interview in Environ 27 ans ou un peu plus, art et féminismes, Sous-sol, Genève
Kültür: Modernisierung, Kunst und Gender in Istanbul MOMA (1996)
Global Food art ad in Vor der Information, Vienna (1996
Free Zone Plan, art ad in geld.beat.sythetik, ID-Archiv, Berlin/Amsterdam (1996)
Strategien der Identität in den 90er Jahren Glarner Nachrichten (August 13, 1996)
Ethno-x-centric reflections on the national expo and the national museum Platzwechsel, Kunsthalle Zürich (1996)
Spaces In-between Problématique, Journal of political studies IV, Toronto (1996)
Foreign Services FAZ (1996)
Postkoloniale Praxis Zyma Art Today (Juni 1996)
Kültür - Modernisierung, Kunst und Gender in Istanbul MOMA (5/1996)
Kunst- und Ausstellungspraxis im postkolonialen Raum and Kulturelle Territorien
Orte der Identität Kültür (1997)
Fighting for representational space – women in the media have to act Zebra, magazine for audiovisual activities, Copenhagen (December 1997)
Gender ist das grosse Ding Interview mit Gayatri Ch. Spivak, WoZ zusammen mit Yvonne Volkart (January 1998)
Performing the Border ANYP Nr. 9, Berlin and Munich (1999)
Performing the Border next Cyberfeminist International, old boys network, boys@obn.org (September 1999)
Politik ist eine kulturelle Domäne interview by Sigrid Weber, iz3W Nr. 240 (September 1999) www.iz3w.org
Performing the Border.Die Grenze als Metapher für Differenz und Gewalt iz3W Nr. 241 (November 1999)
Performing the Border video cult/ures, Museum für Neue Kunst ZKM Karlsruhe and Dumont Köln (September 1999)
Outsourcing and Subcontracting/Auslagerung und Zulieferung Curating Degree Zero,

an international curating symposium, Verlag für moderne Kunst Nurnberg (1999)
Performing the Border Migration findet statt, cfd-dossier (2/1999)
Performing the Border, On Gender, Transnational bodies and Technology Globalization on the Line: Gender, Nation, and Capital at U.S. Borders, ed. by Claudia Sadowsky (2000)
Dread Angel Artistic Practice in the Network, digital museum, New York (2000)
Performing the Border: Gender, bodies and technology at the cross-point of private desire and public space ZED magazine, Center for Design Studies, London (2000)

# Critical Reviews

Kitschobjekte und Hybridkunst Neue Zürcher Zeitung, (8.6.1995)
Aussendienst/Foreign Services by Anke Kempkes, Springerin (Juni 1995)
Das berührt uns doch schliesslich alle by Jochen Becker, TAZ (25. Juli 1995)
Belebung eines Scheintoten – Die Ausstellung "Platzwechsel" zum Zürcher Platzspitz-Areal by Roland Vogler, Tages Anzeiger (12.7.1995)
Platzwechsel by Yvonne Volkart, Springer (4/1995)
Wortbäume und Duftreisen by Verena Mühlberger und Gertrud Vogler, WOZ (Juni 1995)
Der Duft des Fremden, DU (August 1995)
Dekonstruktion der Idylle by Yvonne Volkart, WOZ (28.6.1996)
Wenn die Kunst fremdgeht by Simon Maurer, Tages Anzeiger (28.6.1996)
Strategien der Kunst in den 90er Jahren by Yvonne Volkart, Texte zur Kunst (August 1996)
Just Watch by Hedwig Saxenhuber, Springerin (4/1997)
Jenseits von Bertelsmann by Jochen Becker, TAZ Berlin (22.10.1997)
Just Watch WOZ (September 1997)
Nomaden am Bosporus by Jorg Bader, Tages Anzeiger (13.10.1997)
La 5e Biennial d'Istanbul donne la parole aux femmes. Troublant
by Jörg Bader, Nouveau Quotidien (5 novembre 1997)
Kriegszonen: Körper, Identitäten und Weiblichkeit in der High-Tech Industrie
by Yvonne Volkart, Springerin (Juni-August 1999)
War Zone: Bodies, Identities and Femininity in the global High-Tech Industry
Yvonne Yolkart, n.paradoxa vol. 4 (1999)
War Zone: Bodies, Identities and Femininity in the global High-Tech Industry
Yvonne Yolkart, The Body Caught in the Computer Intestines And Beyond, Women Strategies and/or strategies by women in media, art, theory, edited by Marina Grizinic (Ljubljana) in collaboration with Adele Eisenstein (Budapest/New York/Cologne, 2000)
Kriegszonen: Körper, Identitäten und Weiblichkeit in der High-Tech Industrie
by Yvonne Volkart, WOZ (8.4.2000)

# _BIOGRAPHIES

**Ursula Biemann** studied art and critical theory in Mexico and at the School of Visual Arts and the Whitney Independent Study Program in New York. Her art and curatorial work focuses on gender relations in the media, economy, and the urban space and on rearticulating postcolonial work relations and visual representations. Curatorial projects and publications at Shedhalle Zurich from 1995-1998 include *Aussendienst/Foreign Services, Hors Sol, Kültür*, and the media symposium *Just Watch*.
biemann@access.ch

**Avtar Brah** was born in the Panjab, India, and raised in Uganda. She teaches at Birkbeck College, University of London and lectures internationally. Rockefeller Research Fellow in the Center for Cultural Studies, University of California at Santa Cruz in 1993. She is the author of *Cartographies of Diaspora, Contesting Identities* (1996) and co-editor (with M.J Hickman and M. Mac an Ghail) of Thi*nking Identities: Ethnicity, Racism and Culture* (1999) and *Global Futures: Migration, Environment* (1999).
a.brah@cems.bbk.ac.uk

**Rosi Braidotti** studied English literature and Philosophy at the Australian National University in Canberra and at the University Panthéon-Sorbonne in Paris. Since 1988, she is Chair in Comparative Women's Studies at the Faculty of Arts of Utrecht University. In 1989 she set up the Network Of Interdisciplinary Women's Studies in Europe (NOISE) within the European Union. She is currently working on the politics of feminist postmodernism from a multicultural perspective and on the history of scientific teratology. Among her publications: *Nomadic Subjects* (1994, Columbia University Press), *Patterns of Dissonance* (1991, Polity Press). She co-authored: *Women, the Environment and Sustainable Development* (1994, Zed Books)
Rosi.Braidotti@let.uu.nl

**Simin Farkhondeh** is an independent video producer, artist and educator. She has directed *Labor At the Crossroads*, a TV program about labor issues since 1994, and set up the curriculum for a worker video training course. Multimedia installation *Representing the other - Representing oneself* at Shedhalle Zurich in 1995. Simin is a recipient of the Rockefeller Fellowship Award for the video *Who Gives Kisses Freely from her Lips*, a video about women in Iran. Currently she is working with Ursula Biemann on a video about the global trafficking of women. She is also producing a series of short dramatizations about work issues.
SFarkhondeh@gc.cuny.edu

**Bertha Jottar** is a video artist from Mexico City who lived and worked between Tijuana and San Diego for eight years. From 1988-1991, she was a member of Border Art Workshop/Taller de arte fronterizo. Founding member of the art collective Las comadres and collaborator with the artist and activists from Tijuana. Moved to New York City in the Fall of 1994. Jottar is currently working on an experimental documentary about Afro-Cuban rhumba music in New York. She is finishing her Ph.D. in the Program of Performance Studies at TISCH School of the Arts at New York University.
bjp7185@is.nyu.edu

**Sikay Tang** studied photography and sculpture at the University of Chicago and fine arts at the Jan van Eyck Akademie in Holland. She started making videos in New York City in 1992. Her videos *Untitled*, a two monitor piece, *Phrases*, *Where Did the Music Go* and *In Search of an Allison* were exhibited at Raum Aktueller Kunst in Vienna, Cinema Rex in Belgrade, Shedhalle in Zurich and the International Triennial of Photographic Art in Rovaniemi, Finland. Having worked as a film and video editor in NYC for many years, Tang now works and lives in Hong Kong where she recently curated the exhibition *Dare to Dream*.
muslove@usa.net

**Yvonne Volkart** studied German, Psychology and Art History at the University of Zurich and Vienna. Independent author and curator. She teaches language and new media at the School of Art and Design, Zurich, has a guest lectureship for gender studies at the Art History Department of the University of Zurich and lectures internationally. Co-curator with Ulrike Kremeier of the exhibitions *InterfaceProduction*, Shedhalle Zurich 1998 and *ProductionPublic*, Kunsthalle Exnergasse Vienna, 1999. For Spring 2000, she curates *Tenancity. Cultural Practices in the Age of Bio and Information Technologies* for the Swiss Institute New York.
yvolkart@access.ch